This project was made possible by the generous support of the A.L. Mailman Family Foundation, the William and Flora Hewlett Foundation, and the Lippincott Foundation.

Conflict Resolution in the Middle School: A Curriculum and Teaching Guide
by William J. Kreidler

Editors: Laura Parker Roerden and Eden R. Steinberg

Kreidler, William J.
ISBN 0-942349-07-5

 This book is printed on recycled paper.

Cover design by Lorraine Karcz and Dave Miranda
Page design and layout by Doug Parker Roerden and Christine McGee
Production Editors: Jeremy Rehwaldt-Alexander and Linda Hiltz

Conflict Resolution in the Middle School

A Curriculum and Teacher's Guide

by William J. Kreidler

esr

EDUCATORS
for
SOCIAL
RESPONSIBILITY

23 Garden Street
Cambridge, MA 02138
(617) 492-1764

Contents

Part Two: Working Toward Win-Win

List of Handouts

Acknowledgments

A book like this reflects the contributions of many, many people, and I would like to thank some of them here. *Conflict Resolution in the Middle School* continues to grow and change, based on the needs of middle school students and their teachers. I want to thank all the hundreds of middle school teachers who used the curriculum in earlier editions and gave me feedback, either in writing, at workshops, or through formal and informal conversations. I also want to thank all the middle school students who, in classes, focus groups, and informal conversation, told me what they wanted to learn. This teaching guide would not exist without them.

I would like to thank once again all those people who contributed to the field-test edition of this book. Their thoughtful insights and practical feedback helped create the base upon which this edition of *Conflict Resolution in the Middle School* stands.

My thanks also to the teachers who participated in the national field-test of this guide, especially Jennifer Berry, Donna Krol, Stacey Lieberman, Judith Mimbs, Lauren Ockene, Claudia Schena, Tricia Weyand, and Sandra Weyer. Their experience and honesty immeasurably enriched this book.

I would like to thank my colleagues at Educators for Social Responsibility. It is my great good fortune to work with people who, in part because of their own experience as teachers, are both creative and practical. In particular, I would like to thank:

- the Director of Publications and Communications at ESR, Laura Parker Roerden, for her belief in this project, her creative thinking, and her contribution of "Adolescents and Conflict: A Developmental Overview";

- the editor of this edition, Eden Steinberg, for her endless patience and good humor as I arbitrarily changed deadlines, and for her skill and accuracy in wielding her editor's pen;

- the Executive Director of ESR, Larry Dieringer, who has never stopped believing that this was an important project and who never stopped looking for sources of funding;

- the staff at ESR's Resolving Conflict Creatively Program (RCCP), especially Director Linda Lantieri and Associate Director Jinnie Spiegler, for sharing the practical wisdom that comes from their many years of experience teaching conflict resolution and intergroup relations to adults and young people;

- Rachel Poliner for writing the overview of the infusion section for this edition and for contributing the science and math infusion chapters; Rachel's clear and incisive input did much to shape and improve this book;

- Carol Miller Lieber, who, like myself, has a zeal for developing ways to make abstract concepts concrete and real for young people—I have benefited more than I can say from her innovative thinking about conflict resolution and about schools.

I would also like to thank the many people who, through direct feedback or informal discussions, shaped and influenced my thinking. Their contributions have affected every aspect of this curriculum: Janet Patti, David Hyerle, Sara Goodman, Zephryn Conte, Mara Gross, Jeffrey Benson, Roger Fisher, Pamela Moore, Nancy Schniedewind, Nan Doty, Nancy Grant, Libby Cowles, Yvonne Stone, Donna Crawford, Dick Bodine, and Fred Schrumpf.

Finally, I would like to thank Lisa Sjostrom, for her very useful feedback and her for her contribution to "Adolescents and Conflict: A Developmental Overview." As always, the Kamikaze Associates—Barbara Porro, Susan Beekman, and Jeanne Holmes—provided inspiration, support, and laughs. And, of course, thanks to David Aronstein for his clear thinking, patience, and support.

Introduction

Conflict resolution is one of the most exciting subjects you can teach. And middle school is one of the most exciting places to teach it. That has been our experience, and this curriculum guide is designed to help you have a similar experience as you teach nonviolent conflict resolution skills to middle school students.

Middle school students are hungry to learn new ways to handle conflicts. They are beginning to re-examine their relationships with their peers, their teachers, their parents, their world. Conflict is a natural and necessary part of this process.

Conflict is also a natural and necessary part of life, but that doesn't make it easy to handle. Middle schoolers want to know how to handle conflicts when the old way—getting help from an adult—is no longer acceptable. They scoff at easy or pat answers. They are a demanding audience. But they will eagerly explore and embrace new skills and concepts if they are creditable. And they will eagerly apply what they learn about interpersonal conflict to larger conflicts in the community, the country, and the world.

They are ready to examine such concepts as power, injustice, prejudice, and violence. But they need guidance to do all this, and that is where we, as teachers, come in. This curriculum is designed to help you as you guide students to discover more about conflict, conflict resolution, and related issues. The goal of this curriculum is to help students become more effective at handling conflict nonviolently and to help students use what they have learned about interpersonal conflict resolution to understand conflict in the larger world.

How This Guide is Organized

Conflict Resolution in the Middle School is divided into the following parts:

- Introduction and Preparation
- Part I: Essential Tools
- Part II: Working Toward Win-Win
- Part III: Dealing With Differences
- Part IV: Infusion into the Standard Curriculum

The goal of the *Introduction* is to help you understand how the curriculum is organized, the principles on which the curriculum is based, how to use the lesson plans, and how to best implement the curriculum. The next chapter, *Preparing to Teach This Curriculum*, covers how to create an environment for teaching conflict resolution, how to assess student learning, and how to develop staff and parent support.

Part I: Essential Tools consists of skill lessons one through thirteen. These lessons introduce students to the core conflict resolution concepts and skills. If time for teaching *Conflict Resolution in the Middle School* is limited, teachers should focus on this section of the curriculum.

Part II: Working Toward Win-Win consists of lessons fourteen through twenty-one. This section builds on the core concepts and skills, and helps students to learn to negotiate. Other topics addressed in this section include peer pressure and the concept of personal power and how it can be used and abused.

Parts I, II, and III each end with a group of lessons titled, "Extending the Concepts." In the course of teaching *Conflict Resolution in the Middle School* you may find that your students want or need to explore certain concepts and tools in greater depth. These additional activities will help you do just that. Some of the activities give students more practice with one or two of the tools. In other activities students explore an aspect of the concept that isn't explored in great depth in the main body of the section, such as looking at how a tool can be applied to international conflicts.

Part III: Dealing With Differences helps students better understand diversity and how to deal with conflict that is rooted in diversity. In addition, this unit helps students begin to broaden their understanding of conflict beyond the interpersonal level to the larger societal level.

Part IV: Infusion into the Standard Curriculum describes how to reinforce the skills and concepts introduced in the skill lessons in the context of standard middle school content. This section includes ideas for infusing conflict resolution into English/language arts, social studies, science, and math. The infusion lessons are based on the conflict resolution tools introduced in the skill lessons.

 This symbol sometimes appears in the lesson plans. It represents a mini-lecture containing key concepts. Use the wording provided or cover these points in your own words.

The Peaceable Classroom Model

This curriculum is based on a model that is used in all conflict resolution materials developed by Educators for Social Responsibility. We call this model the Peaceable Classroom. It is an approach to teaching conflict resolution that has been used for over twenty years at all grade levels and in all types of schools: urban, suburban, and rural.

The Peaceable Classroom is a caring classroom community that emphasizes six themes:

- cooperation
- communication
- appreciation for diversity
- the healthy expression of feelings
- responsible decision making
- conflict resolution

These themes influence every activity in this curriculum. There is a heavy emphasis on cooperatively structured activities, and most of the activities encourage students to learn through discussion with each other and with you, the teacher. Students are also encouraged to relate skills and concepts to their own lives and to talk about feelings (although we try to do this in a way that is comfortable and not intrusive). Similarly, the activities try to model appreciation for diversity, and are focused on learning to understand and handle conflict more effectively.

Our experience has shown us that it is not enough to teach students conflict-resolution skills. That alone will not address some important aspects of conflict. The Peaceable Classroom model reminds us of six important components of learning to handle conflict more effectively, and emphasizes that a key aspect of conflict resolution in the middle school is the creation of classrooms and schools that are caring communities.

The Conflict Resolution Tool Kit

Conflict Resolution in the Middle School uses a simple organizing framework we call the Conflict Resolution Tool Kit. Each concept or skill in the curriculum is a "tool." All of us—no matter what age—already have some tools for resolving conflicts. The problem comes when we try to use the wrong tool for the situation. It's like using a hammer when you need to be using a saw. The goal of this guide is to help students acquire more tools and learn to use the right tool for the job.

The conflict resolution tools in this curriculum include:

- The Ability to Identify Conflicts
- The Conflict Escalator
- The Anger Thermometer/The Anger Continuum
- The P.O.V. Glasses
- Active Listening/P.E.A.R.
- "I" Messages
- C.A.P.S.
- Demands and ReallyNeeds*
- Negotiation
- Mediation
- Arbitration
- Conflict Styles
- The Ability to Identify Communication Potholes
- The Conflict Tug O' War Rope
- The Personal Power Package
- The Win-Win Grid
- The Diversity Deck

Options for Lessons

The lessons in *Conflict Resolution in the Middle School* are designed to be both easy to teach and easy to adapt.

Each lesson plan contains the following parts:

- A One-page Overview
- Lesson Activities
- Additional Activities
- Handouts

---

* "Demands and ReallyNeeds" are adapted from Tom Snyder Productions' "Getting to the Heart of It" software (Watertown, MA: Tom Snyder Productions, 1994).

The Workshop Approach

The lessons were designed with two teaching approaches in mind. You will need to decide which approach you want to use. The first is called the "Workshop Approach" and was developed by the Resolving Conflict Creatively Program. The Resolving Conflict Creatively Program, an initiative of Educators for Social Responsibility, is one of the nation's largest and longest-running school-based programs in conflict resolution, violence prevention, and intergroup relations. The Workshop Approach follows the following agenda:

1. A Gathering Activity to bring the class together

2. Reviewing the Agenda

3. The Main Activities

4. An Evaluation and Review of the Key Points in the lesson

5. Closing Activity to end the lesson on a positive note

The Workshop Approach builds community in the classroom and, once students are used to it, helps them engage with the content in a personal and affective way, which is more likely to lead to behavioral change than a heavily cognitive approach.

Lessons take more time with the workshop approach, and some of that time is spent on what seem to be "non-academic" activities. Both teachers and students may need to get used to the kind of personal sharing that the Workshop Approach uses.

The Standard Lesson Approach

The other option is the Standard Lesson approach, which uses this agenda:

1. Reviewing the Agenda

2. The Main Activities

3. An Evaluation and Review of the Key Points in the lesson

The Standard Lesson approach gives more time for the lesson content because the Gathering and Closing activities are eliminated. However, by sacrificing the community building activities used in Gathering and Closing, the discussion may not be as rich and the behavioral change may be less.

We would urge you to at least try the Workshop Approach. It reflects our belief that conflict resolution is best taught in the context of a caring community. The Gathering and Closing Activities are thoroughly classroom tested. Students enjoy them, and we think you will, too.

Choosing the Appropriate Level

All of the activities and materials in this guide are labeled as Level A, Level B, Level C, or some combination of levels, such as Level A/B/C. Level A corresponds roughly to sixth grade, Level B to seventh grade, and Level C to eighth grade. The conflicts that most interest sixth graders are different from the conflicts that most interest eighth graders. These designations reflect the relative sophistication and interest level of the activity or material. However, you should feel free to choose the level you feel will be most appropriate for your students.

Adapting Lessons

The lessons in *Conflict Resolution in the Middle School* can be implemented as presented or adapted to meet particular needs you identify. There are three main ways that pilot test teachers adapted the lessons: timing, role-plays and case studies, and journals.

Timing

Each lesson takes approximately 40-45 minutes. You may choose to give more time to each lesson by allowing discussions to go on or by including some of the additional activities.

Role-plays and Case Studies

The role-plays and case studies in the curriculum are all based on suggestions made to us by middle school students. Their purpose is to give students a chance to apply new skills and understandings to realistic situations. Because of their structured and controlled nature, they challenge students without overwhelming them and are the perfect intermediary step between introducing a new skill or concept and applying it to actual conflict situations.

However, the role-plays and case studies that will mean the most to your students are the ones they develop themselves. Once they have some practice doing role-plays, have students develop their own to supplement or substitute for the ones included in the curriculum. For a more complete guide to running and processing role-plays see Appendix C.

Journals

Another way to help students apply new skills and understandings to real life situations is to have them keep Conflict Journals. Conflict Journals help students observe conflict carefully and analyze different aspects of conflict. This in turn helps them learn to resolve conflict more effectively. In the additional activities section of each lesson, you will find suggestions for journal-keeping activities. The Conflict Journals can be a notebook or folder. You should have students pass in their journals for you to read and comment upon. But don't grade or correct the journals. The focus should be on observing what students are learning about conflict.

You need not have students do all the journal activities in the curriculum. For journal keeping to be successful you will need to vary the assignments, collect and read the journals at least once a week, and, most importantly, have students use their journal entries during class discussions and activities. It is not at all uncommon for students to begin journal keeping with enthusiasm and then lose interest after a few weeks. You can let them take a break from journal keeping and come back to it, or simply end it when student interest wanes. Conflict Journals *will* take extra work on everyone's part, but we think you will find that they are an extraordinarily powerful learning tool.

Implementing the Curriculum

Concerning implementation, the basic question to be answered is: "Who is teaching what, and when are they teaching it?" A variety of methods can be used to implement *Conflict Resolution in the Middle School*. These methods include:

- an exploratory/elective course
- sixth grade orientation
- a team approach
- a core block
- health education
- an advisory period
- cross-graded families

Descriptions of each of these methods along with their strengths and limitations are presented in the chart that begins on p. 7. Whichever approach you use, there are some general guidelines to keep in mind as you plan the implementation of this curriculum.

- Remember that reducing violence and aggressive behavior does not necessarily produce a nurturing, respectful learning environment. Changing a school environment is a process that requires time and conscious intention.

- When planning implementation, keep in mind that it may take up to a year to make any needed adjustments in the school schedule or in teaching responsibilities.

- Try to gain the support of as many staff people as possible. Not everyone needs to teach the curriculum, but it will make your program stronger if other staff know about the curriculum and try to use some of the Conflict Resolution Tools. It would be ideal if your colleagues could participate in a workshop on the curriculum. If that's not possible, try to make at least one presentation about *Conflict Resolution in the Middle School* at a staff meeting. Explain the goals of this conflict resolution program, what students will be learning, and how other teachers can support you. The next chapter, *Preparing to Teach This Curriculum*, provides a sample agenda for a staff meeting and other information about building staff support.

- Start informing parents about the curriculum as soon as possible. See the next chapter for ideas on how to do this. Consider planning some type of presentation for parents where students show some of their work and explain what they are learning from the curriculum.

- Model the skills that you want students to learn and practice. Modeling is the first and most important way we learn.

IMPLEMENTATION MODELS

NAME AND DESCRIPTION	STRENGTHS	LIMITATIONS
Exploratory/ Elective Course The curriculum is used as basis for an elective course that typically meets for about nine weeks with two or three sessions each week.	• Students choose to take the class and are likely to be motivated. • Teachers responsible for an elective course tend to develop a high degree of skill and confidence about teaching the material. • Courses are usually long enough to allow for real depth.	• The course may reach only a few students depending on how often it's offered. • Other faculty and staff are not directly involved and may not feel committed to supporting conflict resolution education.
Sixth Grade Orientation The curriculum is used during the first quarter as an orientation for incoming sixth graders as a way to help students acquire the tools they need for a healthy and productive middle school life.	• This model builds community through a common experience that is shared by all sixth graders at the beginning of their new school experience. • Teachers in other content areas are more likely to infuse conflict resolution into their subject areas if all students have a common learning experience.	• Other topics such as study skills are often taught in sixth grade orientation, leaving less time for conflict resolution. • Sometimes this is the only experience students will have with conflict resolution, so they may gain only a superficial understanding.
Team Approach This approach assumes that a team teaching system is already in place. One teacher on the team acts as the leader and is responsible for teaching the key skill development lessons in this curriculum. The other team members reinforce the tools and themes in their subject areas. (See Part 4, Infusion Into the Standard Curriculum, for information and ideas.) The leader helps other teachers match conflict resolution skills and objectives with curriculum standards.	• The team leader tends to develop a high degree of skill and confidence about teaching this material. • There's flexibility in who teaches the material, so the team can find the best match of skills and interests among them. • The team leader can coach and support team members, helping them develop appropriate lessons in their content areas. • Time for team planning is already scheduled into the day.	• The team leader must sacrifice some instructional time in his or her content area. • Other team members may feel limited responsibility for teaching conflict resolution. • The team leader will need training in order to help other team members match conflict resolution skills and objectives with the curriculum standards in various subject areas. • The team leader needs to be released to meet with other team leaders to facilitate planning.

(continued)

IMPLEMENTATION MODELS

NAME AND DESCRIPTION	STRENGTHS	LIMITATIONS
### Core Block Each core teacher has responsibility for teaching a significant section of the curriculum during the language arts and social studies core block period, which typically lasts one and a half to two hours. Core block teachers at each grade level identify the specific units they will teach.	• Every student has a common experience every year. • Language arts and social studies teachers can deepen the experience by developing infusion activities.	• Not all core teachers may be interested or prepared to teach this material. • Planning is essential: if it is not specified who teaches the curriculum and when, it may not be taught at all.
### Health Education The curriculum is used as a conflict resolution unit during health class.	• Every student is exposed to the material. • Health teachers are often already familiar with the concepts and instructional strategies of the curriculum. • Students often feel comfortable participating in health class discussions.	• The health curriculum is often overloaded already. • The time period allotted for the curriculum may be limited to as little as one or two weeks. • Other faculty and staff are not directly involved and may not feel committed to supporting conflict resolution education.
### Advisory Period The curriculum is used as the basis for conflict resolution focus in an advisory period. Nearly all faculty members are responsible for advisory groups.	• All students are exposed to the material. • Everyone is responsible for delivering the material, so all staff members must become familiar with it. • This model builds community through a common experience.	• The curriculum must be adjusted to fit in short blocks of time, typically 20 to 25 minutes. • There is a need to be selective with topics and lessons, using only those that most staff members can teach comfortably. • It is difficult in such a short time to do sequenced skill building. • Often the purpose of the curriculum must change, focusing on building community, problem solving, building relationships.

IMPLEMENTATION MODELS

NAME AND DESCRIPTION	STRENGTHS	LIMITATIONS
Cross-Graded Families "Family groups" are formed that include approximately 12 to 15 students from different grade levels (all grade levels are represented in each group). Each group includes up to two adult advisors. Both teaching and non-teaching staff can be included as advisors. Groups typically meet regularly—once a week, once every two weeks, or once a month—for a specified length of time. Students stay with their "family" throughout middle school.	• Students and staff are involved in a common experience that involves everyone, including non-teaching staff, creating a strong sense of community. • Not graded, so students often feel they can explore interpersonal conflicts and problems more freely. • Older students can mentor younger students.	• Several people are required to organize this approach. • Planning is required to ensure an engaging experience for all ages.
"Required Elective" Course The curriculum is taught in a course that is "elective" only in the sense that it is not a full-year course. The course lasts nine weeks and is part of a rotation with other "required electives" such as art and music. All students rotate through the course, taking a different elective each quarter.	• Every student is exposed to the material and has a common experience. • Several teachers can teach the course each quarter and can team up for planning. • Teachers responsible for an elective course tend to develop a high degree of skill and confidence about teaching the material. • The course is institutionalized. It becomes part of the formal curriculum so that if the teacher who starts the course leaves, the course continues.	• Other faculty and staff may feel no commitment to supporting conflict resolution education.

CONFLICT RESOLUTION IN THE MIDDLE SCHOOL **9**

Preparing to Teach This Curriculum

A Three-Minute Guide to Conflict Resolution

In this curriculum we define conflict as a dispute or a disagreement between two or more people. This working definition covers most types of interpersonal conflict—from an argument in the hallway to a war between two nations. Sometimes these disagreements are problems, and they need to be solved. Conflict resolution is solving the problems created by conflict situations.

Conflict resolution is an umbrella term. It covers everything from sitting down and talking things out, to a sock in the nose, to running away and hiding. So we need to put some parameters around what makes for "good" conflict resolution. By our definition, good conflict resolution has three qualities:

- it is nonviolent;
- it meets the needs of the people involved;
- it improves the relationship of the people involved.

Of course, you don't always get "good" conflict resolution, but this is our aim both for adults and young people.

There are three key concepts that underlie all conflict resolution education:

First, conflict is a normal and natural part of life. It is not going to go away, nor would that be desirable. Without conflict, there is no growth or progress. Without conflict, there is stagnation. The goal of conflict resolution is to use conflict for its constructive and positive aspects, not its destructive ones. In a middle school, this means using conflict as a learning opportunity.

Second, conflict is not a contest. In a contest, only one person is the winner. Everyone else loses. In conflict resolution we aim for what is called the "win-win" resolution, where both parties are winners. Winning in a conflict means getting what you want or what you need.

Third, there is no one way that is the right way to handle all conflict situations. Basically, there are six ways to handle conflict, and each of them is appropriate in some situations and inappropriate in others. These six conflict styles are discussed more fully in Skill Lesson 12.

- Directing/Competing—"We're doing it my way and that's that."
- Collaborating—"Let's sit down and work this out."
- Compromising—"Let's both give a little."
- Accommodating—"Whatever you want is fine."
- Avoiding—"Let's skip it."
- Appealing to a Third Party—"Let's get some help."

The key to successful conflict resolution is to know when to use which style. For example, as teachers, there are many times when being directive is the most appropriate and the most efficient way for us to handle conflicts. There are also times when avoiding the conflict completely is the most sensible course. And there are times when we want to collaborate and the other party isn't willing. The trick is not to get stuck in one or two styles and use them inappropriately. Conflict resolution is about expanding our options and increasing our skills—and our students' skills—as peacemakers.

Before You Begin Teaching This Curriculum

- Read the guide and be sure you understand what you are going to teach. You will also find that reading other adult resources on conflict resolution will enrich your teaching of *Conflict Resolution in the Middle School*. There is a list of such books in Appendix G, Related Resources.

- Think about personal anecdotes or experiences that you might share with students in the course of discussions. These not only give you an opportunity to model how to share personal experiences, they can also be powerful teaching tools as students listen to your real-life experiences.

- Practice the skills in your daily life: this will give you a deeper understanding of the skills, and it will give you greater insight into just how long it can take to master some of these social skills. In addition, you will probably get some pointed or amusing stories to share with your students.

- Note the teaching strategies that are unfamiliar to you. Some of the strategies in this curriculum, such as discussions, may be like old friends. Others, such as microlabs, may be completely new. Every teaching strategy used in the curriculum is explained either in Appendix D, or in the body of the appropriate lesson.

- In the course of discussions students may share information that is inappropriately personal. Know your school's policies on discussing such issues, and know what your obligations are if you suspect a student is a victim of some kind of abuse. There are certain legal obligations you have in such situations, and your school system may have its own policies as well. Know the "chain of command" in your system—find out to whom you must report what.

- Review the developmental needs of young adolescents. (See Appendix I, Adolescents and Conflict: A Developmental Overview.) This will help you better understand and address the conflicts and concerns of students in this age group.

- Check with the school nurse and the guidance counselors about what resources exist in the school and in the community to help young people deal with problems. These can include mental health agencies, shelters for homeless or abused people, government agencies, and others.

- You may want to modify some activities to make them more appropriate for your students. Some lessons give options or alternatives, others do not. You know the needs of your students, so don't hesitate to make the modifications you feel are necessary.

- Think about how you will arrange the classroom. For example, teachers who participated in the field test of this curriculum found that cooperative activities were facilitated by having desks in clusters of four, and that the quality of discussions improved when students could face each other.

- Plan time for students to reinforce their learning through decorating the room. For example, students can create posters or bulletin board displays on conflict resolution themes. Invite students to look for quotes or articles on any of the themes of the Peaceable Classroom.

- Begin planning how you will keep parents informed about what the students are learning. If students will be making some type of presentation to parents, start planning now. At this point you may only be able to identify when and where the event will take place. Even so, such a decision will shape how you teach the curriculum. Also, think of ways you might want to involve parents and other community people in the program. For example, if you want to have a panel of peacemakers speak to the class, it's never too soon to begin identifying potential participants.

The Limits of Conflict Resolution in the Middle School

Students will learn a great deal about resolving conflict from *Conflict Resolution in the Middle School*, but it is important to have realistic expectations about what the curriculum does and does not do.

- *Conflict Resolution in the Middle School* was developed and tested to meet the needs of average, mainstreamed students. Students with severe behavioral or emotional difficulties will need interventions that are beyond the scope of this guide.

- *Conflict Resolution in the Middle School* can be an important part of a school's violence prevention strategy, but it is not sufficient to be the whole of it. Every school should have a school safety plan, and every staff member and student should know the plan. There should be clear procedures and policies about weapons, racial incidents, sexual harassment, and other types of crises.

- *Conflict Resolution in the Middle School* does not directly address weapons, sexual harassment, child abuse, drug use, gang violence, or domestic violence. However, this curriculum will enhance efforts to address those topics.

Creating a Classroom Environment for Teaching Conflict Resolution

Students may never have experienced activities of the type that are in *Conflict Resolution in the Middle School*. Part of ensuring the success of the curriculum rests in creating a classroom environment where students will feel emotionally safe as they engage in these activities and discussions. Below are some important guidelines for creating such an environment. (See also the Classroom Management Checklist, p. 16.)

- Set the ground rules. This is part of the first lesson in the curriculum. You may be tempted to skip this step or simply to present students with a list of pre-set ground rules. However, involving students in the process of setting ground rules increases their sense of ownership over the rules and their commitment to keeping them. If you have already established ground rules with your students, review them and discuss possible additions or changes before you do any other activities in this guide. Regularly revisiting the ground rules is a good idea. Check in after three or four weeks and ask the students:

1. Are the ground rules working?
2. Does the classroom feel like a safe and productive place?
3. Are there additions or changes that should be made?

You may need to have your students respond to these questions privately on a piece of paper instead of in front of the whole class.

- Whatever ground rules the students develop, be sure to make the following non-negotiable policies clear to students:
  - Everyone has the right to pass. No one will be forced to do anything that makes him or her uncomfortable.
  - Everyone has the right to privacy. Even though there are activities that ask students to share personal experiences, they should share only those they are comfortable discussing publicly.
  - Everyone has the right to be treated with respect, which means no laughing at serious statements and no putting people down.
  - Everyone has the right to confidentiality. Things that students share in the course of discussions should stay in the classroom. They should not be "passed around" to the rest of the school.

- Don't assume that students will know the difference between appropriate and inappropriate behavior. Because the teaching style and activities of *Conflict Resolution in the Middle School* are often very different from what students may be used to, they might assume that "anything goes." You'll need to tell students explicitly what does not "go." For example, at ESR our policy is that young people should not swear or use curse words in school. However, when students are doing role plays about real-life conflict situations they might assume that it's all right to swear. You need to let them know that it's not. In fact, we suggest beginning every role play session with a quick review of what's acceptable and what's not.

- Before you start teaching, and as the course progresses, assess your students' level of competency in such areas as listening, cooperation, respectful behavior, and other social skills. Appendix H contains supplementary activities for addressing these issues. Determine which, if any, of these activities you need to do. For example, if you have a group where some students are prone to putdowns, you may want to do "Putdown Patrol" before you do anything else. Or the need for "Putdown Patrol" may emerge as the course develops. If students are unsure about what is private and what is not, do the "Privacy Lists" activity.

- If your students are not very experienced with cooperative activities, take time to do some of the cooperation skill activities in Appendix H. This will save time later.

- When teaching the lessons, be sure everyone understands the task at hand. Begin by simply asking if everyone understands what they will be doing. It often helps to write the goal of the activity on the board and to ask for a volunteer to review the assignment.

- Keep groups small. Start with pairs and gradually increase group size until you reach four, which we have found to be the optimal group size for most activities.

- Don't hesitate to take a few minutes to discuss cooperation skills if students need it. Ask the class to identify what they think are the key cooperation skills. List these on the board and discuss them.

- If necessary, suggest that each student in the group play a role, such as time keeper, recorder, reader, and/or taskmaster (the one who keeps everyone on task). The lesson will go more smoothly if you do.

- Put students in groups that include people they do not know well. For other ideas about assigning students to groups, see the section titled, "Group Formation" in Appendix D.

- Keep an eye on groups to be sure everyone is participating and that they are solving problems as they arise. As much as possible, let groups solve their problems themselves.

- After every group activity, encourage students to evaluate how they did. Ask each group to identify what they did well and what they could do better next time. Or, another useful set of debriefing questions is (1) Did everyone participate? (2) Did anyone have an idea that was ignored? (3) Did anyone lead? Was that helpful?*

---

* ESR thanks Rachel Poliner for contributing this set of debriefing questions.

Classroom Management Checklist*

In setting up the physical environment in my classroom, I:

❒ Arrange the room to reflect a student-centered approach.

❒ Arrange seating so students can see one another.

❒ Make sure bulletin boards and displays reflect the ethnic and racial diversity of my students.

In establishing a comfortable climate, I:

❒ Learn students' names and use them often.

❒ Give some attention to each student.

❒ Avoid playing favorites.

❒ Model all of the ground rules.

❒ Focus on students' positive qualities and praise their efforts.

❒ Set tasks that are within students' capabilities.

In leading a lesson, I:

❒ Make sure I'm prepared.

❒ Make sure students are ready to learn and have put away unrelated work.

❒ Write the session purpose on the board.

❒ Ask questions throughout the lesson to check for understanding.

❒ Give clear instructions and model tasks when appropriate.

❒ Give guided practice before asking students to apply new skills or knowledge.

❒ Respond promptly to their assigned work orally or in writing.

❒ Use closure questions to help students evaluate their learning.

❒ Make homework assignments and/or notebook entries.

In managing discipline, I:

❒ Encourage students to discuss solutions rather than blame others.

❒ Enforce the ground rules consistently.

❒ Handle problems quickly and discreetly, treating students with respect and fairness.

❒ Share my reactions to inappropriate behaviors and explain why the behaviors are unacceptable.

❒ Talk outside of class with students who continue to disregard the group rules.

Reprinted with permission of Quest International from Lions-Quest *Working Towards Peace* (2nd edition) © 1995 by Quest International.

Developing Staff Support

Your conflict resolution program will be more successful if it is understood and generally supported by all the staff in the school. The topic of conflict resolution is probably fairly new and unfamiliar to your colleagues. The idea of teaching conflict resolution skills may seem either mysterious or frivolous or both. The experience of many field-test teachers was that doing some of the activities from the curriculum at a staff meeting created support and even enthusiasm for the program. One teacher, for example, did one gathering activity from Appendix A at every staff meeting for a year. Another approach that is useful is to provide colleagues with examples of how the conflict resolution tools students are acquiring can enrich the curriculum in other content areas.

What follows is a sample agenda for staff meeting on *Conflict Resolution in the Middle School*. It is based on the Conflict Escalator, but you don't need to feel limited to that. Other good staff meeting activities are the Anger Sort (p. 57), the P.O.V. Glasses (p. 92, with either a historical conflict or a current events conflict), and the Win-Win Grid (p. 118) using the story of "The Zax" by Dr. Suess.

Agenda for a Staff Meeting to Explain *Conflict Resolution in the Middle School*

1. Explain the "Workshop Approach" *(3 minutes)*
   - It is the basis for lesson plans in *Conflict Resolution in the Middle School*.
   - The goal for today's meeting is to experience a few of the key activities and concepts of the curriculum.

2. Gathering Activity: If Conflict Were a Color (p. 338) *(10 minutes)*

3. Overview of Peaceable Classroom *(2 minutes)*

4. Explain the Conflict Resolution Tool Kit *(3 minutes)*
   - List some of the tools on the chalk board.
   - If you can, create a tool kit using props to represent the various tools.

5. The main goals of the curriculum *(2 minutes)*
   - To create a more peaceable and productive learning environment;
   - To help young people acquire more tools for their kits and learn how to use them appropriately.

6. Introduce the Conflict Escalator using a skit *(10 minutes)*
   - Any of the skits in session three of the curriculum will do, but adults seem to particularly enjoy "The Big Betrayal" (p. 42).
   - Ask for two volunteers to act in the skit.
   - When the skit is finished, plot the conflict onto the escalator with the entire group.

7. Questions and Answers *(5 minutes)*

Points to stress in discussing *Conflict Resolution in the Middle School* with your colleagues:

- Conflict is a fact of everyone's life. Skills for handling conflict are life skills.

- All of the lessons in the curriculum have academic objectives as well as social skill objectives. Because conflict is such a pervasive phenomenon, understanding conflict in their personal lives can help students understand conflicts in academic subjects such as literature, history, and current events.

- Studies indicate that schools that spend time teaching conflict resolution skills to students will have more instructional time available during the school year, because less of that time will be used dealing with conflict.

- Getting along, dealing with differences, and problem-solving skills are essential requirements for students who will be job hunting in the 21st century.

- Social and emotional skillfulness has been positively linked to academic and effective learning.

- Increasingly, research tells us that if we focus only on intellectual development stressing "content coverage" at the expense of emotional and social development, we risk disconnecting a majority of young people from meaningful learning experiences.

Sample Introductory Memo to Staff Members

Note: *This memo is just a sample. You will need to tailor the wording to fit your school setting.*

Date:

To:

From:

Re:

As you may know, this year our ___ grade students are participating in a program called Conflict Resolution in the Middle School. This program is designed to help students acquire the skills and understandings they need to deal with their conflicts productively and nonviolently. The course is organized around the concept of a "Conflict Resolution Tool Kit." Here are some of the "tools"—the terms, skills, and concepts that are used in the program.

Conflict Escalator — a method for mapping out how conflicts get worse.

Win-Win Resolutions — solutions to conflicts that meet the needs of everyone involved.

P.O.V. Glasses — looking at all the different points of view in a conflict.

Active Listening — a listening skill that uses paraphrasing to ensure accuracy

"I" Messages —a way to communicate feelings that avoids accusations and attacks.

Anger Thermometer — a technique for gauging the "degree" of one's anger.

One of the exciting things about these tools is that they not only help students understand and resolve their own conflicts, these tools also help students understand conflicts in the community, the nation, and the world.

I'd be happy to show you the Conflict Resolution in the Middle School materials and answer any questions you have. Meanwhile, throughout the year the kids will be participating in various conflict resolution-related projects around the school. Watch for them!

Informing Parents About *Conflict Resolution in the Middle School*

One very simple way to keep parents informed about *Conflict Resolution in the Middle School* is to send home a letter that explains the program and its goals. A sample letter is included below, but feel free to adapt it to the standards and needs of your community.

Don't limit yourself to this one letter. Look for other opportunities to communicate with parents about the curriculum. Taking the time to communicate with parents means there will be fewer misunderstandings that can lead to conflicts. At a parents' night or school open house, share student portfolios with parents (see "Assessing Student Learning," p. 21, for a description of student portfolios) and have students make presentations based on their new learning. If your school has a newsletter, write a paragraph or two periodically to update parents about what students are learning. Homework is another way to reach out to parents. Several of the sessions in *Conflict Resolution in the Middle School* have take-home assignments where students can involve parents.

It has been our experience that most parents are supportive of *Conflict Resolution in the Middle School* and are happy to have their adolescents learning some peaceful conflict resolution skills. When you discuss the curriculum with parents here are some points to stress:

- This curriculum is based on the understanding that middle school is neither an older elementary school nor a younger high school. The needs of early adolescents are unique, and so is the structure of the middle school day. This curriculum was developed with the specific needs of middle school students (and their teachers!) in mind.

- The first stage in developing the curriculum was to interview literally hundreds of middle school students to find out what types of interpersonal problems were on their minds. They told us quite specifically what they wanted to learn, and the curriculum reflects that. We also talked with teachers and parents to find out what they would like from such a curriculum.

- The curriculum has been extensively field-tested and revised based on feedback from teachers. *Conflict Resolution in the Middle School* is now in use in thousands of middle schools across the country. It is in district-wide use in all types of school systems: urban, rural, and suburban.

Sample Letter To Parents

Note: *This letter is just a sample. Adapt it to meet your needs given the standards and concerns of parents in your community.)*

Date:

To:

From:

Re:

As you may know, this year our ___ grade students are participating in a program called *Conflict Resolution in the Middle School*. This program is designed to help students acquire the skills and understandings they need to deal with their conflicts productively and nonviolently. The course is organized around the concept of a "Conflict Resolution Tool Kit." Here are some of the "tools"—the terms, skills, and concepts that are used in the program.

Conflict Escalator —a method for mapping out how conflicts get worse.

Win-Win Resolutions—solutions to conflicts that meet the needs of everyone involved.

P.O.V. Glasses—looking at all the different points of view in a conflict.

Active Listening—a listening skill that uses paraphrasing to ensure accuracy.

"I" Messages—a way to communicate feelings that avoids accusations and attacks.

Anger Thermometer—a technique for gauging the "degree" of one's anger.

One of the exciting things about these tools is that they not only help students understand and resolve their own conflicts, these tools also help students understand conflicts in the community, the nation, and the world. Learning conflict resolution skills enriches the standard curriculum. The students enjoy the active teaching style of *Conflict Resolution in The Middle School* and feel that they are learning useful skills. I appreciate the fact that the program not only teaches skills but enhances academics as well.

Conflict Resolution in the Middle School was developed by Educators for Social Responsibility, a national organization that specializes in producing resources for teaching violence prevention and conflict resolution in schools. This curriculum was extensively field-tested in middle schools around the country, including inner-city, suburban, and rural schools. It is currently being used in thousands of middle schools throughout the United States.

I'd be happy to show you the *Conflict Resolution in the Middle School* materials and answer any questions you have. Meanwhile, throughout the year the students will be participating in various conflict resolution-related projects around the school. Look for these projects when you visit.

Assessing Student Learning

One of the most common questions we are asked is, "How do I evaluate what my students are learning from *Conflict Resolution in the Middle School?*" And students often ask their teachers, "Are we getting a grade in this?" We know that middle school teachers vary in the types of assessment they prefer to use. Field-test teachers used a variety of methods for evaluation. These methods are described below. As you think about assessment, remember that the approaches below are not mutually exclusive. If fact, most field-test teachers preferred a combination of all the approaches.

Meeting Objectives

All of the skill lessons in *Conflict Resolution in the Middle School* list objectives. Through direct questioning, class participation, and discussion, you should be able to get a sense of whether or not your students are grasping the vocabulary, concepts, and key ideas of each session.

Tests

Written tests are useful in helping you determine whether or not students are learning key vocabulary and concepts. Essay/short-answer tests are useful for seeing if students are able to apply the conflict resolution tools. Two sample tests are included in Appendix E. The first test focuses on vocabulary and concepts and uses two formats: fill-in-the-blank and multiple-choice. The second test is an essay/short-answer test focused on applications. Both tests assume that students have completed the entire curriculum. If your students have completed only a portion of the curriculum, feel free to use these tests as models for creating tests that address what you have covered.

Portfolio Assessment

Portfolios are collections of student work that are saved during the course of the year. The purpose is to collect as complete a representation as possible of how a student has grown during the year and how he or she has applied new learnings. There are many assignments and activities in *Conflict Resolution in the Middle School* that are appropriate for inclusion in student portfolios. These include:

- Journal entries
- Self assessments
- Projects, such as art work, written reports, comics, videotaped role-plays, etc.

Students can also choose other examples of their work that they would like included in the portfolio. It's a good idea to have a discussion with the class about what types of assignments are good for inclusion in the portfolio. Emphasize that for the most part they should try to include projects that show how their understanding and use of conflict resolution tools has grown.

Exhibitions, Displays, Performances

Having students create a public exhibition of their learning is a good way to see how students synthesize their learning and apply their understanding of the material in new situations. The process of planning, developing, and presenting a conflict resolution presentation or exhibition will draw on many if not all of the skills students have learned. Furthermore, creating a display—on the qualities of a peacemaker, for example—requires students to review the core concepts of the curriculum. Exhibitions make excellent culminating projects for *Conflict Resolution in the Middle School*, but need not be limited to that. A list of potential exhibition projects is included in Appendix F.

Observation and Anecdotal Assessment

Anecdotal assessment can be accomplished by observing student behavior in school and collecting evidence that students are demonstrating the desired outcomes. This differs from "Meeting Objectives" described above in that you are looking for examples of either how student interactions have changed, or how students are applying their new skills. For example, if a student who usually uses his sarcastic sense of humor to put others down starts to do less of that, that may be a sign that he is internalizing and using what he's learning from the curriculum.

Some of the desired outcomes to look for are:

- fewer physical fights
- fewer incidents of name calling and put-downs
- more incidents of students volunteering to help each other
- students excluding each other less
- students using one or more of the conflict resolution tools
- students making connections between this curriculum and conflicts outside the context of their own lives (for example, bringing in a conflict reported in the newspaper and analyzing it using conflict resolution tools)

Encouraging Self-Evaluation

Self-assessment is a valuable addition to creating a total picture of student learning. Encourage students to reflect on what they have learned and where they think they need to learn more. Journals are an ideal medium for self-reflection, but you might not be using journals as you teach *Conflict Resolution in the Middle School*. Try assigning one or two of the following questions as homework at an appropriate point in the curriculum.

Sample Self-Assessment Questions:

- What are three things you will remember from the conflict resolution course?
- What are the most important things you've learned from this course?
- What is a conflict resolution tool that you've used successfully?
- Describe what you now know about anger management that you didn't know when you started this course.
- List some of the things you say to yourself to keep your anger from getting out of control.
- What conflict style(s) did you use when you started this course? What new ones have you added? Describe how you have used them successfully.
- What's a question you still have about conflict resolution?

Part One: Essential Tools

Getting Started

LESSON IN BRIEF Students are introduced to the conflict unit and establish guidelines for working together.

NOTES This lesson sets the stage for the lessons that follow. Students are introduced to the topic of conflict resolution as they discuss some of the key issues in the unit using an Opinion Continuum. By establishing and discussing guidelines for working together, they are also beginning to put into practice the themes of caring, respect, and community. Finally, the activities raise questions and motivate students to learn more about conflict resolution.

OBJECTIVES Students will be able to:

- define "conflict";
- identify reasons for learning more about conflict and conflict resolution.

CONFLICT TOOL Identifying Conflict, Opinion Continuum

VOCABULARY *Conflict*—A dispute or disagreement between two or more people.

Conflict Resolution—Solving the problems created by conflict situations.

Put Downs—Disrespectful statements or actions that hurt, insult, or mock another person.

LESSON SEQUENCE
- Gathering (Optional)
- Agenda and Vocabulary Review
- Define Conflict and Introduce Unit
- Establish Group Guidelines
- The Opinion Continuum
- Any Additional Activities You May Choose
- Evaluation/Review of Key Points
- Closing (Optional)

TIME NEEDED One class period (minimum 40 minutes), depending on the additional activities you choose.

LEVEL: A/B/C
(5 MINUTES)

Gathering (Optional)

If you desire, choose a Gathering Activity from Appendix A.

LEVEL: A/B/C
(3 MINUTES)

Agenda and Vocabulary Review

Write the agenda on the board and review it with the class. Introduce any vocabulary in the lesson you think will be unfamiliar to your students.

LEVEL: A/B/C
(5 MINUTES)

Define Conflict and Introduce Unit

1. Define "conflict" as a dispute or disagreement between two or more people. Ask students for examples.

2. Give the students an overview of the unit:

For the next few weeks we will be learning more about conflict both in your own lives and in the world. We'll also learn about how to resolve conflicts. Everyone knows some ways of handling conflict, but often we—both young people and grown-ups—get "stuck" handling conflict in ways that aren't effective. Some people always avoid conflict, others always deal with conflict aggressively. In this unit we'll look at three aspects of conflict. Our first few lessons will be about understanding how conflicts start and get worse. The second set of lessons will focus on the skills needed to handle conflicts more effectively. In the third set of lessons we will examine how to use different conflict resolution styles.

3. If you will be continuing with the advanced skill lessons and special units, continue the overview:

After we have the basics down, we'll go into more depth with conflict and conflict resolution skills. We'll also look at how things like diversity, power, peer pressure, and violence are related to conflict.

LEVEL: A/B/C
(10 MINUTES)

Establish Group Guidelines

1. If you have not already done so, establish guidelines with the class for discussions. Explain the need to have clear guidelines for our work together. Talking about conflict can be personal, so no one will be asked to share anything they don't want to share. Also, part of resolving conflict non-violently (without fighting) is treating other people with respect. As a group, we need to be aware of how we treat each other.

2. Introduce the following guidelines for speaking and listening in class:

- Talk one at a time.
- Don't interrupt someone who is speaking.
- Be respectful of other people's opinions. Don't laugh at or put down other people or their contributions.
- Respect the privacy of others. Don't gossip about what others say.

- Try to stay with the topic.
- In small group work, try to stay on task and share the work.
- Say "I" when you speak of yourself.
- When you disagree with someone, state your opinion without attacking the other person.

Discuss each of these guidelines, one at a time. Clarify the meaning of each guideline, and ask students why it would be useful for class discussions.

3. Ask students for additional guidelines that they think should be added to the list. Have students explain why they think their additions are useful.

4. Once a list of guidelines is established, ask the class if they agree to abide by these guidelines.

LEVEL: A/B/C
(15 MINUTES)

The Opinion Continuum

MATERIALS. Either on the board or using tape on the floor, mark a continuum that goes from 1 to 10.

1. Explain that the class will be participating in an Opinion Continuum. You will read a series of statements and the students will place themselves on the Opinion Continuum based on the extent to which they agree or disagree with the statement (10=agree strongly, 1=disagree strongly, and 5=neutral, don't feel strongly one way or the other).

2. Explain that conflict is a part of life that many people—adults and young people—have mixed feelings about and a range of experience with—both good and bad. The statements you will be giving the class are common things people say about conflict. The students should give their own opinion—there are no right or wrong responses to the statements.

3. After you read one of the statements that follow and students have positioned themselves on the continuum, ask one of the students, "What are some reasons you choose that point on the continuum?" After the student has given an explanation, have him or her ask another student the same question. Continue until several students have given the reason for their choices before going on to another statement. After several opinions have been expressed ask, "Is there anyone who would now like to change his or her position on the continuum?"

Statements:

- Conflicts destroy relationships.
- In every conflict there's a winner and a loser.
- It's okay to tease people about how they look or act if you're just joking around.

- Conflict should be avoided at all costs.
- If you lose in a conflict, it's the same as losing face.
- Boys and girls have different styles of handling conflicts.
- It's important to stand up for what you believe in even if other people don't agree with you.
- It's important to stand up for what you believe in even if other people may try to harm you for doing so.
- If someone hits you, it's best to hit back.
- If you are in a conflict, it helps if you keep your feelings to yourself.
- People learn to be prejudiced against people who are different; they are not born prejudiced.

DISCUSSION

- What conclusions would you draw from this activity?
- Did anything happen that surprised you?
- Which statement did you find most challenging?

LEVEL: A/B/C
(5 MINUTES)

Evaluation/Review of Key Points

1. Evaluation: Go around the room and ask students to say one idea that will stay with them from today's class.

2. Review and summarize the key points of the lesson:

   - Conflict is a disagreement or dispute between two or more people.
   - Conflict is a natural part of life; everyone experiences conflict.
   - People have many feelings, opinions, and questions about conflict.

LEVEL: A/B/C
(5 MINUTES)

Closing (Optional)

If you so desire, choose a Closing Activity from Appendix B.

Additional Activity

LEVEL: A/B/C
(10 MINUTES)

Something I'd Like To Learn About Conflict Resolution

MATERIALS Newsprint

Ask students to think of something they'd particularly like to learn about conflict or conflict resolution. It can be in the form of a statement or a question. After a few minutes, have the class brainstorm a list of conflict resolution questions. Write these on newsprint. When the list is finished, post it and say that these are some of the questions that will be answered or that we will try to answer during the conflict resolution unit.

What is Conflict?

LESSON IN BRIEF	Students broaden their personal definitions of conflict as they explore various dimensions of conflict.
NOTES	For many students "conflict" equals "fighting," i.e., physical fighting. While fighting is certainly an aspect of conflict, conflict is much more than that. All too often, as a result of this narrow definition, many students do not even recognize that they are in a conflict until it becomes a fight. If young people are to learn to control their behavior in conflicts and prevent violence, they need a fuller understanding of conflict. The activities in this lesson help students broaden their definitions of conflict by beginning with and then building on what they already know.
OBJECTIVES	Students will be able to:

- define "conflict";
- identify several aspects of conflict that are not physical fighting.

CONFLICT TOOL	Identifying Conflict
VOCABULARY	*Conflict*—A dispute or disagreement between two or more people.
	Conflict resolution—Solving the problems created by conflict situations.
LESSON SEQUENCE	

- Gathering (Optional)
- Agenda and Vocabulary Review
- A Conflict I Saw...
- Web Charts
- Any Additional Activities You May Choose
- Evaluation/Review of Key Points
- Closing (Optional)

TIME NEEDED	One class period (minimum 40 minutes), depending on the additional activities you choose.
HANDOUTS	*Keep a Conflict Journal (Additional Activity)*

LEVEL: A/B/C
(5 MINUTES)

Gathering (Optional)

If you so desire, choose a Gathering Activity from Appendix A.

LEVEL: A/B/C
(2 MINUTES)

Agenda and Vocabulary Review

Write the agenda on the board and review it with the class. Introduce any vocabulary in the lesson with which you think they may need help.

LEVEL: A/B/C
(10 MINUTES)

A Conflict I Saw...

1. Have students work with a partner. Each partner takes two minutes to describe a conflict he or she saw. It can be a conflict at school, in the neighborhood, between adults, or between young people.

2. When both partners have finished, they should take a minute or two to list some of the key aspects of conflict based on their stories. Students will use these lists for the next activity.

Web Charts (Part 1)

> **Note:** *If students are unfamiliar with Web Charts, explain that they are a way of brainstorming that links related ideas. For more information on web charts, see Appendix D.*

LEVEL: A/B/C
(15 MINUTES)

1. Write the word "conflict" on the board and ask students what comes to mind when they hear the word. Use their contributions to create a web chart. For example:

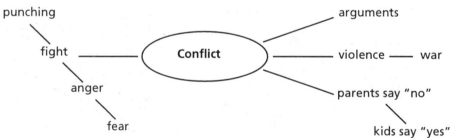

2. Continue the brainstorm as long as energy is high. When contributions begin to slow down, ask if there are any last additions, then discuss.

DISCUSSION

- Do you notice anything about the items in this web chart? (Chances are there won't be many positive things about conflict.)
- What does this tell you about conflict?
- Looking at this chart, what feelings go with conflict?
- Looking at this chart, what feelings do we have about conflict?
- Are there any positive things at all about conflict?

Web Charts (Part 2)

LEVEL: A/B/C
(20 MINUTES)

1. Divide students into working groups of three or four. Have each group create two web charts, one of negative things about conflict and another of positive things about conflict. If your students don't know how to make a web chart, they can create lists.

2. Begin the discussion of the webs by having each group share one item from their negative web. Each group should share something different. As they share, record their contributions on a large web chart on the board. When every group has contributed, go around the room once more and have each group share something else from their chart. Continue to record the contributions. Finally, open it up to anyone to add some final additions to the web chart.

3. Repeat this process with the positive web chart, recording on a new chart. When you are finished there will be a negative and positive chart in view. The pace of this sharing should be very fast.

DISCUSSION

- Looking at both of these web charts, what conclusions can you draw about conflict?
- What kinds of feelings do we have about conflict?
- Which chart was easier/more difficult?
- Why do we tend to think of negative things when we think about conflict?
- Where do we learn such negative ideas about conflict?
- Can you think of an example of a conflict that had a positive result?

4. Conclude with a mini-lecture.
It can be hard to think of positive things about conflict. Most of our lives we learn that conflict is negative and bad. And in fact, conflict can be very negative. This is destructive conflict. But conflict also has the potential to be used in a constructive way. That's one reason we'll be studying conflict and conflict resolution—to identify how to use conflict in a constructive way. The important things to learn from this activity are that conflict is a normal part of life—everyone of every age has conflicts—and that it can be dealt with in ways that are constructive, not destructive.

LEVEL: A/B/C
(5 MINUTES)

Evaluation/Review of Key Points

1. Evaluation: Based on today's discussion, have volunteers say one potential benefit of studying conflict and conflict resolution.

2. Review and summarize the key concepts of the lesson:

    • Conflict is a disagreement or dispute between two or more people.
    • Conflict is a natural part of life; everyone experiences conflict.
    • There are many negative things about conflict, but there are positive things as well.

LEVEL: A/B/C
(3 MINUTES)

Closing (Optional)

If you so desire, choose a Closing Activity from Appendix B.

Additional Activity

LEVEL: A/B/C
(TIME WILL VARY)

Conflict Journals

HANDOUTS   *Keep a Conflict Journal*

MATERIALS   Notebooks or loose pages for Conflict Folders

Throughout this unit it is helpful to have students keep Conflict Journals in which they record both conflicts they see or are involved in. These journals are not to be graded. Keeping a journal will help students become aware of the range of possible conflicts and become better observers of conflict. Journals are also a rich source of the "raw material" for many of the discussions in the conflict skill lessons. Conflicts from student journals can be reworked to substitute for many of the role-plays and case studies in this unit.

In the "Additional Activities" section of each conflict skill lesson, there are suggestions for journals. Have students keep their Conflict Journals in spiral bound notebooks or Conflict Folders by using loose pages of notebook paper kept in a folder. The *Keep A Conflict Journal* handout explains what information students should record in the journal and suggests that they *not* keep records of very personal conflicts, such as conflicts between parents. You will need to use your judgement on this. Do communicate to students that you will not be grading the journals, though you may comment in them, and that no one else will see the journal without the student's permission.

Keep a Conflict Journal

As we study conflict you will need to keep a conflict journal. This will be a record of conflicts you see, hear about, or are involved in. You will need a spiral notebook or loose notebook pages and binder to create a Conflict Folder.

For each conflict:

- Record a brief description of the conflict.
- List who's involved.
- Describe what the conflict is about.
- How did it start?
- How did it escalate or get worse?
- How does each person feel about it?
- What does each person want or need?
- If it has ended, how did it end?
- What type of conflict would you call this?
- Do you think it could have ended differently? If so, how?
- Finally, give your conflict a title.

We may use some of the conflicts in your journal for role-plays and case studies. The journal is a place for you to think about and practice some of the skills and ideas we study.

These journals will not be graded, though I will read them and may make comments in them. You will not be asked to share anything from your journal that you do not want to share. You might want to *not* record conflicts that are too personal to share, such as conflicts between your parents. If you want, feel free to change the names of the people involved.

3 Conflict Escalates

LESSON IN BRIEF	Students are introduced to the "Conflict Escalator" to help them understand how conflicts begin and escalate.
NOTES	When conflicts get worse we say they escalate. Escalation means that the positions of the disputants are more polarized, with more anger and bad feeling. All conflicts escalate in a step-by-step manner. To many students, however, conflict feels more like an express elevator. Once it starts, it goes immediately to the top. In fact, many students don't even recognize that they are in a conflict until it's near the top of the escalator. And unfortunately, the higher the conflict has escalated, the more difficult it is to de-escalate and resolve. The Conflict Escalator introduced in this lesson helps students think about how conflicts begin and what contributes to their escalation. This is an essential part of their learning to control their behavior in conflict situations.
OBJECTIVES	Students will be able to: • plot a conflict on the conflict escalator; • describe how feelings escalate during conflicts.
CONFLICT TOOL	Conflict Escalator
VOCABULARY	*Escalation*—The process by which a conflict gets worse.
LESSON SEQUENCE	• Gathering (Optional) • Agenda and Vocabulary Review • Introduce (or Review) the Conflict Escalator • Practice Using the Escalator • Any Additional Activities You May Choose • Evaluation/Review of Key Points • Closing (Optional)
TIME NEEDED	One class period (minimum 40 minutes), depending on the additional activities you choose.
HANDOUTS	*Going Up the Conflict Escalator; Conflict Escalator Skits (Level A: Missing the Mall, Level B: Three Dollar Dispute, Level C: The Big Betrayal); Conflict Escalator Case Studies (Level A: Hazard in the Hallway, Level B: Tape Player Trouble, Level C: Green-Eyed and Grouchy, Level A/B/C: Street Scene)*

LEVEL: A/B/C
(5 MINUTES)

Gathering (Optional)

If you so desire, choose a Gathering Activity from Appendix A.

LEVEL: A/B/C
(3 MINUTES)

Agenda and Vocabulary Review

Write the agenda on the board and review it with the class. Introduce any vocabulary in the lesson you think will be unfamiliar to your students.

LEVEL: A/B/C
(15 MINUTES)

Introduce (or Review) the Conflict Escalator

HANDOUTS *Conflict Escalator Skits* (Level A, B, or C); *Going Up the Conflict Escalator*

> **Note:** *If this is a review for students, acknowledge at the beginning that they may have been introduced to this concept previously. Explain that this lesson will delve into the concept in more depth.*

1. Introduce the term "escalate," relating it to "escalator." Explain that when a conflict gets worse, we say that it escalates. Distribute the *Going Up the Conflict Escalator* handout. Draw an escalator on the board as follows:

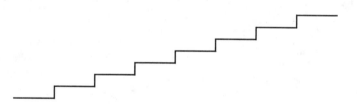

As you draw the escalator, explain that each step on the escalator is a behavior on the part of the people in the conflict that makes the conflict worse.

2. Distribute the appropriate escalator skit (level A, B, or C). Have volunteers act out the skit. Next, ask the class to identify the first step on the escalator, the second step, and so on. Write each step on the escalator you drew on the board. Continue until you reach the top of the escalator.

3. Review each step on the escalator and ask the class: What do you think the person was feeling at this step on the escalator? Write their responses underneath the step. There may be more than one feeling for a particular step. Emphasize that it is not just behavior that escalates during a conflict. Feelings also escalate. In fact, you could say feelings are the energy source that pushes the conflict escalator up.

4. Circle the top step and present the following mini-lecture:

    The higher you go on the escalator the harder it is to come down. The top of any conflict escalator is where the people in the conflict get into trouble, or walk away in a huff, or say they'll never speak to each other again, or get violent. In an international conflict, the top of the escalator is where wars happen. You can get down from the top of the escalator, but it's hard. Try not to go to the top of the escalator!

DISCUSSION

- When you're in a conflict, how do feelings affect the way you behave?
- What feelings most often come up for you in conflicts?
- How do feelings escalate as the conflict escalates?
- What examples have you seen of conflicts escalating?

LEVEL: A/B/C
(20 MINUTES)

Practice Using the Conflict Escalator

HANDOUTS *Conflict Escalator Case Studies* (Level A, B, or C)

Note: *This is a key concept in this curriculum, so allow students plenty of time to practice using the escalator.*

1. Divide students into pairs. Distribute the appropriate *Conflict Escalator Case Study* to each pair. Have them read the case study and plot it on the conflict escalator, placing conflict escalating behaviors on the top of each step and feelings underneath each step.

    Note: *These case studies are designed to fit very neatly onto the conflict escalators. A student may notice this and protest that it is unrealistic. Acknowledge the validity of this, but explain that these case studies are to help them practice the conflict escalator and get a feel for how conflicts escalate. They will be doing other, more "realistic" case studies later.*

    ### DISCUSSION

    - Describe how you plotted your conflict on the escalator.
    - What happens to behavior the higher you go on the escalator?
    - What happens to your feelings as the conflict escalates?
    - How did you and your partner handle any conflicts as you did the activity?

LEVEL: A/B/C
(3 MINUTES)

Evaluation/Review of Key Points

1. Have volunteers say one thing they think they will remember from this lesson.

2. Review and summarize the key concepts of the lesson:
    - When conflicts get worse we say that they escalate.
    - Each behavior in the conflict is a step on the escalator.
    - As conflicts escalate, so do the feelings in the conflict escalate.

LEVEL: A/B/C
(3 MINUTES)

Closing (Optional)

If you so desire, choose a Closing Activity from Appendix B.

Additional Activity

LEVEL: A/B/C
(TIME WILL VARY)

Conflict Journal Activity

As students continue to record conflicts in their conflict journals, ask them to choose one to plot on a conflict escalator. They should follow the guidelines on the *Going Up the Conflict Escalator* handout, plotting the behaviors in the conflict that contributed to the escalation. They should also note the feelings for each step on the escalator.

Going Up the Conflict Escalator

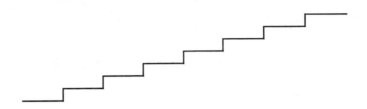

- Every behavior in the conflict is either a step up or a step down the conflict escalator.

- Behavior that makes the conflict worse will take it another step up the escalator.

- Every step up the conflict escalator has feelings that go with it. As the conflict escalates, so do the feelings.

- The higher you go on the escalator, the harder it is to come down.

Missing the Mall

CHARACTERS: Student 1 and Student 2, who have been planning to go to the mall together

SCENE: The sidewalk outside of Student 2's house.

STUDENT 1:   Hi! Are you ready to go?

STUDENT 2:   I'm not sure I want to go.

STUDENT 1:   What do you mean? We've been planning this. You said you wanted to go.

STUDENT 2:   Only because you pressured me. You never want to do anything different.

STUDENT 1:   You always back out of things. You can't be trusted.

STUDENT 2:   You never want to do anything new—or anything I want to do.

STUDENT 1:   I'm going without you.

STUDENT 2:   Fine!

Three Dollar Dispute

CHARACTERS: Student 1 who lent Student 2 three dollars last week.

SCENE: The hallway in school.

STUDENT 1:   Remember the three dollars I lent you? I need it back.

STUDENT 2:   Okay. I'll get it for you.

STUDENT 1:   I need it now.

STUDENT 2:   I don't have it now.

STUDENT 1:   You owe me. Give it to me.

STUDENT 2:   You didn't tell me you needed it today. I don't have it.

STUDENT 1:   You hoped I'd forget about it. You weren't ever going to pay me.

STUDENT 2:   Are you calling me a thief?

STUDENT 1:   You just better get me the money by the end of the day!

STUDENT 2:   Or what?

STUDENT 1:   Or meet me after school!

The Big Betrayal

CHARACTERS: Student 1 and Student 2 who have been close friends.

SCENE: Student 1 confronts Student 2 in the hallway.

STUDENT 1: (Very sarcastically) Thanks a lot!

STUDENT 2: What did I do?

STUDENT 1: I can't believe you told everyone about Ronnie and I breaking up. It was secret!

STUDENT 2: I didn't tell anyone.

STUDENT 1: That is so typical of you. First you betray me, then you deny it.

STUDENT 2: Don't blame me because you can't keep a relationship. I didn't tell anyone.

STUDENT 1: You are such a liar!

STUDENT 2: Oh, right! Like I'm a liar compared to you. No wonder you lost Ronnie. Get out of my way, I'm going to class.

STUDENT 1: I'm going to get you later...

STUDENT 2: (Sarcastically) Oh, I'm so scared!

Hazards In the Hallway

Edward was running down the hall in a hurry to get to his class. He bumped into Marcus who was standing by his locker and knocked the books out of his hand.

"I'm sorry," he said.

"Why don't you watch where you're going," said Marcus.

"I said I was sorry," said Edward. "It was an accident."

"If you're so clumsy, you ought to have a nurse to hold your hand."

Marcus bent over to pick up his books. Edward said, "Oh yeah, like I'm clumsy compared to you. You can't even hold on to your books."

"Everyone knows you're a walking disaster area," Marcus said.

Edward knocked the books out of Marcus' hands and walked into his classroom.

Tape Player Trouble

Sharone lent Rachel her portable tape player. Rachel tried three different tapes in it and it chewed up each of them. The next day at school Rachel confronted Sharone.

"Your tape player ruined three of my tapes. You owe me for those tapes," she said.

"What do you mean it ruined your tapes? It never ruined mine. What did you do to it?" Sharone asked.

"I just tried to play my tapes. That tape player is cheap like all the stuff you have. It ruined my favorite tapes."

"I can't believe this. I lent you my tape player because yours was broken and now you're mad at me? I did you a favor!"

"Some favor. Here's your piece of junk," Rachel said, throwing the tape player on Sharone's desk. The tape player fell off the desk and landed on the floor. The cover broke.

"Look what you did. You're going to buy me a new tape player!" Sharone yelled.

"No I'm not! You're going to buy me new tapes!" Rachel yelled back.

Green-Eyed and Grouchy

James and Darnell have been friends for years, but recently they haven't seen much of each other since Darnell started going with Kindra. James missed hanging out with his friend. He didn't like Kindra that much, but thought that since she and Darnell were definitely a couple, he might as well be friendly towards her. He started going out of his way to be nice to her, talking to her between classes.

One day Darnell confronted him in the hallway. "Don't think I don't know what you're doing," he said angrily.

"What do you mean?" James asked.

"Don't act all innocent with me. I've got eyes. Everyone knows you're coming on to Kindra."

"I was just being friendly," James protested.

"Yeah, sure. You're trying to steal her away. You're just jealous because she's my girlfriend."

"Jealous! You're the one acting like a jealous fool. You're a green-eyed monster. You see things that aren't even there!"

"Man, I thought you were my friend. You've always been jealous of me."

James couldn't stand the superior look Darnell had on his face when he said that. "Jealous of you. There's nothing to be jealous of. You've got nothing I want."

"Well, you'd better stay away from Kindra or you'll be sorry," Darnell warned.

"Like I'm scared of you," James said and walked away.

Street Scene

Jamal and Clare were walking out of school when they spotted a crowd of kids gathering across the street.

"Let's see what's happening," said Clare and the two of them hurried over. At the center of the group were two boys shouting at each other. Different kids in the group were yelling encouragement to each of the boys.

"He's lying, Leroy. He's telling everyone lies about you," said one bystander.

"They're not lies, Andy," countered another. "You're just telling the truth about that boy Leroy."

By this time Andy and Leroy were circling around each other.

"Show him what you can do!" shouted another.

Leroy lunged at Andy, who grabbed Leroy and tried to wrestle him to the ground. The fight was on!

"Fight! Fight!" shouted the crowd. More and more kids joined the group.

"Come on," said Jamal to Clare. "Let's get out of here."

"No, I want to see what happens," said Clare.

The crowd pushed in closer to the two boys, all the while shouting encouragement to both of them. Suddenly someone said, "He's got a knife!"

"Let's go!" Jamal insisted.

"No!" said Clare. "I want to see."

CHAPTER **4**	# What Makes Conflict Escalate?

LESSON IN BRIEF   Students review the Conflict Escalator and identify those behaviors that contribute to conflict escalating.

NOTES   Conflicts escalate or de-escalate because of the behavior of the people involved. Some behaviors, like name-calling, are almost guaranteed to escalate a conflict. Others are more subtle. For young people, learning which behaviors are likely to escalate conflicts is an important step in learning to control their behavior in conflict. A point to emphasize during discussions in this lesson is that we want to avoid escalating conflict—the more a conflict escalates the more difficult it is to de-escalate. This is not the same as avoiding conflict. Conflict is a fact of life and should be dealt with, but in a way that doesn't lead to escalation.

OBJECTIVES   Students will be able to:

- identify behaviors that contribute to a conflict escalating;
- describe how feelings escalate during conflicts.

CONFLICT TOOL   Conflict Escalator

VOCABULARY   *Escalation*—The process by which a conflict gets worse.

LESSON SEQUENCE
- Gathering (Optional)
- Agenda and Vocabulary Review
- Identify Escalating Behavior
- Any Additional Activities You May Choose
- Evaluation/Review of Key Points
- Closing (Optional)

TIME NEEDED   One class period (minimum 40 minutes), depending on the additional activities you choose.

HANDOUTS   *Some Conflict Escalators, Going Up the Conflict Escalator Sort Cards*

MATERIALS   Paper signs for Conflict Escalators (Additional Activity)

<table>
<tr><td>LEVEL: A/B/C
(5 MINUTES)</td><td>

Gathering (Optional)

If you so desire, choose a Gathering Activity from Appendix A.
</td></tr>
</table>

LEVEL: A/B/C
(5 MINUTES)

Gathering (Optional)

If you so desire, choose a Gathering Activity from Appendix A.

LEVEL: A/B/C
(3 MINUTES)

Agenda and Vocabulary Review

Write the agenda on the board and review it with the class. Introduce any vocabulary in the lesson you think will be unfamiliar to your students.

LEVEL: A/B/C
(20 MINUTES)

Identifying Escalating Behavior

1. Have students work in pairs and take two minutes to answer the question: When you are in a conflict, what sends you up the escalator?

2. Have the class come together to brainstorm a list of "Conflict Escalating Behaviors." Record these on chart paper or poster board to keep for later discussions.

3. Organize students into microlab groups. Have each student in the group take two minutes to comment on the following:

   • What conflict escalators do you hear most often at school? At home?
   • Which escalating behaviors really anger you?
   • Which escalating behaviors can you shrug off?
   • Why do some really bother you while others don't?

   DISCUSSION

   • What did you learn about conflict escalators in this activity?

LEVEL: A/B/C
(10 MINUTES)

Classifying Conflict Escalating Statements

HANDOUTS   *Some Conflict Escalators, Going Up the Conflict Escalator Sort Cards*

Note: *For an alternate way to do this activity see "Additional Activities."*

1. Have students remain in their microlab groups. Distribute the *Some Conflict Escalators* handout and ask students to compare the handout with the list they generated.

2. Give each student one of the *Conflict Escalator Sort Cards*. Explain that each card has a statement that represents *at least* one of the behavior types described on the handout. Some contain more than one escalator, and some can fit in more than one category. In their microlab groups have students discuss each statement and classify it in one or more of the conflict escalator categories.

   DISCUSSION

   • How did you classify your statements?
   • When you heard some of these statements, what kinds of feelings did you have?

- What statements did your group disagree about? How did you handle that disagreement?
- Have you ever said a statement like one of these? What happened when you did?

LEVEL: A/B/C
(5 MINUTES)

Evaluation/Review of Key Points

1. Ask students to think about one thing they liked about today's lesson and one thing they would have liked to be better. Ask a few volunteers to share.

2. Review and summarize the key points of this lesson:

   - When conflict escalates it gets worse.
   - Both behavior and feelings escalate.
   - There are specific behaviors that are likely to cause conflicts to escalate.

LEVEL: A/B/C
(5 MINUTES)

Closing (Optional)

If you so desire, choose a Closing Activity from Appendix B.

Additional Activities

LEVEL: A/B/C
(TIME WILL VARY)

Conflict Journal Activities

Using a conflict they've already recorded, have students plot it on an escalator and identify the specific types of conflict escalators that were present. What was the effect of these escalators?

Also, have students look for specific escalating behaviors and statements and record them in their journals. How do people respond to the escalators?

LEVEL: A/B/C
(20 MINUTES)

Classifying Conflict Escalators

HANDOUTS *Some Conflict Escalators, Going Up the Conflict Escalator Sort Cards*

MATERIALS *One paper sign for each of the Conflict Escalators*

Note: *This is a more physically active version of the activity in the lesson. It takes more time than the one in the lesson.*

1. Distribute the *Some Conflict Escalators* handout and ask students to compare the handout with the list they generated. Post the Conflict Escalator signs around the room.

2. Give each student one of the *Conflict Escalator Sort Cards*. Explain that each card has a statement that represents *at least* one of the behavior types described on the handout. Some contain more than one escalator and some can fit in more than one category. Have students think about their statements and how they would classify them in one or more of

the conflict escalator's categories.

3. Once students have decided how they would classify their statement, have students stand and move to the appropriate sign. Once everyone has moved, ask each student to read his or her statement and explain why he or she chose that category.

DISCUSSION

- How did you classify your statements?
- Why did you choose that category?
- What other categories might it have fit in?
- What feelings do these statements bring up?
- Have you ever said a statement like one of these? What happened when you did?

Some Conflict Escalators

When we asked middle school students across the country what sent *them* up the conflict escalator, here are five behaviors that came up again and again:

Bulldozing

Trying to "run-over" and intimidate the other person by accusing, shouting, name-calling, swearing, threatening, taunting, and other kinds of aggressive behavior.

Conflict Archeology

Bringing up past failures or wrongdoing that are not about the current conflict. This keeps people from focusing on the problem at hand.

Global Statements

Using general words like "always," "never," and "every time" instead of being specific. Global statements usually start with the word "you."

Counter Attack

Attacking the other person's personality instead of trying to solve the problem. Thinking of complaints to throw back instead of listening to the other person's point of view.

Above It All

Acting above all this. Not listening or trying to solve the problem. Thinking, "It would be beneath me to deal with this petty little problem."

Going Up the Escalator
Sort Cards

You are always late. I don't know why I even bother planning things with you. You can't be depended upon.

Remember the time you borrowed my basketball and put a hole in it? And when you cracked my C.D. that I just bought? This is just like then.

If you weren't so selfish this never would have happened. You never think of anyone but yourself.

You are such a jerk. No wonder no one wants to be friends with you.

I can't believe you're this upset by this. It's such a little thing.

I don't know how you expect me to talk things out with you when your breath smells the way it does. Have you thought about seeing a dentist about it?

Oh yeah? Well I'll get my friends to help me and you'll see what trouble is.

How about the number of times I've had to wait for you? I can't count them!

I haven't got time for this. I have important things to do.

I suppose in your family people act like that when they're angry.

This is just like the time in the fourth grade when you said you'd help me but then you never showed up.

(Sarcastically) Yeah, like you are known for being able to keep a secret. That's why so many people trust you.

(Shouting) Get out of here or you're going to get it!

Remember when you said we could work together on the science project and you went ahead without me? This it like that. And also the time you promised I could go with your family to the lake, and then you said the car was full. You always break your word.

You started it. This never would have happened if it hadn't been for you.

Oh yeah, like I'm scared of you. You're too chicken to even try it.

Don't blame me. If you'd done what you were supposed to this wouldn't have happened in the first place.

Your mother...

You always get so uptight over such little things. I can't believe you took that seriously.

You can't be trusted. You always back out at the last minute.

Shut up! Shut Up! SHUT UP!

I've trusted you in the past and you've always let me down. I'll never trust you again.

You worry about the stupidest stuff. Why don't you get a life?

This is so typical of you. You only think of yourself.

You're a pig and so's your mother.

Well if you weren't such a clumsy cow it wouldn't have broken in the first place.

You dirty $*&%@*!$#%*&!$!!! (Say, "Blankity, blank, blank!)

Whatever...

This is just like the time in elementary school you borrowed my bike and wrecked it.

S T U D E N T H A N D O U T

You can't be trusted with anything.

Oh yeah, well you're not so perfect yourself. There's lots of times things I wanted got screwed up because of you.

Why don't you quit acting like a third grader and just grow up?

That was your girlfriend you were with? I thought it was your dog.

You're just dumb, dumber, and dumbest all rolled into one.

You ought to run for office. You can be class jerk.

No I'm not going to listen to your side. I'm not interested in talking anything out with you. Just leave me alone.

Why should I listen to you? I'm already bored enough.

(Sarcastically) Oh, you have an idea how we can work it out? Gee, I'm all ears.

Your side? Go tell it to someone who cares.

Listen, I know where you live and I don't forget things, so you diss me and you're just asking for it.

You're just a chicken, that's all.

Are you going to meet me after school or are you going to run home to your mommy-wommy?

This is a nonverbal one: in a very exaggerated way, roll your eyes and make a big sigh.

5 Anger on the Conflict Escalator

LESSON IN BRIEF	Students explore degrees of anger and the role anger and other feelings play in conflict.
NOTES	Of all the possible emotions in a conflict situation, anger is the one that gives students the most trouble. This lesson is based on the premise that anger is a normal and natural emotion and that it is not bad to feel angry. It's how we handle anger that makes it positive or negative. In this lesson, students explore anger by discussing degrees of anger and identifying anger cues and triggers. Anger is not, of course, the only emotion in conflict. You may find that your students need help identifying or talking about a range of feelings. Some of the additional activities can be used in this case.
OBJECTIVES	Students will be able to:

- identify anger triggers;
- identify at least five Degrees of Anger.

CONFLICT TOOL	Anger Thermometer/Anger Continuum
PREREQUISITE	Conflict Escalator (Skill Lesson 3)
VOCABULARY	*Anger cues*—The physical signs of anger.
	Anger triggers—The things that make a person angry.
LESSON SEQUENCE	

- Gathering (Optional)
- Agenda and Vocabulary Review
- Recognizing Anger Cues and Triggers
- Identify Degrees of Anger or the Anger Sort
- Any Additional Activities You May Choose
- Evaluation/Review of Key Points
- Closing (Optional)

TIME NEEDED	One class period (minimum 40 minutes), depending on the additional activities you choose.
HANDOUTS	*Anger Thermometer, Anger Sort Cards, Rate Yourself on the Anger Thermometer (Additional Activity)*
MATERIALS	Masking tape, three sets of five 8 1/2" x 11" cards

LEVEL: A/B/C
(5 MINUTES)

Gathering (Optional)

If you so desire, choose a Gathering Activity from Appendix A.

LEVEL: A/B/C
(3 MINUTES)

Agenda and Vocabulary Review

Write the agenda on the board and review it with the class. Introduce any vocabulary in the lesson you think will be unfamiliar to your students.

INTRODUCTION
LEVEL: A
(15 MINUTES)
REVIEW
LEVEL: B/C
(10 MINUTES)

Recognizing Anger Cues and Triggers

Note: *If this is a review for students, acknowledge at the beginning that they may have been introduced to this concept previously. Explain that this lesson will go into the concept in more depth.*

1. Write the word "anger" on the board and draw a circle around it. Explain that anger is a normal and natural emotion. Everyone feels angry at one time or another. The point is to not let anger become destructive. The first step in calming down is recognizing when you are angry.

2. Explain that anger cues are the physical signs that let you know you're angry. Ask students how they know when they are angry: What are their anger cues? Encourage them to use sensory words. As students make contributions, construct a web chart of anger cues.

   DISCUSSION

   - Do there seem to be categories of anger cues? (e.g.: physical, verbal, facial signs)
   - Which of these anger cues do you associate with a mild form of anger, such as being annoyed or irritated?
   - Which do you associate with more intense anger—being enraged?

3. Have students brainstorm a list of things that make them angry. Record this list on the board next to the anger cues web chart. Label the list "Anger Triggers." This activity can go on for a long time, but keep it short—only five minutes or so. Students will get other chances to discuss anger triggers.

   Note: *If you have time, step 3 and the discussion following this activity makes a good microlab.*

   DISCUSSION

   - Do some anger triggers have more power to make you angry than others?
   - Which ones?
   - (Choose an example from the list that would evoke intense anger.) What kind of anger would this cause?
   - (Choose an example from the list that would evoke mild anger.) What kind of anger would this cause?

LEVEL: A
(15 MINUTES)

Identify Degrees of Anger

HANDOUT   *Anger Thermometer*

MATERIALS   Masking tape; three sets of five 8-1/2 x 11 inch cards with the following words on the cards: annoyed, irritated, angry, furious, enraged.

1.   Explain that different anger triggers lead to different degrees of anger. There are words to describe these degrees of anger, words like irritated, livid, annoyed, furious, etc. Knowing these words can help in handling anger when we get into conflict situations.

2.   Ask for three volunteers to come to the board. Give each volunteer a set of anger vocabulary cards. Have them tape the cards to the board in a vertical line in order from least angry on the bottom to most angry at the top.

3.   When all three have finished, have the class compare the three sets of cards. Discuss as suggested below. After discussion, introduce the Anger Thermometer as a way of thinking about degrees of anger.

4.   Have students find a partner. Distribute the *Anger Thermometer* handout. Give each student two minutes to discuss the following questions.

DISCUSSION

*   What differences and similarities do you see in the three lists of words?
*   What is something from the Anger Triggers list that would make you feel annoyed?
*   What is something from the Anger Triggers list that would make you feel livid?
*   How does the Anger Thermometer compare with the lists on the board?
*   The Anger Thermometer compares being angry to being hot. The angrier you are the hotter you are. Does this comparison make sense to you?

LEVEL: B/C
(20 MINUTES)

Anger Sort

HANDOUTS   *Anger Sort Cards,* cut up and placed in an envelope. You will need one set of cards for each group of three or four students.

1.   Explain that different Anger Triggers lead to different degrees of anger. There are words to describe these degrees of anger, words like irritated, livid, annoyed, furious, etc. Knowing these words can help in handling anger when we get into conflict situations.

2.   Divide students into working groups of three or four. Give each group an envelope of *Anger Sort Cards* and explain the task:

Each envelope contains cards with words on them. All of the words are related to anger. As a group, I would like you to arrange the cards in the order you think represents the least angry to the most angry. If there are some cards that your group thinks do not belong on the list, put them where you think they do belong. Everyone in the group should be ready to explain why each word is placed where it is. For many of these words there is no right answer, so your group will have to discuss and decide what you think.

3. Give students about ten minutes to arrange their words. Circulate to help those that have problems working as a group or who are unfamiliar with the words.

DISCUSSION

- What word did you think was the least angry?
- What word did you think was the most angry?
- What words gave the group the most trouble?
- Did everyone in your group agree?
- What words did you decide didn't belong with the others?
- How do those words relate to anger?
- How does the Anger Continuum compare to your group's arrangement of the words?
- What is something from the Anger Triggers list that would make you feel annoyed?
- What is something from the Anger Triggers list that would make you feel livid?

4. After discussing the activity, introduce the Anger Continuum: Annoyed, Irritated, Angry, Furious, and Enraged positioned on a horizontal line. Explain that the continuum places these words in order from least angry to most angry and is a way students can determine how angry they are.

LEVEL: A/B/C
(5 MINUTES)

Evaluation/Review of Key Points

1. Ask volunteers what's one thing they liked about this lesson? What's one thing they would have liked to be different?

2. Summarize the key points in this lesson:

- Anger is a normal emotion. It is how we express it that makes it "positive" or "negative."
- Calming yourself is the first step in de-escalating conflict.
- Anger that is very intense causes people in conflicts to act impulsively and do things they may later regret.

LEVEL: A/B/C
(5 MINUTES)

Closing (Optional)

If you so desire, choose a Closing Activity from Appendix B.

Additional Activities

LEVEL: A/B/C
(TIME WILL VARY)

Conflict Journal Activities

Note: *These are good homework activities.*

Have students choose a journal entry and describe how anger (and other emotions) played a role. For example, did the participants in the conflict go steadily up the thermometer (or continuum)? Did other feelings precede the anger? How did they calm down?

An alternative journal activity is to have students record ten different examples of people getting angry. When they have ten, have them analyze those examples: What kinds of anger cues did they observe? What were the Anger Triggers? Were other feelings observable besides anger? How did the people calm down?

LEVEL: A/B/C
(15 MINUTES)

More Practice with the Thermometer/Continuum[*]

HANDOUTS   *Rate Yourself on the Anger Thermometer*

Note: *This is a good homework activity.*

Have students complete the handout individually. Then pair them up to compare responses. Have each pair choose four situations and identify ways to cool down the thermometer.

A variation on this activity is to make a sign for each word on the thermometer or continuum. Instead of distributing the handout, read each item aloud and have the students place themselves on the continuum.

---

[*]   This activity is adapted from one developed by Carol Wintle.

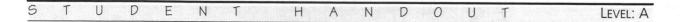

The Anger Thermometer

In some ways anger
is like a thermometer.

It has degrees,
from cool to very hot.

The higher you go
on the Anger Thermometer,
the angrier you are!

Try to cool off
and bring yourself down
the Anger Thermometer.

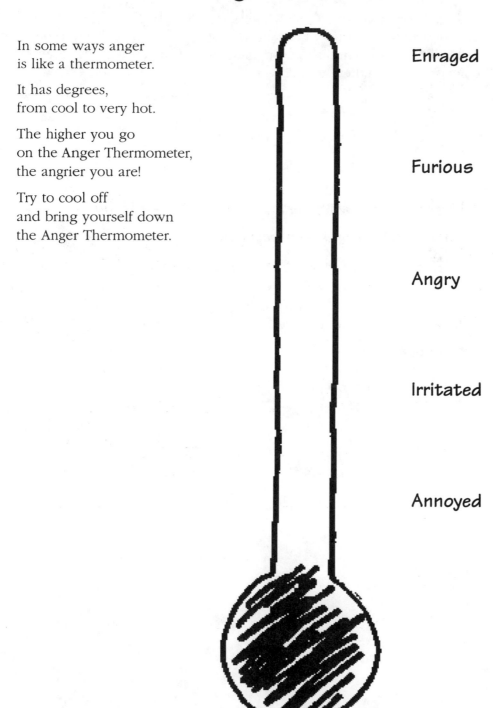

Enraged

Furious

Angry

Irritated

Annoyed

Anger Sort Cards

Angry	Irritated
Annoyed	Enraged
Livid	Mad
Irate	Furious
Grouchy	Helpless

Rate Yourself
on the Anger Thermometer

1. When someone tells on me I feel...

    Annoyed   Irritated   Angry   Livid   Enraged

2. When someone borrows something of mine and breaks it I feel...

    Annoyed   Irritated   Angry   Livid   Enraged

3. When someone gets me into trouble I feel...

    Annoyed   Irritated   Angry   Livid   Enraged

4. When I'm accused of something I didn't do, I feel...

    Annoyed   Irritated   Angry   Livid   Enraged

5. When a friend doesn't listen to me when I talk, I feel...

    Annoyed   Irritated   Angry   Livid   Enraged

6. When someone makes fun of someone in my family, I feel...

    Annoyed   Irritated   Angry   Livid   Enraged

7. When a friend doesn't keep a secret that's important to me, I feel...

    Annoyed   Irritated   Angry   Livid   Enraged

8. Think of one of your own_____

    Annoyed   Irritated   Angry   Livid   Enraged

Dealing with Anger in Conflict

LESSON IN BRIEF Students explore ways of cooling down and handling anger in conflicts.

NOTES This lesson begins the de-escalating sequence in this curriculum. Having talked about going up the conflict escalator, the next few lessons introduce students to the skills they need to come *down* the conflict escalator. Cooling off or getting control over anger is the first step in de-escalating conflict. No one can resolve a conflict when they're enraged. As in the previous lessons, it's important to emphasize during discussions that anger is a normal and natural emotion. What we want students to do is calm down to a point where they can control their destructive impulses when they feel angry. Middle school students often feel, to varying degrees, helpless in the face of their anger and other people's anger. This lesson aims to demystify anger and help students see that they can get it under control.

OBJECTIVES Students will be able to:
- describe how controlling anger contributes to de-escalating conflict;
- discuss positive and negative ways to handle anger;
- identify three Calm Down techniques.

CONFLICT TOOL Anger Thermometer/Anger Continuum

PREREQUISITE Conflict Escalator (Conflict Skill Lesson 3)

VOCABULARY *Anger cues*—The physical signs of anger.

Anger trigger—The things that make a person angry.

LESSON SEQUENCE
- Gathering (Optional)
- Agenda and Vocabulary Review
- Calming Down (Level A or B/C)
- Think/Pair-Share on Dealing With Anger
- Any Additional Activities You May Choose
- Evaluation/Review of Key Points
- Closing (Optional)

TIME NEEDED One class period (minimum 40 minutes), depending on the additional activities you choose.

HANDOUTS *Anger Thought Balloons, Calming Down, More Practice Dealing with Anger*

LEVEL: A/B/C
(5 MINUTES)

Gathering (Optional)

If you so desire, choose a Gathering Activity from Appendix A.

LEVEL: A/B/C
(5 MINUTES)

Agenda and Vocabulary Review

Write the agenda on the board and review it with the class. Introduce any vocabulary in the lesson you think will be unfamiliar to your students.

Calming Down (Level A)

LEVEL: A
(20 MINUTES)

HANDOUTS *Anger Thought Balloons*

1. Explain that calming down is the first step down the escalator, because if we don't calm ourselves we act impulsively in conflicts—that is, we act without thinking through the consequences of our actions. Ask: What are some of the consequences when people in conflicts act impulsively out of anger? (Violence, physical fighting, saying things that will be regretted, etc.)

2. Remind students of the Anger Thermometer. Explain: Calming down or cooling off is like bringing the mercury in the thermometer down. The less "hot" the anger is, the more you can control it. Then you will be ready to deal with the conflict.

3. Have students brainstorm a list of ways they use to calm themselves when they are angry. Before you begin the list, ask them to limit themselves to "healthy ways" to calm themselves, i.e., activities that do not harm either themselves or others.

4. Distribute the *Anger Thought Balloons* handout. Discuss each step of the handout with students, leading them through the appropriate activity, e.g., deep breathing and muscle relaxation. Encourage students to add to the suggestions on the handout in the spaces provided.

DISCUSSION

- How do the ways of calming yourself that you brainstormed fit into these categories?
- What would you add to the suggestions on this handout?

Calming Down (Level B/C)

LEVEL: B/C
(20 MINUTES)

HANDOUTS *Calming Down*

1. Explain that calming down is the first step down the escalator because if we don't calm ourselves we act impulsively in conflicts—that is, we act without thinking through the consequences of our actions. Ask: What are some of the consequences when people in conflicts act impulsively out of anger? (Violence, physical fighting, saying things that will be regretted, etc.)

2. Have students brainstorm a list of ways they use to calm themselves when they are angry. Before you begin the list ask them to limit themselves to "healthy ways" to calm themselves, i.e., activities that do not harm either themselves or others. Record their contributions on the board and refer to them in the next steps.

3. Review the list and have the class determine whether the calming behavior is positive or negative. "Positive" behavior is calming and doesn't hurt oneself or another. "Negative" behavior does hurt or has potential to hurt oneself or another.

4. Distribute the *Calming Down* handout. Present the following mini-lecture:
   Psychologists have determined three main ways of calming down. One is to physically relax the body. On the handout, deep breathing and muscle relaxing are examples for physically relaxing. The other way is to calm the mind by thinking of something else or distracting yourself from the anger. Counting backwards from ten, thinking of peaceful things, and taking a walk are other examples of calming the mind. The third way is to talk to yourself.

5. Discuss the handout with students. As you do, lead them through deep breathing and muscle relaxation. Encourage students to add to the suggestions on the handout.

DISCUSSION

- How do the ways of calming yourself that you brainstormed fit into these categories?
- What would you add to the suggestions on this handout?
- Can you give an example of a time you used one of these techniques when you were in a conflict situation?
- Which calming techniques feel most comfortable to you? Which would you be most likely to use?

LEVEL: A/B/C
(10 MINUTES)

Think/Pair-Share on Dealing with Anger

1. Have students get into pairs. Each student takes two minutes to discuss the following:

- Can you give an example of a time you used one of these calming techniques when you were in a conflict situation?
- Which calming techniques feel most comfortable to you? Which would you be most likely to use?

DISCUSSION

- Is anyone willing to share what they discussed?
- Do you have any reactions to the activity?

LEVEL: A/B/C
(5 MINUTES)

Evaluation/Review of Key Points

Ask students to summarize the following key points in this lesson.

- Anger is a normal emotion. It is how we express it that makes it "positive" or "negative."

- Calming yourself is the first step in de-escalating conflict.

- There are three main ways to calm yourself: relax the body, calm the mind, talk to yourself.

- Calming yourself does not mean you won't be angry or that anger is necessarily bad. It simply means that to deal with the conflict your anger must be under control.

LEVEL: A/B/C
(5 MINUTES)

Closing (Optional)

If you so desire, choose a Closing Activity from Appendix B.

Additional Activities

LEVEL: A/B/C
(20 MINUTES)

More Practice Expressing Anger

HANDOUTS *More Practice Dealing with Anger Cards*, one set for each group

Divide students into work groups. Give each group a set of cards. Have students take turns drawing cards, reading them to the group, and saying how angry they would be (on the thermometer or the continuum), what they would do to calm down, and what they would say to the person. If you have time, you might have each student respond to each situation.

LEVEL: A/B/C
(15 MINUTES)

Guidelines for Dealing with Other People's Anger

Divide students to form microlab groups of three or four. Each group should choose a reporter who will record the group's discussion and report back to the class.

Each student should take two minutes to address the following:

- Tell about a time you were in a conflict with someone who was angry with you...
- How did you deal with that person's anger? What happened?
- What are some ways you've found helpful when other people are angry?

DISCUSSION

- What were some of the ideas your group had about dealing with angry people?
- How were your ideas similar to or different from the conflict escalators we discussed earlier?

LEVEL: A/B/C
(TIME WILL VARY)

Conflict Journal Activity

Note: *This is a good homework activity.*

Have students experiment with different ways of calming down in their daily lives. In their journals they can record their experiences: what was successful, what wasn't, how other people responded, etc.

Anger Thought Balloons

Recognize Anger Cues:

How does my body feel?

Hey, I'm getting angry!!

Distract Yourself:

10-9-8-7-6...

I really liked being at the lake this weekend.

Relax Your Body:

Breathe out the anger...
Breathe in calm...

I am relaxing my muscles.

Talk to Yourself:

I am in control of myself...
I'm not losing it!

I'm coming down the anger thermometer.

Calming Down

Calming Down

Calming Down

Psychologists who have studied anger recommend the following steps in calming down:

1. Recognize the **Anger Cues**—your body will tell you when you're getting angry.

2. There are three basic ways of calming down:

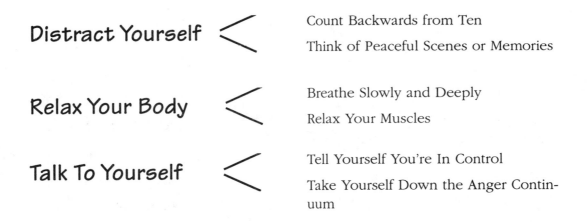

Distract Yourself
- Count Backwards from Ten
- Think of Peaceful Scenes or Memories

Relax Your Body
- Breathe Slowly and Deeply
- Relax Your Muscles

Talk To Yourself
- Tell Yourself You're In Control
- Take Yourself Down the Anger Continuum

3. Name the **Triggers** to your anger, both external and internal.

4. Later, **Reflect**—What can you learn from this experience of anger?

More Practice Dealing with Anger

A friend grabs a CD while you are showing it to another friend.

A classmate never listens when you talk. He/she interrupts and acts like you haven't said anything.

You have a pimple on your chin, and one guy points it out to the whole class.

A classmate keeps calling you "Gumby Head."

A friend won't listen to any ideas other than his or her own. She or he insists on being in charge of every situation.

A friend borrows things from you and doesn't return them.

A teacher jumps on you for talking in class but lets other kids get away with it.

A kid is always putting you down. He says he's joking.

A classmate wants to copy your work.

You know that a classmate has been accusing you of things behind your back.

A friend borrows books, CDs, and clothes, but never returns them.

A classmate is nice to you when some students are around, but not others.

De-escalating Conflict with "I" Messages

LESSON IN BRIEF	Students practice making "I" Messages and discuss their value in de-escalating conflict.
NOTES	"I" Messages or "I" Statements are a way of communicating feeling without blaming or being aggressive. They are based on a simple format that goes: "I feel_____when_____ because_____." Speaking from one's own perspective in this manner can communicate the feeling without escalating the conflict. This is very different from "You" Messages, which are often blaming, accusing, or in some way aggressive and escalating. Some middle school students have had extensive experience with "I" Messages. If this is true for your students, this lesson can be made a review. Many subsequent lessons make use of "I" Messages, so be sure your students have a good grasp of this skill.
OBJECTIVES	Students will be able to: • explain what an "I" Message is; • compare the effects of "I" Messages to other ways of communicating feelings; • make "I" Messages for a hypothetical conflict situation.
CONFLICT TOOL	"I" Message
PREREQUISITE	Conflict Escalator (Conflict Skill Lesson 3)
VOCABULARY	*De-escalate*—The process by which conflicts become less volatile. *"I" Message*—A sentence format to communicate feeling: "I feel _____ when _____ because _____."
LESSON SEQUENCE	• Gathering (Optional) • Agenda and Vocabulary Review • Introduce (or Review) "I" Messages • Practice Using "I" Messages • Any Additional Activities You May Choose • Evaluation/Review of Key Points • Closing (Optional)
TIME NEEDED	One class period (minimum 40 minutes), depending on the additional activities you choose.
HANDOUTS	*Roommate Rumpus, Part 1; Roommate Rumpus, Part 2; More Practice Making "I" Messages (Additional Activity)*

Level: A/B/C
(5 minutes)

Gathering (Optional)

If you so desire, choose a Gathering Activity from Appendix A.

Level: A/B/C
(2 minutes)

Agenda and Vocabulary Review

Write the agenda on the board and review it with the class. Introduce any vocabulary in the lesson you think will be unfamiliar to your students.

Level: A/B/C
(15 minutes)

Introduce (or Review) "I" Statements

Handouts *Roommate Rumpus, Part 1 and 2*

> **Note:** *If this is a review for students, acknowledge at the beginning that they may have been introduced to this concept previously. Explain that this lesson will go into the concept in more depth.*

1. Ask two female volunteers to act out the skit *Roommate Rumpus, Part 1*. When they have finished, discuss it with the class.

Discussion

- How do you think Carol felt about Aikiko in this skit?
- How do you think Aikiko felt about Carol?
- Do you think Carol communicated well? Why or why not?
- Do you think Aikiko will try to keep the room neater? Why or why not?
- What kinds of escalating statements did you hear in the skit?

2. Have the same two volunteers act out *Roommate Rumpus, Part 2*. When they have finished, discuss it with the class.

Discussion

- How do you think Carol felt about Aikiko this time?
- How do you think Aikiko felt about Carol?
- Do you think Aikiko might make an effort to keep the room in order? Why or why not?
- What were some of the comments made in the first skit? In this skit?
- What kinds of non-verbal behaviors were used in the first skit? In this skit?
- What differences did you observe in the way Carol tried to communicate?
- How was her communicating more effective in the second skit?

3. Explain that the first skit contained "You" messages, and the second contained "I" Messages. Give the following mini-lecture:

"You" Messages attack, threaten, or blame another person. Whether you mean to or not, "You" Messages tend to escalate conflicts. The other person feels attacked so they try to defend themselves or retaliate with a counterattack. "You" Messages are like a big finger pointing and poking at the other person. That person tries to defend themselves from the poking, pointing finger.

With an "I" Message the speaker communicates his or her feelings and identifies a problem to be solved instead of attacking the other person. "I" Messages usually have the following format (write this on the board):

1. I feel_____

2. when_____

3. because_____.

This formula helps show the parts of an "I" Message and helps in learning to create "I" Messages.

4. Have students work with a partner to create "You" Messages and "I" Messages for the following situation: One of you promised to call the other with a homework assignment, and forgot to do it.

DISCUSSION

- What were some of the "You" messages you used?
- What were some of the "I" Messages you used?
- How did it feel to receive an "I" Message compared to a "You" message?

Note: *Students may protest that "I" Messages are too artificial or feel uncomfortable to use. Reassure them that many new skills feel artificial or uncomfortable at first. With time and practice they will feel more natural. Also, over time they will not need to strictly follow the format for the "I" Message, they will make it part of their own communication style.*

LEVEL: A/B/C
(15 MINUTES)

Practice Using "I" Messages

1. Have everyone find a partner and choose to be either person A or person B. Ask students to stand back-to-back with their partners. Describe one of the following situations, then have the students face their partners and enact the situation:

   - Person A is standing in line in the cafeteria when person B pushes right in front of him or her.

   - Person A walks past person B in the hall and calls B a name under his or her breath.

2. Call "Freeze" after a minute or two. Have character A express his or her feelings about B's behavior using an "I" Message. When students have had a chance to deliver their "I" Messages, stop the role-play and discuss.

DISCUSSION

- What was person A's first reaction in the situation? What was your impulse?
- What feelings came up?
- What "I" Messages did you use?
- How did the Bs feel when they heard the "I" Message?

3. Repeat the activity so that the Bs have a chance to use "I" Messages. Some possible situations are:

- Person B lets person A wear an expensive bracelet and she or he loses it.
- Person B trips over person A's foot in the cafeteria and thinks person A stuck it out on purpose.

LEVEL: A/B/C
(5 MINUTES)

Evaluation/Review of Key Points

1. Have volunteers respond to this statement—"Something I found challenging in today's lesson. . ."

2. Review and summarize key points in this lesson:

- "You" Messages attack and blame the other person.
- "You" Messages are escalating.
- "I" Messages are less likely to escalate conflict.
- "I" Messages can be based on a format "I feel ___ when ___ because ___."

LEVEL: A/B/C
(5 MINUTES)

Closing (Optional)

If you so desire, choose a Closing Activity from Appendix B.

Additional Activities

LEVEL: A/B/C
(TIME WILL VARY)

Journal Activity

Note: *This makes a good homework assignment.*

Have students try using "I" Messages and record their experiences in their journals. In what situations did they use an "I" Message? What did they find easy or difficult about using the "I" Message? How did the other person respond? What could they do differently next time?

LEVEL: A/B/C
(15 MINUTES)

More Practice with "I" Messages

HANDOUTS   *More Practice Making "I" Messages*

Note: *This handout makes a good homework assignment.*

Have students work in pairs. Distribute the *More Practice Making "I" Messages* handout. Have them complete the handout, then discuss.

DISCUSSION

- What were some of the "I" Messages you wrote?
- How did it feel to develop these "I" Messages?
- Did the process feel more natural the more you did it?

Advertising "I" Messages

LEVEL: A/B/C
(TIME WILL VARY)

To practice the components of an "I" message and think of reasons why "I" messages might be an important skill to use in conflict situations.

1. Divide students into work groups.

2. Have the groups develop one minute "public service announcements" to present to the class. These PSAs should explain what "I" messages are and how and why to make them.

3. If video equipment is available, make a tape of each group's PSA.

S T U D E N T   H A N D O U T   LEVEL: A/B/C

Roommate Rumpus, Part 1

CHARACTERS: Carol and Aikiko who are sharing a room.

SCENE: Their room.

CAROL: I can't stand sharing a room with you.

AIKIKO: What are you talking about?

CAROL: You're just a slob. Every time I try to straighten up in here so I can find my things, you mess it up again.

AIKIKO: Where do you get off calling me a slob? You think you're so perfect.

CAROL: Where do you get so much junk? There's no room for me in here. You only think about yourself.

AIKIKO: Just because I don't want to spend all my time cleaning like you do. You're the one who's selfish. You think the whole world revolves around you and everyone should live the way you say.

CAROL: I can't live with you, that's for sure. I hope you plan on living alone because nobody in the world is going to put up with this stuff.

AIKIKO: I clean up plenty. If you can't live with me it's because of your personality, not my cleaning.

Roommate Rumpus, Part 2

CHARACTERS:	Carol and Aikiko who are sharing a room.
SCENE:	Their room.

CAROL: I'm really having trouble living in this room.

AIKIKO: What do you mean?

CAROL: I mean it really makes me upset when I come in here looking for a little peace and there's stuff all over the place. I can't think when there's a mess around me.

AIKIKO: It doesn't seem like a mess to me. I've actually been neater than I usually am. I thought I was doing a pretty good job.

CAROL: It's not like I'm super neat, but I can't find my things when I need them. They get buried in your things. I really need more order in here.

AIKIKO: I'm sorry. I didn't know it was a problem. Look, is there some way we can divide the room so my clutter doesn't get in your way? We could clear a space that's just yours.

More Practice Making "I" Messages

Make "I" Messages for the following situations. Remember the format:

"I feel _____ when _____because _____."

1. A classmate always makes fun of a group of students who don't speak English well.

2. One of your good friends has been ignoring you lately. You don't know if something's wrong.

3. A student you don't know keeps staring at you in the library. It's getting on your nerves and making it hard to study.

4. A classmate keeps teasing you about the clothes you wear. You think it's probably good natured teasing, but it bothers you just the same.

5. A friend wants you to join in spray-painting graffiti on the side of a building.

6. You find out a student you don't know well is spreading gossip about you that isn't true.

Listening to De-escalate Conflict

LESSON IN BRIEF   Students practice listening skills and discuss how listening can de-escalate conflicts.

NOTES   Listening is one of the more important skills needed to de-escalate conflicts. Unfortunately, when we are in the middle of conflicts, listening is often the last thing we want to do. In this lesson students are introduced to the process known as Active Listening. To teach the process we use an acronym: PEAR— Paraphrase Facts, Encourage Talking, Pay Attention, Reflect Feelings. Students practice paraphrasing as the first part of Active Listening. Many middle school students have had experience with Active Listening. If this is true for your students, this lesson can be combined with the following lesson and made a review lesson, with the emphasis on de-escalation and Communication Potholes.

OBJECTIVES   Students will be able to:

- identify elements of Active Listening;
- paraphrase in a communication exercise.

CONFLICT TOOL   Active Listening/P.E.A.R.

VOCABULARY   *Active Listening*—A listening technique that involves paraphrasing or reflecting the speaker's content and feelings.

LESSON SEQUENCE
- Gathering (Optional)
- Agenda and Vocabulary Review
- Introduce (or Review) Active Listening
- Practice Paraphrasing and Reflecting
- Any Additional Activities You May Choose
- Evaluation/Review of Key Points
- Closing (Optional)

TIME NEEDED   One class period (minimum 40 minutes), depending on the additional activities you choose.

HANDOUTS   *Active Listening Guidelines, Paraphrase Practice Cards*

<table>
<tr><td>

LEVEL: A/B/C
(5 MINUTES)

</td><td>

Gathering (Optional)

If you so desire choose a Gathering Activity from Appendix A.

</td></tr>
<tr><td>

LEVEL: A/B/C
(3 MINUTES)

</td><td>

Agenda and Vocabulary Review

Write the agenda on the board and review it with the class. Introduce any vocabulary in the lesson you think will be unfamiliar to your students.

</td></tr>
<tr><td>

LEVEL: A/B/C
(10 MINUTES)

</td><td>

Introduce (or Review) Active Listening

HANDOUTS *Active Listening Guidelines*

</td></tr>
</table>

Note: *Many middle school students have had experience with Active Listening. If this is true for your students, you need only review the Active Listening Guidelines. As you do the other activities, emphasize their usefulness in de-escalating conflict.*

1. Before beginning the lesson, arrange with a student to role-play a conflict over a grade with you.

2. Explain to the class that listening is an important skill in conflicts and is one of the ways to de-escalate conflict. Describe that you will be role-playing with a student to demonstrate Active Listening. Ask the class to observe how listening affects the conflict.

3. Role play the student coming to you to complain about a low grade. Model active listening.

DISCUSSION

- How could you tell I was listening?
- When you've been in situations where you felt someone was really listening to you, how did you know that?
- How might I have acted if I were not listening?
- What was the effect of my listening on the conflict?
- Have you ever been in a conflict situation where listening helped de-escalate it?

4. Distribute the *Active Listening Guidelines* handout and discuss each of the behaviors.

Note: *As you discuss the handout with students, be sure they understand that Active Listening is not something you do all the time. It is useful in conflicts to help clarify perceptions and understand other points of view.*

<table>
<tr><td>

LEVEL: A/B/C
(20 MINUTES)

</td><td>

Practice Paraphrasing and Reflecting

HANDOUTS *Paraphrasing Practice Cards*, one set for each group of three or four students.

</td></tr>
</table>

1. Divide students into working groups of three or four. Everyone in the group should have a number from one to three or four.

2. Explain the task. Each group will receive a pile of Paraphrase Practice Cards. Student 1 draws a card and reads it to student 2. Student 2 paraphrases what he or she heard, reflecting back both the facts and the feelings. When student 1 feels the paraphrase is complete, she or he says, "Okay."

3. Student 2 then draws a card and reads it to student 3, who paraphrases what he or she heard, reflecting back both the facts and the feelings. When student 2 feels the paraphrase is complete, she or he says, "Okay." And so on until all the students in the group have had two turns.

DISCUSSION

- What did you notice trying to paraphrase?
- What was easy about this activity?
- What was hard about this activity?
- What feelings did you hear being expressed? Did you paraphrase or reflect the feelings?
- How might paraphrasing help in a conflict?

LEVEL: A/B/C
(20 MINUTES)

Alternative Activity for Practicing Paraphrasing and Reflecting

Divide students into microlab groups of three or four. Have group members designate themselves as "A," "B," "C," and "D." "A" should begin by talking for two minutes on the following:

- What I find most frustrating about middle school is...

As "A" talks, "B" should listen and paraphrase what he or she says. "A" should verify the accuracy of the paraphrase. After two minutes give a time signal, and "B" talks for two minutes with "C" paraphrasing. Continue until everyone has had a chance to participate.

DISCUSSION

- What did you notice trying to paraphrase?
- What was easy about this activity?
- What was hard about this activity?
- What feelings did you hear being expressed? Did you paraphrase or reflect the feelings?
- How might paraphrasing help in a conflict?

LEVEL: A/B/C
(5 MINUTES)

Evaluation/Review of Key Points

Review and summarize the key points of the lesson. As you do, have a volunteer paraphrase what you say.

- Listening is a way to de-escalate conflicts.
- PEAR is the acronym for Active Listening.
- PEAR stands for Paraphrase, Encourage, pay Attention, and Reflect feelings.

LEVEL: A/B/C
(5 MINUTES)

Closing (Optional)

If you so desire, choose a Closing Activity from Appendix B.

Additional Activity

LEVEL: A/B/C
(TIME WILL VARY)

Journal Activity

Ask students to experiment with using paraphrasing in their day to day interactions. Have them record the results in their journals. What was difficult or easy about the paraphrasing? How did people respond to the paraphrasing? Was it helpful?

Active Listening Guidelines

Listening can help you de-escalate a conflict. Here are some guidelines for Active Listening. Just remember **PEAR:**

P

Paraphrase the facts

- "So you want to go to the party and your parents won't let you."
- "You thought we were going to meet at your house before going to the rally."

E

Encourage the other person to talk

- "I'm willing to listen to your side."
- "Do you want to talk this out?"

A

Pay *Attention*

- Look at the speaker.
- Encourage them by nodding or other positive signs.

R

Reflect feelings

- "You sound upset about not being able to go to the party."
- "How do you feel when she says those kinds of things?"

Paraphrase Practice Cards

To a Friend:

I was late for practice twice and now the coach won't let me play in Saturday's game. It's completely unfair. She wouldn't even listen to why I was late.

To a Friend:

My parents have grounded me for three weeks because of my report card. I admit I've got to work harder, but not letting me go out on weekends isn't going to help my grades. I won't study. I'll just stay home and do nothing. That will show them.

To a Friend:

I did a really stupid thing. I let Chris copy my test answers and the teacher caught us. Now we both get a failing grade, and my parents are going to find out why. I've never done anything like this before, and I let Chris talk me into it. My reputation will be shot.

To a Friend:

You and I have been friends since elementary school. Now everyone in school is talking about this big party you're having next weekend, and I can't believe that you didn't even invite me. That really stinks!

To a Friend:

Jamie and I were playing catch and the ball went through Mrs. Coleman's window. Jamie ran away, but I went up to her door to tell her. No one was home though, so I left her a note and apologized and offered to pay for it and gave my phone number. She called and said she was so impressed with my honesty she wouldn't ask me to pay for the window.

S T U D E N T   H A N D O U T

To a Friend:

You keep saying things to me about how I dress and how I'd fit in more if I dressed like those kids. I think you're trying to help me and all, but I like the way I dress, If they don't like me because of my clothes, too bad. You're supposed to be my friend, so let up on me.

To a Friend:

It really bugs me the way you guys always pick on that new kid. I mean he's not my favorite person or anything, but I just stay away from him. I don't see the point of this scapegoating you do.

To Parents:

I have more chores around the house than anyone else. It's not fair. Just because they're younger they have less to do. And they're not even that young! Between homework and practice and chores I don't get any time to hang out with my friends except on weekends. They just lie around after school and watch TV.

More On Communicating in Conflict

LESSON IN BRIEF	Students practice listening skills and discuss some of the problems related to communicating.
OBJECTIVES	Students will be able to:
	• use the skill of Active Listening;
	• explain how listening can de-escalate conflicts;
	• identify "Communication Potholes."
CONFLICT TOOL	Active Listening/P.E.A.R.
VOCABULARY	*Active Listening*—A listening technique that involves paraphrasing or reflecting the speaker's content and feelings.
LESSON SEQUENCE	• Gathering (Optional)
	• Agenda and Vocabulary Review
	• More Practice With Active Listening
	• Discuss Communication Potholes
	• Any Additional Activities You May Choose
	• Evaluation/Review of Key Points
	• Closing (Optional)
TIME NEEDED	One class period (minimum 40 minutes), depending on the additional activities you choose.
HANDOUTS	*Active Listening Guidelines* (from Skill Lesson 8), *Communication Potholes*

LEVEL: A/B/C
(5 MINUTES)

Gathering (Optional)

If you so desire, choose a Gathering Activity from Appendix A.

LEVEL: A/B/C
(3 MINUTES)

Agenda and Vocabulary Review

Write the agenda on the board and review it with the class. Introduce any vocabulary in the lesson you think will be unfamiliar to your students.

LEVEL: A/B/C
(15 MINUTES)

More Practice with Active Listening

HANDOUTS *Active Listening Guidelines* from Conflict Skill Lesson 8

1. Review the *Active Listening Guidelines*. Remind students that in the previous lesson they practiced the paraphrasing aspect of Active Listening. Today they will practice the whole process of Active Listening.

2. Divide students into microlab groups of three or four. Have group members designate themselves as "A," "B," "C," (and "D"). "A" should begin by talking for two minutes on the following:

    *   What are some of the strongest feelings you have experienced in the last two weeks?
    *   What are some reasons for those feelings?

3. After "A" talks, "B" should use the Active Listening Guidelines and take about a minute to paraphrase the facts and reflect feelings. After two minutes give a time signal, and "B" then talks for two minutes with "C" Active Listening. Continue until everyone has had a chance to participate.

DISCUSSION

*   Did you feel that you were heard by the other person?
*   What was easy about this activity?
*   What was hard about this activity?
*   How did you feel when you had to restate what someone else said?
*   Did Active Listening help or hinder the discussion?

Note: *Students may protest that Active Listening is too artificial a process, that they don't feel comfortable with it. Explain that most new skills feel artificial or uncomfortable at first. With time and practice, the skills will feel more natural. During a conflict, the most important thing is to listen as well as you can.*

LEVEL: A/B/C
(15 MINUTES)

Discuss Communication Potholes

HANDOUTS *Communication Potholes*

1. Ask students what some "Not Listening" behaviors are. Note these on the board.

2. Distribute the *Communication Potholes* handout and discuss how the behaviors students mentioned fit in these categories. (Not all of them

will.) The three behaviors are called potholes because when you fall into them communication stops or gets a sharp jolt.

3. Working in their microlab groups from the previous activity, have students take two minutes each to address one of the following:

- A personal experience I had with a Communication Pothole...
- A time I was in a conflict and Communication Potholes were a problem...
- The Communication Pothole that I dislike the most is...

DISCUSSION

- What did you notice as you did this activity?
- In what ways are the potholes like the escalators?
- What potholes do you hear most often around school?
- How can you respond to someone who is using Communication Potholes?

LEVEL: A/B/C
(2 MINUTES)

Evaluation/Review of Key Points

1. Ask volunteers to respond—What's one thing you learned from this lesson? What's one thing you need to practice?

2. Summarize the key points in this lesson:

- Listening is one of the ways to de-escalate conflict.
- Active listening involves PEAR—Paraphrase Facts, Encourage Talking, Pay Attention, Reflect Feelings.
- There are Communication Potholes we can fall into when we to listen. They are: Giving Advice, Passing Judgement, and Avoiding the Issue.

Additional Activities

LEVEL: A/B/C
(TIME WILL VARY)

Journal Activities

Have students look for examples of Communication Potholes in their interactions during the next few days. How do those Communication Potholes sound? What effect do they have on communication? How do people get out of the potholes?

LEVEL: A/B/C
(TIME WILL VARY)

Playing with Communication Potholes

Have students develop short skits that illustrate the Communication Potholes in conflict situations. The skits should not name the potholes being used. Have groups act out their skits for the class. The rest of the class can guess what pothole(s) is being illustrated.

Communication Potholes

Even with the best of intentions, we can start out on the road of Active Listening and fall into a Communication Pothole. When that happens communication gets a big jolt, and it may even stop.

Three of the big Communication Potholes to watch out for are:

Giving Advice

Telling the other person what to do instead of really listening. Trying to solve the problem *for* them instead of *with* them.

- "Listen, don't you take that from him or her."

- "You ought to..."

- "If I were you I'd..."

Passing Judgement

Criticizing, blaming, being sarcastic. It doesn't help solve the problem, it just makes the other person feel bad and can escalate the conflict.

- "I can't believe you let this happen. It's all your fault."

- "Oh swell. This is another of your great jobs."

- "It's your own fault."

Avoiding the Issue

Making jokes, interrupting, changing the subject instead of listening and dealing with the problem.

- "Just ignore it."

- "What a pain she is. Do you want to go shopping?"

- "Read a book for awhile, then you'll feel better.

10 Points of View in Conflicts

LESSON IN BRIEF	Students explore the various points of view (P.O.V.) on conflict situations and discuss how those P.O.V. affect how the disputants behave in conflict.
NOTES	Understanding other people's perspectives, or points of view, is an essential component of defining conflicts and resolving them. The differences of perception in a conflict *are* what the conflict is about. This lesson introduces the concept of P.O.V. and the P.O.V. glasses, i.e., the lenses through which we see the world. Our P.O.V. lenses are colored by our experiences, our goals, our feelings, our values, and our needs.
OBJECTIVES	Students will be able to:

- identify various points of view in conflict situations;
- describe what influences someone's point of view;
- define the central problem in conflict situations based on hearing the points of view of the disputants.

CONFLICT TOOL	P.O.V. Glasses
VOCABULARY	*Needs*—The physical, emotional, or psychological drives people want to fulfill.
	Values—The beliefs or personal ethics that guide one's behavior.
	Perspective—The viewpoint or outlook of a disputant.
LESSON SEQUENCE	

- Gathering (Optional)
- Agenda and Vocabulary Review
- Introduce (or Review) P.O.V. Glasses
- Practice Identifying P.O.V. in Conflicts
- Any Additional Activities You May Choose
- Evaluation/Review of Key Points
- Closing (Optional)

TIME NEEDED	One class period (minimum 40 minutes), depending on the additional activities you choose.
HANDOUTS	*The P.O.V. Glasses; P.O.V. Role Plays (Level A: Lunch Line Laments, Level B: French Class Fracas, Level C: Phys. Ed. Fracas); Looking at Conflict Through the P.O.V. Glasses (Additional Activity)*

LEVEL: A/B/C
(5 MINUTES)

Gathering (Optional)

If you so desire, choose a Gathering Activity from Appendix A.

LEVEL: A/B/C
(10 MINUTES)

Agenda and Vocabulary Review

Write the agenda on the board and review it with the class. Introduce any vocabulary in the lesson that you think will be unfamiliar to your students.

LEVEL: A/B/C
(3 MINUTES)

Introduce (or Review) P.O.V. Glasses

HANDOUTS *Conflict Skits* (Level A, B, or C) from Conflict Skill Lesson 2

> **Note:** *If this is a review for students, acknowledge at the beginning that they may have been introduced to this concept previously. Explain that this lesson will go into the concept in more depth.*

1. Write P.O.V. on the board and explain that it is an abbreviation for Point of View. Point of View means how a person sees a situation—their perspective on the situation or, in a conflict, their side of the story.

2. Ask for two volunteers to act out the appropriate conflict skit—either level A, B, or C. As the volunteers are reading the script, ask the class to look and listen to figure out the P.O.V. of each person. When the actors are ready, have them present the skit.

DISCUSSION

- What do you think ___'s P.O.V. is? What did she do and/or say that makes you think that?
- What do you think ___'s P.O.V. is? What did she do and/or say that makes you think that?
- Did anyone express strong beliefs or values?
- What goals does each person in the conflict have?
- What escalating behavior did you see?
- What do you think each of them is feeling? Why do you think that?
- How do their feelings affect their P.O.V.?

LEVEL: A/B/C
(10 MINUTES)

Introduction (or Review) to P.O.V. (Alternative)

MATERIALS Before class, arrange for two students to come in late, having a noisy argument about whose fault it is that they are late. (You may also use one of the disputes suggested below.)

1. Write P.O.V. on the board and explain that it is an abbreviation for Point of View. Point of View means how a person sees a situation—their perspective on the situation or, in a conflict, their side of the story.

2. As you are explaining P.O.V., the "late" students should enter. When you tell them they are late, they should role-play their argument. As the incident reaches the top of the escalator, call "Freeze!"

DISCUSSION

- What did you see happen?
- Did anyone see something different than was just described?
- Who started this incident?
- What do you think ___'s P.O.V. is? What did she do and/or say that makes you think that?
- What do you think ___'s P.O.V. is? What did she do and/or say that makes you think that?
- What escalating behavior did you see?
- What do you think each of them is feeling? Why do you think that?
- How is this like actual conflicts you've been involved in?

ALTERNATE SITUATIONS

- Three students enter late. You tell them they are late and tell them to sit. They sit on the floor at the front of the classroom. You say, "Not there," and two of them run around the classroom until they get to their seats. The third student goes to his or her seat on hands and knees.

- Two students seated next to each other at the front of the class poke at each other. A third student behind them stands and swats both (gently) with a rolled up paper. Then they each stand up and sit down three times.

LEVEL: A/B/C
(10 MINUTES)

Discuss P.O.V. Glasses

HANDOUTS   *P.O.V. Glasses*

1. Distribute the *P.O.V. Glasses* handout and refer to it as you present the following mini-lecture on the P.O.V. Glasses:

   Each of us looks at the world through an invisible pair of sunglasses called the P.O.V. Glasses. Everything we see and experience is filtered through these glasses. Several things in our lives contribute to the color of these lenses. Five of the shadings on the P.O.V. Lenses are Needs, Goals, Experiences, Feelings, and Values.

   Needs are the physical and psychological drives that we want to fulfill. Goals are the things we want to accomplish. Experiences are the things that have happened to us. Feelings are the emotional reactions we have to what we're seeing. Values are a combination of our beliefs and the things we think are important.

   For example, let's say that you are hungry right before your last period class. That's a physical need that's contributing to your P.O.V. on going to your last period class. You develop a goal to meet that need before you get to class. You want to find something to eat. You know from experience that your friend has some cookies in his or her locker, and you know from experience that your friend is generous. So you find that friend, who says, "No, I only have a few left, and I'm saving them." Your emotional reaction is one of hurt and anger, and it turns to outrage because you strongly believe that friends should share with each other. Your P.O.V. on the conflict then is that your friend has let you down when you needed him or her, and you are disappointed and angry and feel your friend is wrong.

2. Have students work in pairs and take two minutes each to identify a few examples of how these five things have colored their P.O.V. lenses using the following questions as guides. Be sure to signal when two minutes has elapsed.

    DISCUSSION

    -   What types of experiences colored your P.O.V. glasses?
    -   What people in your life have contributed to your P.O.V. glasses?
    -   How have your P.O.V. glasses changed since you've been in middle school?

LEVEL: A/B/C
(15 MINUTES)

Practice Identifying P.O.V. in Conflicts

HANDOUTS *Role-Play Cards*

1. Divide students into two groups (As and Bs) for Hassle Line Role-Plays. Explain that this time they will be using a technique called "Role Reversal" where they will start out playing one role and then switch and play the other. They will have two minutes to play each role; before they switch roles they will trade *Role-Play Cards*.

2. Distribute *Role-Play Cards* to all the As and all the Bs. Give them a minute to read their role, then have them present their case. Let the role-play go for two minutes, then freeze.

    DISCUSSION

    -   How would you describe your character's P.O.V.?
    -   How would you describe your opponent's P.O.V.?
    -   What clues did your opponent give you?

3. Have students trade cards, and give them a minute to read the second role. Then have them role-play for two minutes and freeze.

    DISCUSSION

    -   Now that you've switched roles, how would you summarize each P.O.V.?
    -   What was easy or hard about changing roles? What did you learn from it?
    -   In an actual conflict, how would you go about finding out what the other person's P.O.V. was?
    -   How would you combine the P.O.V.s to define the problem in this conflict?

LEVEL: A/B/C
(2 MINUTES)

Evaluation/Review of Key Points

1. Have volunteers say something they liked about today's lesson.

2. With the class, summarize the key points in this lesson:

   - There are always several P.O.V.s in every conflict situation.
   - Our individual P.O.V.s are like a pair of sunglasses through which we see the world.
   - Many things go into coloring the lenses of our P.O.V. Glasses.

LEVEL: A/B/C
(5 MINUTES)

Closing (Optional)

If you so desire, choose a Closing Activity from Appendix B.

Additional Activities

LEVEL: A/B/C
(TIME WILL VARY)

Conflict Journal Activity

Have students go over some of the conflicts in their journals and summarize the main points of view that they see in the conflicts. Discuss how those differing P.O.V.s lead to conflict.

LEVEL: A/B/C
(20 MINUTES)

Looking at Conflict Through the P.O.V. Glasses

HANDOUTS *Looking at Conflict Through the P.O.V. Glasses*

> **Note:** *This makes a good homework assignment.*

Distribute the *Looking at Conflict Through the P.O.V. Glasses* handout. Have students work either in pairs or in work groups of three or four to complete the handout. Discuss their answers to the questions, then ask the discussion questions, either in pairs or with the whole class.

DISCUSSION

- Have you ever had a conflict like this?
- What colored your P.O.V. Glasses?
- How did you feel about having such a different P.O.V. from your friend?
- How did it affect your friendship?
- Were you able to resolve the conflict?

The P.O.V. Glasses

Each of us looks at the world from our own point of view. It's as if we look through an invisible pair of sunglasses called the P.O.V. Glasses. Everything we see and experience is filtered through these glasses. Many things in our lives contribute to the color of these lenses.

Five of the shadings on the P.O.V. Lenses are:

Experiences:

Values:

Goals:

Needs:

Feelings:

© 1997 Educators for Social Responsibility

Lunch Line Laments

The Conflict: Student A is angry because Student B keeps cutting in the lunch line. Student A confronted Student B and the Lunchroom Monitor has sent them to a corner table to work things out.

Student A: Almost every day Student B cuts in the lunch line. It's really unfair. The rules say no cutting. You've told the teachers in charge, but there are new ones on duty every day so nothing has changed. Also, it seems to you that Student B gets whatever he or she wants by pushing other people around. She or he has this attitude that they're better than anyone else. Well, you're tired of being pushed around. You've had it!

Lunch Line Laments

The Conflict: Student A is angry because Student B keeps cutting in the lunch line. Student A confronted Student B and the Lunchroom Monitor has sent them to a corner table to work things out.

Student B: Everyday you have a friend save a place for you in line so that you can eat early. You have a stomach problem, and you have to eat your lunch very slowly or you get sick. So you have to get your lunch and start eating early. The teachers and lunchroom aides know this and let you do it. A couple of your friends know it, but you don't want every-one to know. Student A really bugs you. He or she really has a big mouth and is always minding other people's business.

French Class Fracas

The Conflict: Student A and Student B had a loud argument in French class. The teacher separated them and sent them to the hall to work things out.

Student A: Student B is in your French class and is always getting on your case. She or he stares at you, laughs when you make mistakes, groans when you ask questions, and today, pushed your books on the floor. You've had it. You already feel stupid in this class. French is hard for you and you feel like the other kids put you down a lot, especially Student B. But you really want to learn French, because your grand-parents speak French, and you want them to be proud of you.

French Class Fracas

The Conflict: Student A and Student B had a loud argument in French class. The teacher separated them and sent them to the hall to work things out.

Student B: You have an easy time with French and want to learn as much as you can. You have French-speaking relatives and you want them to be proud of you. You hate having to wait for slower students like A that just hold up the whole class. Student A should be in a special class for stupid students. You know that you should have more patience with students like A. After all, you aren't that great at math, but nobody puts you down in math class. All the same, you get frustrated with Student A because you really want to learn.

Phys. Ed. Fracas

The Conflict: Student A and Student B were getting ready to fight in the locker room. The phys. ed. teacher stepped in and took them to his office to cool off. Then he ordered them to talk things out.

Student A: In the locker room after class, Student B came up to you, called you a jerk, and spit on your shirt. You want him to apologize, and you want the shirt cleaned. You don't really know Student B, but you didn't do anything to deserve this. You have been teased in P.E. before, but this time it's gone too far.

- -

Phys. Ed. Fracas

The Conflict: Student A and Student B were getting ready to fight in the locker room. The phys. ed. teacher stepped in and took them to his office to cool off. Then he ordered them to talk things out.

Student B: In class today, Student A shoved you during the game. He also shoved one of your friends. After class you told him to watch out next time. You didn't spit on him, you spit on the floor. You're not going to apologize or clean his shirt. He thinks he's better that anyone else and has a real attitude.

Looking at Conflict
Through the P.O.V. Glasses

The Conflict: Gail believes strongly that people shouldn't fight with each other. She had a cousin who was killed in a fight and she thinks fighting never solves anything. In fact, she's involved in a peer leadership project to make the school a more peaceful place. This morning her good friend Renee came up to her and told about being challenged to fight by a third girl. Renee wants Gail's help with this fight. Gail wants to help her friend, but told Renee she wouldn't help her fight. Renee is now very angry at Gail for letting her down.

Experiences:

Values:

Goals:

Feelings:

Needs:

- What is Gail's P.O.V. in this situation?

- What things color Gail's P.O.V. Glasses?

- What do you think Renee's P.O.V. is?

- How might Gail and Renee solve their dispute?

De-escalating Conflict with CAPS

LESSON IN BRIEF	Students explore the concept of de-escalating conflict and learn the CAPS formula for de-escalation.
NOTES	So far students have learned about conflict and some of the skills needed to de-escalate conflict. In this lesson, they begin putting all that information into practice to de-escalate conflicts. De-escalating conflict refers to reversing the process of conflict escalation so that the conflict can be resolved. This lesson focuses on the CAPS formula for de-escalating conflict. CAPS is an acronym for C-Calm Down, A-Agree to Work It Out, P-Point-of-View on the Problem, and S-Solve the Problem. This acronym gives students a way to think about how to de-escalate conflicts.
OBJECTIVES	Students will be able to:

- explain the acronym CAPS;
- identify the skills needed for de-escalating conflict using CAPS;
- apply the CAPS approach to a hypothetical conflict.

CONFLICT TOOL	CAPS, "I" Messages, Active Listening/P.E.A.R.
PREREQUISITES	Conflict Escalator (Skill Lesson 3)
VOCABULARY	*De-escalate*—The process by which conflicts become less volatile.
LESSON SEQUENCE	

- Gathering (Optional)
- Agenda and Vocabulary Review
- Introduce (or Review) CAPS
- Demonstrate CAPS
- Practice Using CAPS
- Any Additional Activities You May Choose
- Evaluation/Review of Key Points
- Closing (Optional)

TIME NEEDED	One class period (minimum 40 minutes), depending on the additional activities you choose.
HANDOUTS	*Coming Down the Conflict Escalator; De-Escalating Conflict Case Studies (Level A: Broken Bracelet Bonds; Level B: Canoes, Camping, and Conflict; Level C: Too Cool Compadres)*

LEVEL: A/B/C
(5 MINUTES)

Gathering (Optional)

If you so desire choose a Gathering Activity from Appendix A.

LEVEL: A/B/C
(3 MINUTES)

Agenda and Vocabulary Review

Write the agenda on the board and review it with the class. Introduce any vocabulary in the lesson you think will be unfamiliar to your students.

LEVEL: A/B/C
(5 MINUTES)

Introduce (or Review) CAPS

HANDOUTS   *Coming Down the Conflict Escalator*

Note: *If this is a review for students, acknowledge at the beginning that they may have been introduced to this concept previously. Explain that this lesson will go into the concept in more depth.*

1. Review the conflict escalator, i.e., as conflicts get worse, they escalate, which is like going up to the top of an escalator. In order to resolve conflict, we have to get it to come down the escalator. This is called de-escalating the conflict.

2. Draw an up escalator and then add four steps down. Distribute the *Coming Down the Conflict Escalator* handout. Using this diagram, and the handout, give the following mini-lecture to explain CAPS:

    There is a formula for coming down the escalator that is called CAPS. (Label the down steps C, A, P, S.) These letters stand for Calm Down, Agree to Work It Out, Point of View on the Problem, Solve the Problem.

    The *first* step down the escalator is *Calm Down*, because no one can resolve a conflict if they are furious. The *second* step is *Agree to Work It Out*, because it would be almost impossible to come up with a mutually agreeable solution if one of the people in the conflict refused to try to work it out. *Third*, the two people need to share their perspective or *Point-of-View on the Problem*. *Fourth*, once they agree on what conflict they are trying to solve, they *Solve the Problem* in a way that leads to a mutually agreeable solution, or as close to one as possible.

LEVEL: A/B/C
(10 MINUTES)

Demonstrate CAPS

1. Read the following conflict situation to the class:

    Maria and Sondra are sisters who are at the top of the escalator. Maria was talking on the telephone to a friend. Sondra kept asking her to get off the phone. After the fourth time, she walked in and hung up the phone on Maria. Now they are yelling at each other.

2. Have the students find partners and take two minutes to discuss how Maria and Sondra might use CAPS to come down the escalator. After two minutes, bring the class back together to discuss the conflict as sug-

gested here. As students make suggestions for each step, record their suggestions on the diagram on the board.

Discussion

- How might Maria and Sondra calm down? (Emphasize that they can still be angry, but they must be reasonably calm in order to discuss the conflict at all.)
- What could they say to each other to agree to work it out? What might be the first thing one of them says?
- How would each girl describe the problem?
- What are some ways they could solve the problem?

Level: A/B/C
(20 minutes)

Practice in Small Groups

HANDOUTS *CAPS Conflicts* (Level A, B, or C)

Note: *As students do this activity in small groups, circulate to provide assistance and to observe which aspects of the CAPS approach give them the most trouble. This will help you determine where to put emphasis in future lessons.*

1. Divide students into work groups of three or four. Distribute the appropriate *CAPS Conflicts* handout to the groups. Have each group devise a plan for de-escalating the conflict using the CAPS formula. Give them about ten minutes for this, then have them discuss with the whole class.

Discussion

- How did you de-escalate your conflict?
- What were some ideas you had about calming down?
- What were some ways to Agree to Work it Out?
- What were the various perspectives on the problem?
- What possible solutions did your group come up with?

2. Optional Variation: Have students role-play for the group how they would use the CAPS approach to de-escalate conflicts in the case studies. Then discuss as above.

Level: A/B/C
(5 minutes)

Evaluation/Review of Key Points

1. What's something you think you will remember from this lesson?

2. Summarize the key points in the lesson:

- CAPS stands for C-Calm Down, A-Agree to Work It Out, P-Point-of-View on the Problem, and S-Solve the Problem.
- Various skills are needed at each step down the escalator. We have discussed Calm Down skills.
- The next few lessons will be devoted to other aspects of de-escalating and resolving conflict.

LEVEL: A/B/C
(5 MINUTES)

Closing (Optional)

If you so desire, choose a Closing Activity from Appendix B.

Additional Activity

LEVEL: A/B/C
(TIME WILL VARY)

Conflict Journal Activity

Have students choose several conflicts from their Conflict Journals. These should be conflicts that were resolved or in some way de-escalated. Ask them to describe how the de-escalation took place. Did it follow the CAPS formula or can they identify pieces of the CAPS approach? How did the disputants calm down? Agree to work it out? Share points of view on the problem? Solve the problem? What other specific de-escalating behaviors did they see?

Coming Down
the Conflict Escalator

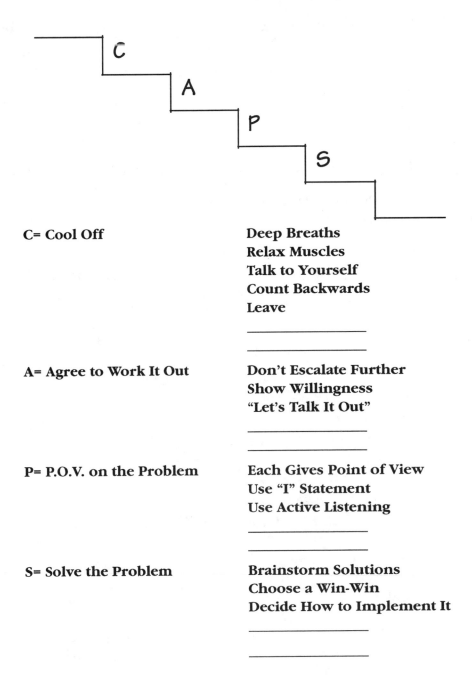

C= Cool Off

Deep Breaths
Relax Muscles
Talk to Yourself
Count Backwards
Leave

_____

_____

A= Agree to Work It Out

Don't Escalate Further
Show Willingness
"Let's Talk It Out"

_____

_____

P= P.O.V. on the Problem

Each Gives Point of View
Use "I" Statement
Use Active Listening

_____

_____

S= Solve the Problem

Brainstorm Solutions
Choose a Win-Win
Decide How to Implement It

_____

_____

Broken Bracelet Bonds

Use CAPS to come up with a plan to *De-escalate* the following conflict:

Marie gave Chee a friendship bracelet a few weeks ago. At first, Chee wore it everyday. But lately she hasn't been wearing it much. While Marie and Chee still do things together, they don't spend as much time together as they did. Chee says this is because she has to go to Chinese school now every Monday, Wednesday, and Thursday. But Marie saw her on Saturday at the movies with Joyce.

On Monday morning she went up to Chee and demanded the friendship bracelet back. "You don't deserve a friendship bracelet, because you don't know how to treat friends."

"Well, you're no kind of friend if you just take back gifts like that," said Chee. "Take your stupid bracelet. Only kids give friendship bracelets anyway, and you act just like a kid."

Canoes, Camping, and Conflict

Use CAPS to come up with a plan to *De-escalate* the following conflict:

Chester and Juan have been friends ever since they've been in middle school. Juan doesn't have brothers or sisters, and he likes Chester's energetic ways and the fact that Chester always has an idea for something to do.

Lately though, Juan has noticed that Chester only wants to do the things he suggests. He never seems to take Juan's ideas seriously.

Yesterday when they were planning a weekend camping trip, Chester wasn't listening to Juan's idea for renting canoes. Juan decided that he wouldn't give in. This time they were going to do what he wanted.

"You never even listen to me, " Juan accused Chester.

"Your ideas aren't worth listening to," said Chester. "Who wants to paddle a canoe anyway. It's stupid."

"Fine," said Juan. "Go camping by yourself then." And he left Chester alone.

Too Cool Compadres

Use CAPS to come up with a plan to *De-escalate* the following conflict:

Guillermo and Carlos have been friends since fourth grade. Lately, Guillermo feels like Carlos has been hanging around with the cool kids at school. When it's just the two of them, Carlos is fine—the same good guy he's always been. But when other people are around, especially kids from this cool crowd, Carlos either doesn't talk to him or puts him down.

This morning he said, "You all know my buddy Guillermo, don't you? We call him 'Goodwill Guillermo' because that's where he shops!" Everyone laughed and Guillermo laughed too, pretending it didn't bother him.

Later Guillermo confronted Carlos. "Man, if I'm not good enough for you and your cool friends just say so. I don't need you, and I don't need this crap from you."

Styles of Handling Conflict

LESSON IN BRIEF	Students examine six styles of conflict resolution.
NOTES	Conflict resolution education is about helping students learn that they have many options and choices in conflict situations. In this lesson, students explore six styles of conflict resolution: Aggression, Collaboration, Compromise, Giving In, Avoiding/Delaying, and Appealing to Authority. Each of these styles has potential uses and limitations. This is a point to emphasize with students—not all conflict styles will work in all situations. You need to know your options.
OBJECTIVES	Students will be able to:

- name six conflict styles;
- describe situations in which each might be appropriate.

CONFLICT TOOL	Conflict Styles
VOCABULARY	*Aggression*—Attacking or attempting to hurt another person with actions or words.
	Compromise—Resolving conflict by both sides giving up some of what they want.
	Win-Win—Resolving conflict in a way that meets the needs or goals of all the parties.
LESSON SEQUENCE	

- Gathering (Optional)
- Agenda or Vocabulary Review
- Introduce (or Review) Conflict Styles
- Microlab: Discuss Conflict Styles
- Any Additional Activities You May Choose
- Evaluation/Review of Key Points
- Closing (Optional)

TIME NEEDED	One class period (minimum 40 minutes), depending on the additional activities you choose.
HANDOUTS	*Six Ways of Handling Conflict, Conflict Resolution Styles Skits*

LEVEL: A/B/C
(5 MINUTES)

Gathering (Optional)

If you so desire, choose a Gathering Activity from Appendix A.

LEVEL: A/B/C
(3 MINUTES)

Agenda and Vocabulary Review

Write the agenda on the board and review it with the class. Introduce any vocabulary in the lesson you think will be unfamiliar to your students.

LEVEL: A/B/C
(20 MINUTES)

Introduce (or Review) Conflict Styles

HANDOUTS   *Six Ways of Handling Conflict; Conflict Styles Skits*

> **Note:** *If this is a review for students, acknowledge at the beginning that they may have been introduced to this concept previously. Explain that this lesson will go into the concept in more depth.*

1. Present the following mini-lecture/discussion:

    All animals, including humans, are equipped with two possible responses or ways of dealing with conflict. One is "fight" and the other is "flight," or running away. When we say "fight" we tend to think of physical fighting, but humans have ways of fighting other than physically.

    - Some of those ways of fighting are...?

    Whatever form fighting takes it is almost always a Win-Lose approach to conflict. One person will almost always win the fight while the other will lose.

    Similarly, while flight might be physically running away, it could take other forms as well.

    - Some forms of flight that are not physically running away are...?

    Flight is almost always a Lose-Win approach to conflict. One person deliberately loses so therefore the other automatically wins.

    There are times when everyone uses some form of fight and flight. But humans have other ways of handling conflict other than fight and flight.

    - What are some examples of Working-It-Out approaches to conflict that you have used?

2. Distribute the *Six Ways of Handling Conflict* handout. Review the styles.

3. Have volunteers read or act out each conflict style skit. After each skit, have students identify the style they think was demonstrated.

    DISCUSSION

    - What would be the potential advantages to each style?
    - What would be the potential disadvantages?
    - What styles do you see most often in school?

- If you were going to name each style after an animal, which animals would you use?

LEVEL: A/B/C
(10 MINUTES)

Microlab: Discuss Conflict Styles

HANDOUTS *Six Ways of Handling Conflict*

1. Have students form microlab groups of three or four. Give each student in the group two minutes to respond to the following:

   - What style do you think you use most often? Does it work for you?
   - Are there one or two responses that you use all the time?
   - Are there any responses you never use?

   Give the groups a signal when two minutes is up so that the next person can begin sharing. When everyone has had a chance to talk, discuss the activity.

   DISCUSSION

   - Did you notice anything as you did the activity?
   - Are there ways you handle conflict that are not represented on this sheet?
   - What are some examples of Collaborative approaches to conflict that you have used?
   - What are some examples of Compromise that you have used?
   - What are some of the benefits of each style?
   - What are some of the drawbacks of each?

LEVEL: A/B/C
(5 MINUTES)

Evaluation/Review of Key Points

Summarize the points in this lesson:

- There are four main types of conflict resolution: Win-Win, Win-Lose, Lose-Win, and Lose-Lose.
- There are different styles of dealing with conflict and these fit the broad categories of Fight, Flight, and Working It Out/Collaboration, and Compromise.

LEVEL: A/B/C
(5 MINUTES)

Closing (Optional)

If you so desire, choose a Closing Activity from Appendix B.

Additional Activities

LEVEL: A/B/C
(TIME WILL VARY)

Conflict Journal Activities

Have students look for specific examples in their journals that illustrate one or more of the various conflict resolution styles. Have them describe the conflict to the class. Other students can respond by saying what style or styles they think were being used. A variation on this activity is to have students look for each specific style for a week and an example of each in their journals.

LEVEL: A/B/C
(TIME WILL VARY)

Illustrating Styles

After students are familiar with the *Six Ways of Handling Conflict* handout, divide the class into six groups. Assign each group a conflict style, without the rest of the class knowing what it is. Ask them to develop a short skit that illustrates that style being used. When they're finished, have the groups present their skits to the rest of the class. Then, ask the class to guess the style being portrayed.

LEVEL: A/B/C
(TIME WILL VARY)

The Best Conflict Style Is...*

This activity is similar to the one above, except instead of developing a skit illustrating the conflict style, ask each group to develop an advertisement to "sell" its style as the best way to handle conflicts. When they are finished, the groups present their advertisements to the class. This is a good way to reinforce the point that all conflict styles have some uses.

---

* This activity was suggested by Sandi Adams of Denver, Colorado.

Six Ways of Handling Conflict

AGGRESSION

- Physical Fighting
- Yell
- Make the Other Person Feel Bad

COLLABORATE

- Problem-Solve Together
- Talk It Over
- Come Up with a Solution You Both Like
- Negotiate

COMPROMISE

- Everyone Gives a Little
- No One Gets Exactly What They Want

GIVE IN

- Let Them Have Their Way
- You Don't Care That Much
- The Other Person Has All the Power

AVOID or DELAY

- Pretend Nothing's Wrong
- Run Away
- Stay Away from the Other Person

APPEAL TO AUTHORITY

- Get an Authority to Decide or Settle the Dispute

Conflict Resolution
Styles Skits

1. Theresa and Denisha in the school library:

Theresa: Hey, that's my book. I reserved it last week!

Denisha: Then why was it on the shelf? I got it first.

Theresa: (Walking away angrily) Okay, then. She's so pushy! I reserved it first.

2. Theresa and Denisha in the school library:

Denisha: I need this book for class.

Theresa: I reserved it and I need it, too. Can we work something out?

Denisha: I need to have it read by Friday. When do you need it?

Theresa: Let me have it first, and I'll have it finished by Wednesday.

Denisha: I was hoping to have it a little longer, but I can live with that.

3. Theresa and Denisha in the school library:

Denisha: I need this book for class.

Theresa: But I reserved it! I can prove it.

Librarian: Yes, Theresa reserved it. Denisha, you can have it next week.

4. Theresa and Denisha in the school library:

Denisha: I need this book for class.

Theresa: I reserved it, and I need it, too. Can we work something out?

Denisha: I'm writing a paper, and I need it for research. It's due Friday.

Theresa: I have to write a book report on this book. And it's due Friday. Do you have to use this book or could you get the information from another book?

Denisha: Sure, if there was another book with this information.

Theresa: Actually, I know of a couple. Come here, I'll show you.

5. Theresa and Denisha in the school library:

Theresa: Hey, give me that book. I reserved it last week!

Denisha: Too bad. I got it first.

Theresa: Give it to me. (She grabs at it and knocks Denisha's notebook out of her hands.)

Denisha: Look what you did! What a jerk you are!

Theresa: (Sarcastically) Thanks for the book.

6. Theresa and Denisha in the school library:

Theresa: Denisha, don't take that book. I reserved it last week. I need it for class.

Denisha: Okay. I was just looking at it. It looks good. Let me know when you've finished.

CONFLICT RESOLUTION IN THE MIDDLE SCHOOL   **115**

Win-Win Resolutions in Conflict

LESSON IN BRIEF	Students use the Win-Win Grid to solve conflicts.
NOTES	In conflict resolution education we emphasize helping students see that they have many options. But we also encourage them to use approaches to conflict that lead to Win-Win resolutions, where all parties get what they want or need. The concept of Win-Win conflict resolution is very abstract for many middle school students. The Win-Win Grid gives students a concrete way to think about the various types of solutions possible in conflicts.
OBJECTIVES	Students will be able to:

- define Win-Win, Win-Lose, and Lose-Lose resolutions to conflict;
- give examples of each type of resolution.

CONFLICT TOOL	Conflict Styles, Win-Win Grid
VOCABULARY	*Confrontation*—Facing the problem or situation; taking action.
	Compromise—Resolving conflict by both sides giving up some of what they want.
	Win-Win—Resolving conflict in a way that meets the needs or goals of all the parties.
LESSON SEQUENCE	

- Gathering (Optional)
- Agenda and Vocabulary Review
- Introduce (or Review) the Win-Win Grid
- Practice Using the Win-Win Grid
- Any Additional Activities You May Choose
- Evaluation/Review of Key Points
- Closing (Optional)

TIME NEEDED	One class period (minimum 40 minutes), depending on the additional activities you choose.
HANDOUTS	*The Win-Win Grid; Win-Win Conflict Case Studies (Level A: Twin Television Troubles, Level B: Science Project Problems, Level C: What Are Friends For?)*
MATERIALS	Win-Win Grid Overhead (optional)

LEVEL: A/B/C
(5 MINUTES)

Gathering (Optional)

If you so desire, choose a Gathering Activity from Appendix A.

LEVEL: A/B/C
(3 MINUTES)

Agenda and Vocabulary Review

Write the agenda on the board and review it with the class. Introduce any vocabulary in the lesson you think will be unfamiliar to your students.

LEVEL: A/B/C
(15 MINUTES)

Introduce (or Review) the Win-Win Grid

HANDOUTS   *The Win-Win Grid*

MATERIALS   Win-Win Grid overhead (optional)

> **Note:** *If this is a review for students, acknowledge at the beginning that they may have been introduced to this concept previously. Explain that this lesson will go into the concept in more depth.*

1. Review the definition of conflict: a dispute or disagreement between two or more people. Sometimes these disputes or disagreements cause problems, then people try to solve the problems. Conflict resolution is trying to solve the problems created by conflict. People approach conflict resolution in many different ways.

2. Read the following situation to the class:

    Abe and Ricco are friends who spend every Friday evening together. Usually they rent a video and relax. This week Abe has said he wants to go to the dance at the Youth Center. Ricco has to baby-sit for his young cousin who is too young to go to the dance.

    "Man, you said you would help me out with this," he says to Abe. "I thought we'd hang out together at least."

    "I don't want to miss the dance just to baby-sit some little kid," says Abe. "This is a chance to do something different."

    DISCUSSION

    *   What would you say was the problem in this situation?
    *   What does Abe want?
    *   What does Ricco want?
    *   How might they try to solve it?
    *   Would that solution help or hurt their friendship?

3. Explain that there are several ways to solve a problem like this. It's helpful to think in terms of what would help each person "win" or get what they want out of the situation. Write the following chart on the board, or use the Win-Win Grid overhead:

	RICCO GETS WHAT HE WANTS	RICCO DOESN'T GET WHAT HE WANTS
ABE GETS WHAT HE WANTS	Win-Win	Win-Lose
ABE DOESN'T GET WHAT HE WANTS	Lose-Win	Lose-Lose

4. Place the class solutions onto the Win-Win Grid. If there are blanks on the grid, ask for possible solutions. If students are stuck, here are some possibilities for you to suggest:

WIN-WIN	Hire another baby-sitter. Do something together on Saturday night. Ricco gets another friend to come over on Friday.
WIN-LOSE	Abe goes to the dance and leaves Ricco to baby-sit alone.
LOSE-WIN	Abe skips the dance and stays with Ricco.
LOSE-LOSE	Abe doesn't go to the dance but helps Ricco and is resentful. Abe and Ricco stop being friends. The dance is canceled.

DISCUSSION

- What approach do people use most—Win-Win or Win-Lose?
- Why do you think that?
- Where do people learn to use Win-Lose?
- Have you ever been in a conflict you resolved in a Win-Lose way? A Win-Win way? A Lose-Lose way?

LEVEL: A/B/C
(15 MINUTES)

Practice Using the Win-Win Grid

HANDOUTS   *The Win-Win Grid, Conflict Case Studies* (Level A, B, or C)

MATERIALS   Win-Win Grid overhead (optional)

1. Divide students into work groups of three or four. Distribute *The Win-Win Grid* handout and *Conflict Cases* (Level A, B, or C). Have each group choose a conflict case and fill out the *Win-Win Grid* for that conflict.

DISCUSSION

*   What was one of your Win-Lose solutions? Win-Win solutions?
*   Which types of solutions were easiest to come up with?
*   Which were the hardest?
*   How did you "test" the Win-Win solutions to determine if both parties would be satisfied with them?

LEVEL: A/B/C
(5 MINUTES)

Evaluation/Review of Key Points

1. What's something you liked about today's class? What's something that might have been different?

2. Summarize the points in this lesson:

    *   There are four main types of conflict resolution: Win-Win, Win-Lose, Lose-Win, and Lose-Lose.
    *   The Win-Win Grid is a tool to help us think of different types of solutions.

LEVEL: A/B/C
(5 MINUTES)

Closing (Optional)

If you so desire, choose a Closing Activity from Appendix B.

Additional Activity

LEVEL: A/B/C
(TIME WILL VARY)

Conflict Journal Activity

Have students choose a conflict from their journal and use the Win-Win Grid to analyze the conflict. They can write the actual resolution in the appropriate square, then develop solutions for the other squares.

The Win-Win Grid

WIN-WIN	WIN-LOSE
Both people get what they want.	Person 1 gets what he or she wants but person 2 doesn't.
LOSE-WIN	LOSE-LOSE
Person 1 doesn't get what he or she wants but person 2 does.	Neither person gets what he or she wants.

Twin Television Troubles

Terry and Deena are twin brother and sister. They are both in middle school.

Deena was lying on the couch watching TV. "This movie will be great," she thought. "Just what I need to forget those mean kids in homeroom." Suddenly, Terry came rushing in.

"Deena, I've got to use the TV now. There's a show on that I need to watch for my social studies class, and it started five minutes ago."

Deena laughed. "Oh, give me a break. Like you're supposed to watch TV for Mrs. Reed. She'd be the last person to assign a TV show."

"Well, she did," Terry insisted. "It's about the Civil War and if I don't report on it I'm in trouble. She gave me the assignment because I need the extra credit. I'm really doing lousy in her class, and if I don't do this she'll kill me. You know how she is!"

"Well, I was here first, so for once I get to be in charge. Besides, you can watch it on Mom and Dad's TV. Or tape it. I've had a tough day and I really want to watch this movie."

"Their TV is on the blink and you're using the VCR to watch your movie. Come on, Deena. I really need your help."

Science Project Problems

Mara and Reggie have been assigned to work together on a cooperative project for science class. They've known each other for several years, but they haven't worked together before. They haven't been very friendly either.

The project is due in two weeks, and they will receive a joint grade. Part of the grade will be based on the content of the project and part of it will be based on how well they work together.

Two days into the project, Reggie is already upset with Mara. Reggie likes to plan ahead, and he hates doing things at the last minute. But he can't get Mara to commit to anything. They agreed the first day that the project would be about solar energy, and they're both doing research. But they haven't decided what their project will be, who will do what, how big a project it will be, when each piece will be done, anything. It's making Reggie crazy.

"I'm not doing this whole thing myself," he said to Mara.

"Will you relax? We have a week and a half. We'll get it done," Mara said.

"When are we going to get it done? We only have a week and a half!"

"My style is different from yours," Mara said. "I need to read my book and think about how the project might look. I get good ideas just letting things percolate in the back of my head. Don't worry, I always get things done."

What Are Friends For?

Christopher and Suzanne are friends who hang around with the same group of friends. One day they were talking together after school when Suzanne started talking about a problem she was having with Ouida, a girl Christopher likes and has just asked out Friday night.

Christopher said, "You know, she's really nice."

"I'm not saying she's not nice," protested Suzanne. "I'm saying I have a problem with her. She has an attitude sometimes."

"Well it makes me mad when you talk that way about someone I like. You're disrespecting her and me."

"So when I have a problem with someone I can't talk to you about it, even though we've been friends for years. Is that what you're saying? It makes me mad when someone who is supposed to be my friend won't listen to me."

Christopher felt very frustrated. "I just don't want you talking that way about Ouida!"

"You can't tell me what to talk about!" Suzanne snapped.

Extending the Concepts of Part One: Additional Activities

CONFLICT TOOLS

Identifying Feelings and Managing Anger

Feeling Feet

ACTIVITY IN BRIEF   Students review affective vocabulary by acting out feeling words.

MATERIALS   A sheet or blanket

1. Have the group stand and watch as you pantomime a feeling word. Ask them to mimic what you are doing, then guess what feeling you are miming. After you have done the first feeling, have a student volunteer come to the front of the room and mime another feeling. Have the other students first mimic the volunteer, then try to guess what the feeling is.

2. Vary the activity by asking for a volunteer who would be willing to be covered with the sheet or blanket. Have the volunteer sit in a chair and cover his or her head and body with a sheet or blanket. Only the legs should show.

3. Whisper a feeling word into the volunteer's ear. He or she should pantomime the feelings you name using only his or her legs and feet.

    DISCUSSION

    *   What did you learn about feelings from the pantomime?
    *   How do feelings affect our bodies?
    *   What are some of the ways we know what other people are feeling?

Feelings Relay

ACTIVITY IN BRIEF   Teams of students review the meaning of feeling words by pantomiming the feelings in a relay.

MATERIALS   Feelings Cards made of 3x5 cards with feeling words written on them such as "happy," "sad," "angry," "scared," "suprised," etc. (you will need approximately 5 cards for each group)

1. Divide the group into teams of 4-5. Have each group stand at equal distances away from you. Explain that each team will be given a set of five feelings cards. They must discover what these cards are by having one person in the group act out the feeling on the card for the others. The actor is not allowed to talk. The first group to guess all their cards wins.

2. The group then sets up the order they will act in so that each person in

the group gets a chance to act.

3. When everyone is ready, say "go." One person from each team runs to you and gets a card. They then each read the card and leave it on the floor by your feet, returning to their group to act out the feeling for the group. Once the group guesses the feeling correctly, a new group member can come to you for a new card. This relay continues until one team gets five. (Note: If a group gets really stuck on a word or the person acting does not know what the word is, pull that card out and substitute a new one.)

Discussion

- Think of a time when you couldn't describe how you felt. What happened?
- To whom were you trying to describe how you felt?
- How did you eventually resolve the conflict?

Reflecting on any Feelings Activity

Activity in Brief
Students use Feelings Cards to express their feelings about a particular activity.

Materials
Feelings Cards (see the Feelings Relay activity on p.125)

1. Upon completion of an activity, such as a role play or game, ask the group to form a circle. Spread out a set of Feelings Cards in the center of the circle where students will be able to see as many of them as possible.

2. Give students 5 minutes to find 3 cards (each) that represent how they felt at the beginning of the activity, how they felt at some point in the middle, and how they feel now. (Feel free to vary the number of cards, for instance, you might have them choose only one or two cards that represent their feelings now that the activity is complete.)

3. Once each person has his cards, go around the group. Allow each person to share his or her cards and say why he or she chose each card.

Discussion

As the group is sharing, look for common themes or interesting comments. Return to these themes or comments once the go-round is complete.

More Practice Expressing Anger

Activity in Brief
Students practice effective ways to express anger.

Handouts
More Practice with Anger Cards, one set for each group

1. Divide students into work groups. Give each group a set of cards.

2. Have students take turns drawing cards, reading them to the group, and saying how angry they would be. Have them put themselves on the anger thermometer (see page 60). Have each student also say what she or he would do to calm down, and what she or he would say to the person. If you have time, you might have each student respond to each situation.

More Practice
Dealing with Anger

A friends grabs a CD while you are showing it to another friend.

A classmate never listens when you talk. He/she interrupts and acts like you haven't said anything.

You have a pimple on your chin, and one guy points it out to the whole class.

A classmate keeps calling you "Gumby Head."

A friend won't listen to any ideas other than his or her own. She or he insists on being in charge of every situation.

A friend borrows things from you and doesn't return them.

A teacher jumps on you for talking in class but lets other kids get away with it.

A kid is always putting you down. He says he's joking.

A classmate wants to copy your work.

You know that a classmate has been accusing you of things.

A friend borrows books, CDs, and clothes, but never returns them.

A classmate is nice to you when some students are around, but not others.

Exploring/Understanding Conflict

Conflict Dialogues*

To give students an opportunity to examine a conflict they have experienced. They can then use this conflict as the source for a case study, role play, discussion, etc.

1. Have students think of a conflict. It may be a conflict they were involved in or one they observed. It can be from school, home, the neighborhood, or wherever. It should, however, be a conflict students will feel comfortable talking about with other students.

2. Have each student work with a partner. If there is an extra student, form a group of three. Each student then briefly describes his or her conflict to the other. Allow about two and a half minutes for each student. When they have finished sharing their stories, they should choose one of the conflicts to work on.

3. Have students use the conflict they have chosen as the basis for a short dialogue they will write. They need not stick to what really happened. They may condense the action or exaggerate it. The dialogue is like a short play or video clip, a back and forth exchange that will show how the conflict started and how it escalated or got worse. For example:

Daughter: Hi, Mom. I'm home.

Mom: Where have you been? I thought I told you to be home for supper.

Daughter: I tried, but the game took a really long time.

Mom: I don't care if it took all night! You were supposed to be home by 6:30!

And so on......

Explain to students that they should not show how the conflict was resolved. Right now they are concentrating on how conflicts begin and how they escalate.

4. When students have finished, have each pair join with another and read their dialogues for the other pair. Before they read, they should offer a line or two of background explaining who is involved and where they are. The students who are not reading are observers and will watch and listen for how the conflict started and how it escalated. Students should not try to solve the conflict.

5. When the first pair finishes reading, all four identify the escalating

---

* Adapted, with permission, from Richard Cohen, School Mediation Associates.

behaviors they observed in the conflict. Then the second pair explains who is involved in their conflict and where the conflict takes place. Following the same procedures for sharing as identified above, this pair will then read their dialogue and identify escalating behaviors.

DISCUSSION

- What things did you notice about how this conflict started? What got it going?
- What behaviors or statements contributed to its escalation? What did the characters do that made the conflict worse?
- What did the characters *not* do that made the conflict worse? What behaviors might have prevented the escalation?
- What happened to the characters feelings during the conflict? How did this affect their behavior in the conflict?

CAPS Practice Using "Conflict Dialogues"

ACTIVITY IN BRIEF

If students did the Conflict Dialogues activity, they can use those conflicts and apply the CAPS approach to the situations, describing how they would de-escalate the conflicts. Focus on de-escalating the conflicts using CAPS, but encourage students to identify several specific behaviors that contribute to de-escalation.

Baggage on the Conflict Escalator

ACTIVITY IN BRIEF

To explore some of the issues people bring to conflicts that lead to conflicts escalating.

1. Explain that nobody gets onto the conflict escalator empty handed. We all carry a suitcase or baggage with us. This baggage influences how far and how quickly the conflict will escalate. Some of the things that go into our baggage are:

   - past relationship with the person,
   - current feelings about the person,
   - past experiences with conflict,
   - current feelings about conflict,
   - feelings about self,
   - mood that day,
   - and more.

2. Help the students form groups and have them discuss: "A time I carried a lot of baggage onto the conflict escalator and how it affected the conflict."

3. Refer students to the case studies in Skill Lesson 3. What baggage is referred to in the case studies? Is there baggage that is implied or that might be inferred from the text?

De-escalating Conflict/CAPS

Quick Decision De-escalation

To identify strategies for de-escalating conflicts and to practice de-escalating conflicts quickly.

Have students work in groups of three or four. Explain that you are going to read them a conflict situation and they will have 60 seconds to de-escalate the conflict. They may use all or part of the CAPS approach or any other de-escalation ideas they may have.

- You accidentally bumped into another student in the hall. Now he or she wants to fight you. How would you de-escalate the situation?

- You're at a basketball game and the other school lost. After the game, a student from that school says, "You guys think you're so tough. Let's see you fight." How would you de-escalate the situation?

- You said something to the new student during class to encourage him or her. You meant it as a compliment, but he or she thought you were being insulting. Now he or she is threatening you in the hall. How would you de-escalate the situation?

- A student who used to be a good friend of yours is now accusing you of spreading rumors about his or her family members. How would you de-escalate the situation?

- A student you don't know very well comes up to you and says she or he heard you've been calling her or him a "gumbyhead." "I'll meet you after school," she or he threatens and stalks off. How would you de-escalate the situation?

- A friend of yours comes up and says, "I've had it with you. You can't keep a secret no matter how important it is. You're not my friend anymore." Then he or she stalks off. You have no idea what this friend is talking about. How would you de-escalate the situation?

Practice "Agreeing to Work It Out"

To practice in-depth how to "Agree to Work It Out" as part of de-escalating conflict.

Five Ways to Make an Offer

One of the most common sticking points in conflict resolution is Agreeing to Work It Out. Many times young people simply don't know how to turn the conflict around. They may not know what to say, how to indicate their willingness to talk, or even how to avoid escalating the conflict further. There are three parts to Agreeing to Work It Out: Avoiding Behavior that Escalates, Willingness to Work It Out, and Making an Offer.

AVOIDING FURTHER ESCALATION

1. Remind students of the Lesson 3 and the discussion about how conflicts escalate. Ask: "What are some of the behaviors that cause conflicts to escalate?" Record responses on the board.

2. Explain that to work out conflicts and come to win-win solutions, we must avoid behavior that makes them escalate further. Ask for two volunteers to be in a skit. (Use one of the scripts from Conflict Skill Lesson 3.) While the volunteers are reading over the script, explain to the class that the two players have been in a conflict and have calmed down. They think they are ready to work things out. But the class should listen and watch for escalating remarks and behaviors.

3. Have the players present the skit.

DISCUSSION

- What escalating remarks did you hear?
- What escalating behaviors did you see?
- What remarks/behaviors were the worst or most escalating?
- How did these remarks/behaviors affect the chances for working it out?
- How could the disputants have said what they needed to say without escalating the conflict?

ASSESSING WILLINGNESS

Explain that to work out conflicts, people must be willing to work them out. If they say escalating things, they probably are not willing to work things out. Ask: "What are some other signs people might not be willing to work things out?" (Not being willing to listen, interrupting, blaming, or other escalating behavior.)

INTRODUCING MAKING AN OFFER

Distribute the *Five Ways to "Make an Offer"* additional handout. Explain that to start the process of Working Things Out someone has to Make an Offer. Go over the handout with the class and discuss:

DISCUSSION

- What are some of the things that get in the way of Making an Offer?
- Can you give an example of a time you Made an Offer using one of these?
- What are some other ways to Make an Offer?

PRACTICING MAKING AN OFFER/ROLE-PLAY

4. Divide students into two groups to role-play using a Hassle Line (have the two groups line up facing each other). Designate the lines

as "A" and "B." Using a role-play from Conflict Skill Lesson 20, explain the situation to the class, then give each line their role. Their goal is to de-escalate the conflict by making an offer using one of the possibilities on the worksheet. They will have two minutes after the starting signal to do so. If they Agree to Work It Out, they should begin to problem solve.

5. Start the role-play. After two minutes, stop the role-play and discuss.

DISCUSSION

- Who made an offer first?
- How did it feel to use these words?
- What made it hard to Make an Offer?
- Did anyone get into problem solving? What did you do or say?

BLOCKS TO MAKING AN OFFER

6. Explain that it's easier to talk about Making an Offer than to do it. Ask for volunteers to stand in the front of the room to read the handout. Huddle with volunteers first, so the class cannot see what you are doing. Give each volunteer a piece of tape to put over his or her mouth. Tell them that when you give the signal they should try to read one of the phrases on the handout through the tape. The class will try to guess which phrase they are reading. Emphasize that they should not move their mouths so hard that the tape comes off.

7. Give a signal and have the volunteers face the class. One by one have them read a phrase from the handout while the class tries to guess which phrase they are reading. When everyone has finished, tell the volunteers to carefully remove the tape from their mouths. They should not tear it off as this may hurt.

DISCUSSION

- How did it feel to Make an Offer with tape on your mouth?
- What made it difficult?
- How is trying to Make an Offer like trying to talk with tape on your mouth?
- What are some of the things that make it hard for us to Make an Offer? (Or what gets in the way of Making an Offer?)
- What would help make it easier? (Or what would help you "take the tape off"?)

Five Ways
to "Make an Offer"

- "Do you want to work it out?"

- "I'll listen to you if you listen to me."

- "Let's try to work this out."

- "I'm listening."

- "Do you want to tell me your side?"

- _____

CONFLICT TOOL

Conflict Styles

Uses and Limitations of Styles

ACTIVITY IN BRIEF

To examine in greater depth various conflict resolution styles by looking at what behaviors are associated with each style; to identify potential uses and limitations of each style.

NOTE

This activity focuses on the handout *Six Ways of Handling Conflict* on p. 113. This makes a good homework assignment.

1. Explain that each conflict resolution style has potential uses and potential limitations.

2. Have students work in groups to complete the following chart:

STYLE	HOW IT SOUNDS	HOW IT LOOKS	POTENTIAL USES	LIMITATIONS

3. When they've completed the chart, discuss the specific behaviors of each style by looking at the "How It Sounds" and "How It Looks" columns.

4. Next, discuss the uses and limitations students identified, and the kinds of situations in which the style would or would not be useful.

CONFLICT TOOL

Point of View

More Practice Identifying and Synthesizing P.O.V. in Conflicts

ACTIVITY IN BRIEF

Students practice identifying points of view in conflict situations and see how different points of view affect how a conflict is described.

HANDOUTS

Conflict Skits or *Role-Play Cards* from previous lessons.

1. Divide students into work groups of four for role-plays. Distribute *Role-Play Cards* or skits from previous lessons.

2. Two group members act out the role-play. The other two describe what Needs, Goals, Experiences, Feelings, and Values they heard in each disputant's dialogue. They then try to combine the two P.O.V.s into a

single problem statement.

3. When they have finished, the role-players become the listeners/problem identifiers, and vice versa. Once they have experience with this activity, students can make up their own P.O.V. conflicts.

Part Two:
Working Toward Win-Win

14 The Personal Power Package

LESSON IN BRIEF   Students identify the components of personal power and explore positive and negative uses of power.

NOTES   One of the key issues for young adolescents is their growing sense of personal power—how much power they have, how to use their power, and how to get more. However they rarely get an opportunity to talk directly about power, so it's not surprising that adolescents often wield their power in ways that are clumsy and ineffective. The next two lessons introduce the topic of personal power and how it can affect relationships and conflicts. We return to the concept of power in Lesson 26, Understanding Clout. In that lesson power is addressed in a larger, societal context.

OBJECTIVES   Students will be able to:

- Define "power,"
- Identify several key components of personal power,
- Distinguish between positive and negative uses of power,
- Define and distinguish between "power over" and "power with."

CONFLICT TOOL   Personal Power Package

VOCABULARY   *Power over*—Using power to dominate or control another person or group; withholding power completely from another person or group or just dispensing part of the power; making decisions that affect another person or group without that person or group's consent.

Power with—A collaborative or shared approach to power where, as much as possible, the people affected by a decision are involved in the decision making.

LESSON SEQUENCE
- Gathering (Optional)
- Agenda and Vocabulary Review
- Discuss Personal Power Packages
- Brainstorm: Positive and Negative Uses of Power (Level A)
- Power Plays: Skits for Examining Personal Power (Level B/C)
- Evaluation/Review of Key Points
- Closing (Optional)

TIME REQUIRED   One class period (Minimum 40 minutes) depending on the additional activities you choose.

HANDOUTS   *Personal Power Packages, Power Plays (Level B/C: Homework Helper, Group Ground Rules, Questions About the Quarry)*

LEVEL: A/B/C
(5 MINUTES)

Gathering (Optional)

If you so desire, choose a Gathering Activity from Appendix A.

LEVEL: A/B/C
(2 MINUTES)

Agenda and Vocabulary Review

Write the agenda on the board and review it with the class. Introduce any vocabulary in the lesson you think they may need help with.

Note: *This lesson has several options. You will need to choose which aspects of power you wish to emphasize. For Level A we suggest that you start with the Discuss Personal Power Packages activity then move to Brainstorm: Positive and Negative Uses of Power. For Level B and C students, we suggest that you start with Discuss Personal Power Packages then do the Power Plays.*

LEVEL: A/B/C
(5 MINUTES)

Discuss Personal Power Packages

HANDOUT: *Personal Power Packages*

1. Ask the students what words come to mind when they hear the word "power." What is power? Who is powerful? How do people become powerful? Record responses on the board. After you have heard from several volunteers, explain, "Today we are going to look at some of the ways that you, as individuals, have power."

2. Deliver the following mini-lecture:

   All of us, even very young children, have some personal power. Power is particularly important for kids your age. Adolescence is a time when you can gain more personal power and learn to use it in ways that are constructive and ways that will help you and other people. Power is not just one thing; it is a collection of qualities like the ones you just brainstormed. Together these qualities make up another tool for our conflict resolution tool kits. This tool is the "Personal Power Package."

3. Distribute and review the handout *Personal Power Packages*. Elaborate on the handout using the following mini-lecture.

   As you can see on this handout, Personal Power Packages consist of elements we can choose and control, elements we are born with, and elements we are given. As you get older society gives you more power in the form of rights and responsibilities. The more you know about your own values and spiritual beliefs, the more personal power you have. You can choose to increase your power by developing your strengths, talents, and interests, and by choosing to use the power you have in responsible ways. With more power comes more responsibility.

   Another thing to be aware of is the question of who holds your Personal Power Package. As you get older you will assume more and more responsibility for your Personal Power Package. But there will always be times when you share your Personal Power Package.

4. Ask the following questions:

- Who are some of the people to whom you give your personal power?

- Do you give your power to people at school?

- Do you give it to them or do they take it?

5. Continue the mini-lecture:

Sometimes we give up our personal power voluntarily. For example, if you were hospitalized with a serious illness or injury, it would probably make good sense to give up part of your power temporarily to the doctors and nurses. You may give up power involuntarily because adults believe that is what's best for you at a certain time of life. School is the best example of that. You don't choose to go to school. That's an example of someone having power over you, and you have to surrender part of your Personal Power Package. But you still keep some of your power; for example, you might choose to work hard while you're in school because what you learn there will give you more power later on.

These are positive examples of giving up control of your Personal Power Package. There are also negative examples. Doing something you know is wrong so that you can be part of the group is a negative example. Peer pressure is handing over your personal power to other people when it doesn't help you in the long run.

Always think before you hand someone your Personal Power Package. That's a power you always have and like all power, it can be used positively or negatively.

Brainstorm: Positive and Negative Uses of Power

LEVEL: A
(15 MINUTES)

1. Make two columns on the chalkboard. Label one "Positive Uses of Power" and the other "Negative Uses of Power." Have the class brainstorm each list. If the class needs help ask some of the following prompting questions:

- How have you seen kids at school using power positively/negatively?
- When have people used power positively/negatively with you?
- Have you ever used your power positively/negatively?

2. Summarize and conclude the brainstorming by asking the following questions:

- If someone were visiting us from another planet, what would you say to him or her about using power on this planet?
- How would you summarize these two lists?

LEVEL: B/C
(15 MINUTES)

Power Plays: Skits for Examining Personal Power

Handouts *Power Plays*

1. Ask for volunteers to present the Power Play entitled, "Homework Helper." Explain the background information to the class, then have the actors present the skit. When they have finished, discuss how power is used in the skit.

   DISCUSSION:
   - What kind of power does Chris have or lack in this skit?
   - What kind of power does Pat have or lack?
   - How did you see power being used in this skit?
   - Would you call them positive or negative uses of power?
   - What makes it positive? What makes it negative?
   - The next time Chris goes to divide fractions, what do you think will happen?
   - How could Chris or Pat change the power dynamic?

2. During the discussion, introduce the concepts "power over" and "power with." Write these terms on the board. Ask students what they think these terms mean. If they cannot figure out the meanings, explain as follows:

   Power over—A way of holding power that dominates or controls another person or group; having power and either withholding it completely from another person or group or just dispensing part of the power; making decisions that affect another person or group without that person or group's consent. Power over is similar to an aggressive or directing conflict resolution style.

   Power with—A collaborative or shared approach to power where, as much as possible, the people affected by a decision are involved in the decision-making.

   Both styles have potential uses and limitations. For example, if you were babysitting and the children started playing with matches, you would want to use your power in a power-over manner and take the matches away. Then you might discuss with the children why playing with matches is dangerous, which would be "power with" because it shares information with them.

3. Choose one of the remaining *Power Plays* and ask volunteers to act it out. Ask the class to pay attention to the ways that power is being used. After the skit is finished, lead a discussion.

   DISCUSSION
   - How did you see power being used by the various characters?
   - What would be an example of "power over" in this skit? What made it either a positive or negative use of power?

- What would be an example of "power with" in this skit?
- If you were in this situation, how would you change it into a positive use of power?

LEVEL: A/B/C
(5 MINUTES)

Evaluation/Review of Key Points

1. Have volunteers say one thing they think they will remember from this lesson.

2. Review and summarize the key concepts of the lesson:

   - Everyone has a Personal Power Package.
   - The Personal Power Package is made up of Skills and Knowledge; Social Position; Social Skills; Abilities, Strengths, and Talents; Rights and Responsibilities; and Self-knowledge.
   - Power can be used in ways that are positive and negative.
   - It's important to be aware of when and how we are asked or forced to give up our Personal Power Package.

Additional Activities

LEVEL: A/B/C
(TIME WILL VARY)

Conflict Journal Activity

Have students write on one of the following topics in their conflict journals:

- Throughout the day, when are you asked to give up all or part of your Personal Power Package? Is giving it up voluntary or are your forced to give it up? When you do give it up, what power do you keep?

- Throughout the day, what examples do you see of positive and negative uses of power? Which are examples of Power Over? Which are examples of Power With? What are the consequences in each type of situation?

LEVEL: A/B/C
(TIME WILL VARY)

Microlab

The concept of power is a rich one and lends itself well to a microlab. Set up microlab groups of four and present them with a few of the following questions. If your students are interested and time allows, repeat the microlab with a new set of questions.

- What choices have you made with your Personal Power Package? Are there changes you would like to make?
- What rights do you have? How do you exercise those rights?
- What responsibilities do you have? How do you perform them?
- Do you think of yourself as a "responsible person"? Do other people think of you as a responsible person? Why or why not?
- What knowledge and skills are you gaining that will increase your Personal Power Package? What knowledge and skills could you add?
- Describe a time you felt powerful and why. Describe a time you felt powerless and why.

The Personal Power Package

Your Personal Power Package is made of several components. Some components overlap, and in every component there are aspects you control, and aspects you do not control. You are always making choices about what you will do with the power you have.

SOCIAL SKILLS

These are your skills at interacting with other people. They include how you communicate, resolve conflicts, work cooperatively, deal with differences, and make decisions. You can choose to develop and improve these skills.

SOCIAL POSITION

This includes your age, gender, race, ethnicity, and social class. You don't control these, and these may be used to either increase or limit your power. You may choose to resist the limitations imposed on you by your social position.

ABILITIES, STRENGTHS, AND TALENTS

Examples include talents in areas such as the arts, athletics, and public speaking. You may be born with many of these, but you can choose to develop and use them.

RIGHTS AND RESPONSIBILITIES

As a citizen of a nation you have rights, but you also have responsibilities that go with them, and you choose how to use your rights and execute your responsibilities. You also have rights and responsibilties as a member of this class, of a club, a religious group, and a community.

SKILLS AND KNOWLEDGE

This includes standard academic skills such as reading, writing, math, science, and critical thinking. This also includes technical and job-related skills such as the ability to use computers. You may be required to learn some sets of knowledge and skills, but you choose how well you learn them. Having skills and knowledge makes you more powerful.

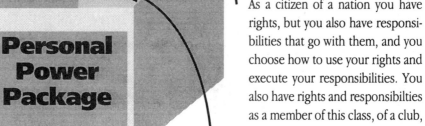

SELF-KNOWLEDGE

Understanding and respecting yourself gives you power. Knowing your spiritual beliefs, your values, and your priorities also gives you power.

Power Play: Homework Helper

The Scene: Pat is a middle school student. Pat's younger sibling is Chris, a fifth grade student. They are sitting together at the kitchen table, doing homework.

CHRIS: (Slams table in frustration) I give up!

PAT: What's the matter?

CHRIS: It's this math homework. I'll never get how to divide fractions.

PAT: Let me see if I can help you. (Pat starts doing the homework)

CHRIS: Wow, that's great how fast you do them! How did you get the first answer?

PAT: Well it's a little complicated to explain. Why don't you just let me do them, then you'll be off the hook.

CHRIS: But what will I do the next time?

PAT: You'll probably get it by then. If not, I'll be here to help you again.

Power Play: Group Ground Rules

The Scene: It is the beginning of the year in a middle school health class. The health teacher is asking the class to participate in establishing some ground rules.

MS. POOLE:	I thought it would be a good idea to talk about some ground rules for our time together. Let's create some guidelines about what to do and not do in this class to help us have a more successful time together. Any suggestions?
STUDENT #1:	Don't interupt others when they're talking?
MS. POOLE:	Sounds good to me, what do the rest of you think?
STUDENT #2:	No tests!
MS. POOLE:	I meant what do you think about "No interupting."
STUDENT #3:	(Interupting her) No papers either!
MS. POOLE:	Come on guys, be serious.
STUDENT #1:	How about the right to say "I pass." We have that in Ms. Alexander's class. We can decide if we want to participate in a discussion.
MS. POOLE:	Hmmm. I don't know about that one.
STUDENT #2:	Come on, what are you afraid of?
STUDENT #3:	The right to pass is important. I mean, you can't force people to talk about things they don't want to talk about.
MS. POOLE:	That's true, but frankly I'm afraid it will be abused. Some kids will pass all the time.
STUDENT #2:	That doesn't happen in Ms. Alexander's class. She trusts us.

STUDENT #3:   Yeah, don't you trust us?

MS. POOLE: It's not about trust. If everyone passes all the time then I won't have the information I need to grade you.

STUDENT #3:   See? She doesn't trust us.

MS. POOLE: I said that it's not about trust, but I'm saying "no" to the suggestion of establishing a right to pass. (Students groan.) Let's continue. Does anyone else have a guideline or rule they'd like to suggest?

Power Play: Questions About the Quarry

The Scene: It's a hot summer afternoon. Marcus, Larry, Jerome, and Randell are hanging out, trying to decide what to do.

MARCUS:	Let's go hang out at the old quarry.
LARRY:	Yeah, we can go swimming and stuff.
JEROME:	No, I don't want to.
MARCUS:	Come on. What are you, chicken?
JEROME:	No, but it's dangerous there. Last year a kid was really hurt on the rocks, and the police have been stopping people from swimming and hanging out.
RANDELL:	(Imitates chicken) Squawk, squawk squawk!
JEROME:	Very funny. Cut it out.
MARCUS:	You're such a wimp. You never want to do anything.
JEROME:	I just don't want to get in trouble over something stupid.
MARCUS:	Fine with me chicken boy.
RANDELL:	Chicken wimp boy.
LARRY:	Knock it off you guys. Let's find a place we all want to go.
MARCUS:	What? Are you a chicken, too?
LARRY:	Forget it then, let's just go to the quarry. We'll see you later Jerome.
MARCUS:	So long, wimp!
RANDELL:	Squawk, squawk, squawk squawk!

15 Power Struggles

LESSON IN BRIEF	Level B and C students (seventh and eighth grades) analyze a power struggle and explore the concepts of "power over" vs. "power with" in conflicts.
OBJECTIVES	Students will be able to:

- Define and distinguish between "power over" and "power with,"
- Identify strategies for "dropping the rope" in power struggles,
- Explain why no one really wins a power struggle.

CONFLICT TOOL	Conflict Tug O' War Rope
VOCABULARY	*Coercion*—The act of dominating or restraining by force; making something happen by force or threat.

Power Struggle—A conflict over who holds power; usually involves an attempt to dominate another person or group.

LESSON SEQUENCE

- Gathering (Optional)
- Agenda and Vocabulary Review
- Analyze a Power Struggle
- Mini-lecture on Power Struggles
- Conflict Tug O' War Demonstration
- Evaluation/Summary of Key Points
- Closing (Optional)

TIME REQUIRED	One class period (Minimum 40 minutes) depending on the additional activities you choose.
HANDOUT	*Drama Trauma*
MATERIALS	Clothes line (25 feet in length)

LEVEL: B/C
(5 MINUTES)

Gathering (Optional)

If you so desire, choose a Gathering Activity from Appendix A.

LEVEL: B/C
(2 MINUTES)

Agenda and Vocabulary Review

Write the agenda on the board and review it with the class. Introduce any vocabulary in the lesson you think they may need help with.

LEVEL: B/C
(15 MINUTES)

Analyze a Power Struggle

MATERIALS: Two copies of the handout *Drama Trauma*

> **Note:** *If your students were not introduced to "power over" and "power with" in the previous lesson, do so now. (See p. 142.)*

1. You will need two boys and one girl to act in the skit, as well as one student of either gender to be the narrator. Any two of these students can also help you with the demonstration in the Conflict Tug O' War activity, but it often has more dramatic impact if you use the same two boys who act out the dispute. It's helpful to explain the demonstration to the participants beforehand.

2. Have the players act out the skit as written. Then discuss.

   * How can you tell this is a power struggle?
   * Where does Marcus get his power?
   * Where does Tom get his power?
   * Where does Ms. Cohen get her power?
   * What makes Marcus and Tom powerful people in this situation?
   * What negative uses of power did you see in this interchange?
   * What positive uses of power did you see?

LEVEL: B/C
(5 MINUTES)

Mini-Lecture On Power Struggles

1. Give the following mini-lecture

   Power plays a role in every conflict. Some conflicts are mostly about power, such as getting someone to do something he or she doesn't want to do. These are called "power struggles." Power struggles often lead to people using power in a "Power Over" way that is negative. In the long run, no one wins a power struggle. They may win in the short run by getting someone to do what they want, but at the same time they sow seeds of resentment, hostility, and revenge. That's because the person who wins the power struggle often has to resort to "Power Over" tactics such as force or coercion to make the other person do what they don't really want to do.

LEVEL: B/C
(10 MINUTES)

Conflict Tug O' War Demonstration

MATERIALS   Clothes line (about 25 feet)

Note: *It heightens the impact of this demonstration if you take a few minutes ahead of time to explain to the participating students what you are trying to do. It also helps if these are the same two students who participate in the role-play at the beginning of this session.*

1.   Hold up the loose rope and explain:

A power struggle is like a tug o' war. This conflict resolution tool that I'm holding is called the "Conflict Tug O' War Rope." Student X and Y are going to show you how it works. As you watch this demonstration, think about the play you just read/saw.

2.   Have one of the students hold the rope at the end. Have the other student hold the rope about six feet along. You should hold on to the rest of the rope. Have the students enact a tug o' war and say the following words as they pull: first student pulls and says, "Yes you will!" The second student pulls and says "No I won't!" First student pulls and says "Yes you will!" and so on, back and forth until you tell them to stop. Let the tug o' war go for a few pulls, then as they continue pulling, take your end of the rope and begin wrapping it around the warring students. When the rope is all used up, stop the tug o' war and say: "The problem with a power struggle is that everyone involved can end up tied in a big knot."

3.   Continue explaining:

A power struggle is like a tug o' war. It begins when someone offers the other end of a rope (do so to one of the students) and that person picks it up. Then the back and forth begins, usually leading nowhere. The trick then is to recognize when someone is trying to get you to pick up the other end of the rope. By doing this they are trying to control you. You don't have to be controlled. You can't have a power struggle if one person refuses to pick up the other end of the rope. If you pick it up without realizing it, drop it as soon as you can. Remember the phrase "Drop the rope." When you "drop the rope," you and your opponent can choose a more constructive way to handle the conflict. You open the way to use "power with" instead of "power over."

DISCUSSION

- What are some ways you've been handed a rope and then participated in a power struggle?
- Can you think of an example of a power struggle that someone won in the short run but lost in the long run?
- Can you think of an example of a power struggle that led to a "Power With" solution?

LEVEL: B/C
(5 MINUTES)

Evaluation/Summary of Key Points

1. Have volunteers say one thing they think they will remember from this lesson.

2. Review and summarize the key concepts of the lesson:

    *   Power can be used in ways that are positive and negative.
    *   Power struggles are based on a power-over approach and in the long run no one wins a power struggle.
    *   A power struggle is like a tug o' war.
    *   Be aware of when someone is trying to get you to pick up the other end of the rope. If you do pick it up, try to drop it.

Additional Activity

LEVEL: A/B/C
(TIME WILL VARY)

Conflict Journal Activity

Have students write about power in their conflict journals. Ask them to look for examples of power struggles throughout the day. Have them analyze these examples using one or two of the following questions:

*   How are these struggles handled, "Power Over" or "Power With"?
*   Who wins and who loses?
*   Have you seen anyone drop the rope? What's the effect of that?

Drama Trauma

Roles:

Narrator

Marcus—A middle school student

Tom—A middle school student

Ms. Cohen—the drama club advisor

NARRATOR:	Marcus and Tom are members of the drama club and are the only members of the selection committee. Plays are chosen by the selection committee and in the past month they have read over 30 plays. As we join them they are trying to make their final selection.
MARCUS:	I don't think there's any question about it. *On With Your Life!* is the play to do.
TOM:	Oh barf!
MARCUS:	What do you mean "barf"?
TOM:	I mean that it's a really lousy play—just about the worst of all the ones we read.
MARCUS:	I thought it was great and I think we should do it.
TOM:	You just like it because your girlfriend wrote it!
MARCUS:	Oh give me a break! That had nothing to do with it.
TOM:	Yeah, right.
MARCUS:	I say we do *On With Your Life!*
TOM:	And I say never in a million years.
MARCUS:	I'm the director, and I should get the most say in which play we do.
TOM:	That's not what the rules say. The rules say we have to agree. So what's your second choice?
MARCUS:	*On With Your Life!*
TOM:	Forget it.
MARCUS:	You know, I've done lots of favors for you.

TOM: This isn't about favors. It's about finding a good play.

MARCUS: This is a good play.

TOM: Don't bother talking about it anymore. We're not doing that play.

MARCUS: Yes we are.

TOM: No we're not!

MARCUS: Yes

MS. COHEN: (Pokes her head into the room) How's it coming guys?

MARCUS: Terrible! We can't agree on what play to do.

MS. COHEN: Do you want me to decide for you?

16 Making Responsible Decisions

LESSON IN BRIEF	Students discuss responsible decision making, then learn and practice a decision-making method.
OBJECTIVES	Students will be able to:

- Identify steps in decision making,
- Name criteria for determining whether a decision is "responsible,"
- Apply steps and criteria to a decision.

CONFLICT TOOLS	ABCDE Decision Making; Personal Decision-Making Guidelines
VOCABULARY	*Evaluate*—To determine the importance, size, or value of something; to judge, analyze, assess.
	Criteria—The standards used to make a decision; guidelines for judgments and decisions.
LESSON SEQUENCE:	

- Gathering (Optional)
- Agenda and Vocabulary Review
- Discuss Responsible Decision Making
- Introduce the ABCDE Approach
- Guidelines for Responsible Decision Making
- Evaluation/Review of Key Points
- Closing (Optional)

TIME REQUIRED	One class period (Minimum 40 minutes) depending on the additional activities you choose.
HANDOUTS	*ABCDE Decision Making, Personal Decision-Making Guidelines*

<table>
<tr><td>

LEVEL: A/B/C
(5 MINUTES)

</td><td>

Gathering (Optional)

If you so desire, choose a Gathering Activity from Appendix A.

</td></tr>
</table>

LEVEL: A/B/C
(2 MINUTES)

Agenda and Vocabulary Review

Write the agenda on the board and review it with the class. Introduce any vocabulary in the lesson you think they may need help with.

LEVEL: A/B/C
(10 MINUTES)

Discuss Responsible Decision Making

1. Have students brainstorm a list of decisions that they have made today. List these on the board. Point out that we are always making decisions about what we do and say.

2. Ask: How do we make decisions? Is there a process you use to make decisions such as,

   - Whether or not you will do homework?
   - Whom you will sit with at lunch?
   - What activities you will do with friends?

LEVEL: A/B/C
(5 MINUTES)

Introduce the ABCDE Decision-Making Process

Note: *If students have been introduced to ABCDE in previous years, simply review the steps then go to the microlab on responsible decision making.*

1. Give the following mini-lecture.

   Anytime we make a decision we go through several steps. We may not even be aware of going through the steps, but we do. You've probably seen problem-solving or decision making procedures before. Problem solving and decision making are pretty much the same. They both involve defining what the problem is, thinking of ways to solve the problem, choosing a solution and implementing it, then evaluating your decision.

2. Distribute the handout, "ABCDE Decision Making." This is a variation on the problem-solving process. It's been adapted to an ABCDE format to make it easy to remember. The steps are:

   A Assess the situation and ask, "What's my problem?"

   B Brainstorm possible solutions.

   C Choose a solution according to the Decision-Making Guidelines.

   D Do it—act on your decision.

   E Evaluate the decision once it has been implemented.

3. Lead a discussion about the decision-making process.

- Do you tend to make decisions quickly or do you think about them for a long time? How might the process on the handout change that?
- Why do you think the handout specifies "personal" decisions? Would this process be different if a group was making the decision? How?

LEVEL: A/B/C
(10 MINUTES)

Guidelines for Responsible Decisions

Note: *If students have discussed responsible decision making in previous years, go to the microlab activity.*

1. Ask students to think about some of the decisions they have made recently.

2. Ask the class: What is a "responsible" decision? Have them brainstorm a list of words and phrases that describe responsible decisions.

3. Distribute the handout, *Personal Decision-Making Guidelines*. Read the handout together then ask the following questions:

- How does this list compare with our list?
- Do any of these criteria seem more or less important than the others?
- Which of these criteria have you used?
- Where do these guidelines fit in to the decision-making process? (Emphasize that they are used at steps C and E.)
- Why do you think the handout specifies "personal" decisions? Would these questions be different if a group was making the decision? How would they be different?

LEVEL: B/C
(15 MINUTES)

Microlab: Responsible Decision Making

1. Divide the class into microlab groups of four.

2. Write the following questions on the board. Each group member should take a total of three minutes to describe:
   - A time when I made a responsible decision and how I know it was responsible.
   - A time I made an irresponsible decision and how I know it was irresponsible.
   - A time I couldn't figure out what decision to make.
   - A time I made a decision to please my friends and regretted it.
   - A decision I made that pleased my parents.

   You should take responsibility for signaling at the end of each three-minute period.

3. Bring the class back together for a dicussion:

    - What similarities emerged as your group shared decision-making experiences?
    - What are the main factors you consider before making a decision?
    - How is personal decision making related to personal power?

LEVEL: A/B/C
(5 MINUTES)

Evaluation/Review of Key Points

1. Have volunteers say one thing they think they will remember from this lesson.

2. Review and summarize the main points of the lesson:

We make decisions all the time.

Decision making can be helped by a process called ABCDE:

A   Assess the situation and ask, "What's my problem?"

B   Brainstorm possible solutions.

C   Choose a solution according to the Decision-Making Guidelines.

D   Do it—act on your decision.

E   Evaluate the decision once it has been implemented.

Decisions need to be evaluated according to some criteria or guidelines before calling them "responsible." Some guidelines for responsible decisions are:

- Is it legal?
- Is it against the rules of the place where I am?
- Is is moral? Is it consistent with my religion or values?
- Does it help or hurt myself and others?
- Will I feel good about it afterwards?
- Is it safe?
- How would I feel if someone did this to me?

Additional Activity

LEVEL: A/B/C
(TIME WILL VARY)

Conflict Journal Activity

Have students write on one of the following topics in their conflict journals:

- A decision I've made that backfired and why I think that happened.
- A decision I made that pleased or didn't please my friends and what happened to my relationship as a result.
- A time I was stuck making a decision and why I think I got stuck.

ABCDE Decision Making

This is a process for making personal decisions:

A   **Assess** the situation and ask, "What's my problem?"

B   **Brainstorm** possible solutions.

C   **Choose** a solution according to the Personal Decision-Making Guidelines.

D   **Do** it—act on your decision.

E   **Evaluate** the decision once it has been implemented.

Personal Decision-Making Guidelines

These are criteria to use to determine whether a personal decision is responsible.

1. Is this legal or is it against the law?

2. Is this acceptable here or is it against the rules?

3. Is it moral? Is it against my beliefs and values or the teachings of my religion?

4. Does it help myself and others, or is it harmful to myself and others?

5. Will I feel good about it afterwards or will I feel sorry afterwards?

6. Is it safe or is it dangerous?

7. How would I feel if someone did this to me?

Demands and ReallyNeeds*

LESSON IN BRIEF   Students learn to distinguish Demands from "ReallyNeeds."

NOTES   This lesson takes students to a greater level of understanding of Point of View by helping them learn to identify Demands and ReallyNeeds. (These are also known in conflict resolution language as Positions and Interests.) Demands (or positions) are what people in a conflict say that they want. ReallyNeeds (or interests) are why they want them, their "needs, desires, concerns, and fears." Demands are often mutually exclusive, and people in conflict get stuck at this level, not knowing how to progress further. Being able to distinguish ReallyNeeds from Demands is a powerful tool for students to help them move past the Demands Impasse.

OBJECTIVES   Students will be able to:

- define Demands and ReallyNeeds;
- identify Demands and ReallyNeeds in conflict situations;
- re-frame negative ReallyNeeds into positive language.

CONFLICT TOOL   Demands and ReallyNeeds

VOCABULARY   *Demands*—What people in conflicts say that they want.

ReallyNeeds—The reasons why they are making those demands; their needs, desires, concerns, and fears.

LESSON SEQUENCE
- Gathering (Optional)
- Agenda and Vocabulary Review
- Introduce (or Review) Demands and ReallyNeeds
- Practice Identifying Demands and ReallyNeeds
- Any Additional Activities You May Choose
- Evaluation/Review of Key Points
- Closing (Optional)

TIME NEEDED   One class period (minimum 40 minutes), depending on the additional activities you choose.

HANDOUTS   *Demands and ReallyNeeds Case Studies (Level A: Twin Television Troubles, Level B: Science Project Problems, Level C: What Are Friends For?); Demands and ReallyNeeds Role Plays (Level B: Class Clown Conflict; Level C: Choosing Sides Conflict)*

* The terms "Demands" and "ReallyNeeds" are adapted from Tom Snyder Productions, *Getting to the Heart of It,* (Watertown, MA: Tom Snyder Productions, 1994), Computer software. They in turn are adapted from the concepts of Positions and Interests in Roger Fisher and William Ury, *Getting To Yes: Negotiating Agreement Without Giving In* (New York: Viking Penguin, 1981,1991).

MATERIALS

Demands and ReallyNeeds Overheads (Level A: "I need to watch this show on T.V."; Level B: "I'm doing all the work."; Level C: "You can't talk that way about Ouida.")

LEVEL: A/B/C
(5 MINUTES)

Gathering (Optional)

If you so desire, choose a Gathering Activity from Appendix A.

LEVEL: A/B/C
(3 MINUTES)

Agenda and Vocabulary Review

Write the agenda on the board and review it with the class. Introduce any vocabulary in the lesson that you think will be unfamiliar to your students.

LEVEL: A/B/C
(15 MINUTES)

Introduce (or Review) Demands and ReallyNeeds

HANDOUTS   *Case Studies* (Level A, B, or C)

MATERIALS   Demands and Really Needs Overhead, overhead projector (if an overhead projector is not available, write the Demands and ReallyNeeds on the board).

> **Note:** *If this is a review for students, acknowledge at the beginning that they may have been introduced to this concept previously. Explain that this lesson will go into the concept in more depth.*

1. Explain to students that this lesson will help them understand more about P.O.V.s. Distribute the appropriate case studies, reminding students that they originally looked at these cases in Skill Lesson 13 when they used the Win-Win Grid. Have students review the case studies.

2. Show the Demands and ReallyNeeds Overhead (Level A, B, or C as appropriate), making sure that the thought balloons are covered up. Read the two Demands. Explain that these are Demands, that is, what the two people in the conflict say that they want. (If you are not using the overheads, write the Demands on the board.)

3. Ask: Why do you think they each are making these Demands? For each .character have students suggest some possible reasons for their Demands. After students have made suggestions, read the appropriate case study. Then show the thought balloon for each disputant and compare what's written with what students suggested.

4. Write the terms "Demands" and "ReallyNeeds" on the board and explain that Demands are what people in a conflict say that they want. ReallyNeeds are why they want them—their needs, desires, concerns, and fears. Often people get stuck by insisting on their Demands when they could solve their conflict by looking at ReallyNeeds. Today's lesson focuses on how to identify Demands and ReallyNeeds.

DISCUSSION

- What are some examples of common Demands you hear in school?
- What might be the ReallyNeeds behind those Demands?
- How could looking at ReallyNeeds help the people in our example solve their conflict?
- How do feelings affect ReallyNeeds?

LEVEL: B/C
(15 MINUTES)

Practice Identifying Demands and ReallyNeeds

HANDOUTS *Demands and ReallyNeeds Role Plays* (Level B or C)

1. Ask for two volunteers to act out a conflict for the group. While the actors are reading over their roles, read the first paragraph to the class on the role-play card, which explains what the conflict is about. Ask the actors to confront each other in their conflict. Also ask them to try to reveal through their dialogue all the information on their cards.

2. When the role-play is complete, have the following discussion.

DISCUSSION

- What were the Demands in this role-play?
- How could they solve this conflict based on the Demands?
- What ReallyNeeds could you identify?
- Think of the definition of ReallyNeeds: needs, desires, concerns, fears. Can you think of other possible ReallyNeeds?
- What's difficult about determining ReallyNeeds?
- If you were one of these disputants, how would you find out the other person's ReallyNeeds?
- How would you let them know your own ReallyNeeds?

3. Challenge students to come up with a solution that incorporates some of the ReallyNeeds of both disputants. Give them two minutes for this.

DISCUSSION

- What solutions did you come up with?
- How were they different from the kinds of solutions that were based on Demands?
- In what ways was looking at ReallyNeeds helpful?

LEVEL: A/B/C
(2 MINUTES)

Evaluation/Review of Key Points

1. Have volunteers say something they learned in today's lesson.

2. Summarize the key points in this lesson.

- Demands are what people in a conflict say that they want.
- ReallyNeeds or Interests are why they want them, their needs, desires, concerns, and fears.

LEVEL: A/B/C
(5 MINUTES)

Closing (Optional)

If you so desire, choose a Closing Activity from Appendix B.

Additional Activities

LEVEL: A/B/C
(TIME WILL VARY)

Conflict Journal Activity

Have students choose a conflict from their journal and describe the Demands and ReallyNeeds of the disputants. Did the disputants stay at the level of Demands, or did they move to discuss ReallyNeeds? How might they have resolved the conflict by sharing ReallyNeeds?

LEVEL: A/B/C
(TIME WILL VARY)

Writing ReallyWant Comics

Note: *This is a good homework assignment.*

Have students create Conflict Comics where the characters talk about their Demands and ReallyNeeds. They should first state the ReallyNeeds for each character in thought balloons. Then the comic strip should show how the characters get beyond arguing about Demands and explain their ReallyNeeds to each other.

Twin Television Troubles

Terry and Deena are twin brother and sister. They are both in middle school.

Deena was lying on the couch watching TV. "This movie will be great," she thought. "Just what I need to forget those stuck-up girls in gym." Suddenly, Terry came rushing in.

"Deena, I've got to use the TV now. There's a show on that I need to watch for my social studies class, and it started five minutes ago."

Deena laughed. "Oh, give me a break. Like you're supposed to watch TV for Mrs. Reed. She'd be the last person to assign a TV show."

"Well, she did," Terry insisted. "It's about the Civil War, and if I don't report on it I'm in trouble. She gave me the assignment because I need the extra credit. I'm really doing lousy in her class, and if I don't do this she'll kill me. You know how she is!"

"Well, I was here first, so for once I get to be in charge. Besides, you can watch it on Mom and Dad's TV. Or tape it. I've had a tough day, and I really want to watch this movie."

"Their TV is on the blink, and you're using the VCR to watch your movie. Come on, Deena. I really need your help."

Science Project Problems

Mara and Reggie have been assigned to work together on a cooperative project for science class. They've known each other for several years, but they haven't worked together before. They haven't been very friendly either.

The project is due in two weeks and they will receive a joint grade. Part of the grade will be based on the content of the project and part of it will be based on how well they work together.

Two days into the project, Reggie is already upset with Mara. Reggie likes to plan ahead, and he hates doing things at the last minute. But he can't get Mara to commit to anything. They agreed the first day that the project would be about solar energy, and they're both doing research. But they haven't decided what the project will be, who will do what, how big a project it will be, when each piece will be done, anything. It's making Reggie crazy.

"I'm not doing this whole thing myself," he said to Mara.

"Will you relax? We have a week and a half. We'll get it done," Mara said.

"When are we going to get it done? We only have a week and a half!"

"My style is different from yours," Mara said. "I need to read my book and think about how the project might look. I get good ideas just letting things percolate in the back of my head. Don't worry, I always get things done."

What Are Friends For?

Christopher and Suzanne are friends who hang around with the same group of friends. One day they were talking together after school when Suzanne started talking about a problem she was having with Ouida, a girl Christopher likes and has just asked out for Friday night.

Christopher said, "You know, she's really nice."

"I'm not saying she's not nice," protested Suzanne. "I'm saying I have a problem with her. She has an attitude sometimes."

"Well it makes me mad when you talk that way about someone I like. You're disrespecting her and me."

"So when I have a problem with someone I can't talk to you about it, even though we've been friends for years. Is that what you're saying? It makes me mad when someone who is supposed to be my friend won't listen to me."

Christopher felt very frustrated. "I just don't want you talking that way about Ouida!"

"You can't tell me what to talk about!" Suzanne snapped.

Demands and ReallyNeeds Overhead

I need to watch this show on T.V.!

I'm watching this movie so forget it!

I need the extra credit from this report.

Mrs. Reed gave me this chance. I want to protect my reputation with her.

I need to feel my sister supports me when I'm in a jam.

I need to relax after today.

Those girls hurt my feelings and I want to forget them for awhile.

I want to get *my* way once in a while.

Demands and ReallyNeeds Overhead

I'm doing all the work!

My style is different from yours!

I want a good grade.

I hate working at the last minute. I feel sick.

I like to work steadily all along.

I want a good grade.

I need to let things percolate for a while.

I like to work at my own pace, sometimes fast, sometimes taking my time.

Demands and ReallyNeeds Overhead

You can't talk that way about Ouida!

You can't tell me what to talk about!

I like Ouida.

I want her to be respected.

I'm afraid she'll think I agree with Denise.

I don't want to feel like I'm caught in the middle.

I want to like Ouida, but she's making it hard.

I need someone to talk to.

I'm afraid she's taking my friend away from me.

Class Clown Conflict

The Conflict (explain to the group): The Teacher has a conflict with Student A, who talks and jokes a lot in class. Yesterday the Teacher yelled at Student A, who then stormed out of the class. Now they are meeting in private.

Teacher: You have a large class with several troublesome students. Student A in particular is the class clown, always talking and fooling around. This encourages other students to fool around. You feel very frustrated with the lack of respect you receive. Even though you dislike shouting and prefer to treat students calmly and maturely, yesterday you lost it. You yelled at Student A in front of the whole class. Student A stomped out shouting that she or he was never coming back. Now things have calmed down, and you are meeting with Student A in private.

- -

The Conflict: The Teacher has a conflict with Student A, who talks and jokes a lot in class. Yesterday the Teacher yelled at Student A, who then stormed out of the class. Now they are meeting in private.

Student A: You feel that the Teacher is always blaming you for every problem and outburst that anyone makes. It seems like the Teacher has it in for you, and no matter what kind of work you do, you get a poor grade. Sure you joke a lot, but you have a good sense of humor. Your joking around keeps other students from making fun of how short you are. You like getting attention, but on your terms, not by being yelled at. When the Teacher yelled at you yesterday, you were embarrassed in front of everyone. You weren't going to take that.

Choosing Sides Conflict

The Conflict (explain to the group): Student 2 has a boyfriend/girlfriend that his or her parents don't like. Student 2 wants Student 1 to help him or her lie to the parents. They are talking about it now.

Student 1: Your friend, Student 2, has a boyfriend/girlfriend of whom his or her parents don't approve. Student 2 keeps asking you to lie to his or her parents about where he or she is. You did lie for him or her once, but you didn't feel good about it. You want to keep your friend, but you don't believe it's right to lie. Besides, you think the parents have a point about this boyfriend/girlfriend. You think Student 2 could do much better.

- -

The Conflict: Student 2 has a boyfriend/girlfriend that his or her parents don't like. Student 2 wants Student 1 to help him or her lie to the parents. They are talking about it now.

Student 2: Your parents don't want you to see your boyfriend/girlfriend. You have asked your best friend, Student 1, to help you lie about your whereabouts to your parents. You think it's okay to lie if a situation is unfair. Besides, friends should stick together and help each other out. You'd do the same for Student 1. He or she did it once, why not again?

18 Demands and ReallyNeeds in Conflicts

LESSON IN BRIEF	Students practice distinguishing demands from "ReallyNeeds" and use this information in resolving conflicts.
NOTES	Learning to identify and use demands and ReallyNeeds is an important skill for anyone who wants to learn to handle conflict more effectively. It can also be a difficult skill to master. This lesson provides students with more practice in identifying demands and ReallyNeeds, both in case studies and in their own lives.
OBJECTIVES	Students will be able to:

Students will be able to:

- identify demands and ReallyNeeds in conflict situations;
- discuss demands and ReallyNeeds in their own lives.

CONFLICT TOOL	Demands and ReallyNeeds
VOCABULARY	*Demands*—What people in conflicts say that they want.

ReallyNeeds—Why they are making those demands; their needs, desires, concerns, and fears.

LESSON SEQUENCE

- Gathering (Optional)
- Agenda and Vocabulary Review
- Find the Hidden Demands
- Microlab: Identifying Demands and ReallyNeeds
- Any Additional Activities You May Choose
- Evaluation/Review of Key Points
- Closing (Optional)

TIME NEEDED

One class period (minimum 40 minutes), depending on the additional activities you choose.

LEVEL: A/B/C
(5 MINUTES)

Gathering (Optional)

If you so desire, choose a Gathering Activity from Appendix A.

LEVEL: A/B/C
(3 MINUTES)

Agenda and Vocabulary Review

Write the agenda on the board and review it with the class. Introduce any vocabulary in the lesson that you think will be unfamiliar to your students.

LEVEL: A/B/C
(15 MINUTES)

Find the Hidden Demands

1. Explain that demands can sometimes seem like ReallyNeeds. Read the following situation to students:

   Shawna and Mark are working together on a social studies project about everyday life just prior to the Civil War. They found some diaries from the period and feel like they really understand how young people lived then.

   Shawna wants them to put the information into a skit. She enjoys getting up in front of people and performing. In fact, she plans on becoming an actress. Mark hates this idea of a skit. He hates getting up in front of people, and he's no performer. He's always afraid that people will laugh at him and tease him. He's been teased before and tries to avoid putting himself in situations where it might happen again. Mark wants them to write a report—no big dramatics, but no risks either.

   Shawna really dislikes this idea. Actually, she's a good writer, but frankly, her grades in social studies haven't been too good this term. She thinks that if they do something big and dramatic the teacher will be sure to give both of them an "A."

2. Write the following on the board:

Shawna says "I want to..."	**Mark says "I want to..."**
Get a good grade.	Get a good grade.
Put on a skit.	Avoid being teased.
Get attention from my classmates.	Do something safe.
Do something I'm good at.	Write a nice, safe report.
Perform in front of the class.	Not do a skit.
	Avoid risks.

3. Discuss which of the statements listed are demands and which are ReallyNeeds. Remind them of the definition of each.

   DISCUSSION

   - Looking at Shawna's statement, which do you think might be a Demand? (Put on a skit; perform in front of the class.)

   - Which of Mark's list might be demands? (Write a nice, safe report;

not do a skit.)

- Why is it important to distinguish between the two? (If they start negotiating based on these lists, Shawna and Mark could end up just going back and forth about whether or not to do a skit and never solve the conflict in a way that meets their important ReallyNeeds.)

**LEVEL: A/B/C
(15 MINUTES)**

Microlab: Identifying Demands and ReallyNeeds

1. Have students form microlab groups of three or four. Have each student take two minutes to address the following:

   - My demands and ReallyNeeds in a conflict were...
   - The demands and ReallyNeeds of the person I was in conflict with were...
   - How our demands and ReallyNeeds affected our conflict was...

   Be sure to give a signal every two minutes.

2. Bring the group together for a discussion.

   DISCUSSION

   - What did you observe as you did the activity?
   - How did it feel to talk about demands and ReallyNeeds?
   - Did you have any difficulty determining demands and ReallyNeeds?

**LEVEL: A/B/C
(5 MINUTES)**

Evaluate/Review of Key Points

1. Have volunteers say something they liked about today's lesson and something they wish had been different.

2. Summarize the key points in this lesson:

   - Demands are what people in a conflict say that they want.
   - ReallyNeeds are why they want them—their needs, desires, concerns, and fears.
   - It is usually more productive to negotiate around ReallyNeeds than demands. Demands are often mutually exclusive.

**LEVEL: A/B/C
(5 MINUTES)**

Closing (Optional)

If you so desire, choose a Closing Activity from Appendix B.

Additional Activities

**LEVEL: A/B/C
(TIME WILL VARY)**

Conflict Journal Activity

Have students choose a conflict from their journal and describe the demands and ReallyNeeds of the disputants. Did the disputants stay at the level of demands, or did they move to discuss ReallyNeeds? How might they have resolved the conflict by sharing ReallyNeeds?

LEVEL: A/B/C
(TIME WILL VARY)

Writing ReallyNeed Comics

Note: *This is a good homework assignment.*

Have students create Conflict Comics where the characters talk about their demands and ReallyNeeds. They should first state the ReallyNeeds for each character in thought balloons. Then the comic strip should show how the characters get beyond arguing about demands and explain their ReallyNeeds to each other.

LEVEL: A/B/C
(15 MINUTES)

The Voice of ReallyNeeds

Have a volunteer come to the front of the room and pretend to be a person in a conflict. Ask the volunteer to face the class and give a Demand. Once the Demand is given, other students take turns standing behind that student and say possible ReallyNeeds behind the Demand, using as much as possible an "I ReallyNeed..." format. For example, if the Demand is, "You better stop saying stuff about me or else!" the ReallyNeeds might be, "I ReallyNeed to have a good reputation," "I ReallyNeed to feel respected," "I ReallyNeed to feel like I can trust my friends," "I ReallyNeed to _____."

19 Beginning to Negotiate

LESSON IN BRIEF	Students use a negotiation process based on separating Demands from ReallyNeeds and developing solutions that meet the important ReallyNeeds of both or all parties.
NOTES	Negotiation is a collaborative process where people work out their disputes together. Students will need to handle most conflicts in their lives without third-party assistance, so negotiation is an important process to learn and a process that students can use all their lives.
OBJECTIVES	Students will be able to:

- identify the steps of win-win negotiation,
- practice negotiation in a role-play,
- name the five negotiation guidelines,
- describe how negotiation might be used in a real-life conflict.

CONFLICT TOOL	Negotiation
PREREQUISITE	Demands and ReallyNeeds (Conflict Skill Lesson 17)
VOCABULARY	*Negotiation*—A collaborative approach to problem solving.
LESSON SEQUENCE	

- Gathering (Optional)
- Microlab: Introduce (or Review) Informal Negotiation
- Introduce (or Review) Formal Negotiation
- Practice Negotiating
- Evaluation/Review of Key Points
- Closing (Optional)

TIME NEEDED	One class period (minimum 40 minutes), depending on the additional activities you choose.
HANDOUTS	*Win-Win Negotiation*

LEVEL: A/B/C
(5 MINUTES)

Gathering (Optional)

If you so desire, choose a Gathering Activity from Appendix A.

LEVEL: A/B/C
(3 MINUTES)

Agenda and Vocabulary Review

Write the agenda on the board and review it with the class. Introduce any vocabulary in the lesson that you think will be unfamiliar to your students.

LEVEL: A/B/C
(10 MINUTES)

Microlab: Introduce (or Review) Informal Negotiation

Note: *If this is a review for students, acknowledge at the beginning that they may have been introduced to this concept previously. Explain that this lesson will go into the concept in more depth.*

1. Explain that negotiation is a type of conflict resolution where the disputants talk things out in order to reach an agreement. There isn't a third party helping them negotiate, they do it on their own. People negotiate informally all the time.

2. Divide the class into microlab groups of three or four. Each group should choose one person to be a reporter. Each student in the group has two minutes to address the following:

   • A time I negotiated with a friend or family member was...
   • The solution was...
   • How I felt about negotiating and the solution was...

3. Have the whole class discuss the experience with the reporters responding to the following discussion questions:

   DISCUSSION

   • What types of negotiating were talked about in your group?
   • Did negotiating lead to satisfactory solutions?
   • Where did people have trouble negotiating?
   • What did people like about negotiating?

LEVEL: A/B/C
(5 MINUTES)

Introduce (or Review) Formal Negotiation

HANDOUTS   *Win-Win Negotiation*

Note: *If this is a review for students, acknowledge at the beginning that they may have been introduced to this concept previously. Explain that this lesson will go into the concept in more depth.*

1. Explain that one way to get better at informal negotiation is to practice a more formal or structured type of win-win negotiating.

2. Distribute the *Win-Win Negotiation* handout, explaining that the class will be following this negotiation procedure to resolve a conflict. Discuss the steps of win-win negotiation.

DISCUSSION

- How are these steps similar to or different from the CAPS approach?
- Are there steps that are unclear or confusing?

LEVEL: A/B/C
(15 MINUTES)

Practice Negotiating

1. Have students rejoin their microlab groups to participate in this activity. Explain the situation:

   Each group has just won an all-expenses-paid vacation anywhere they want to go for two weeks. There are only three conditions:

   1) You must use the win-win negotiating process to decide where you are going.

   2) You can only go to one place, and you must go together and stay together.

   3) You must all agree that you want to go there, and you must agree on how you will get there.

   (In other words you *can't* divide the two weeks by saying: we'll spend three days in Florida, then three days in Italy, then three days at Marcia's grandmother's house. And two of us are going to fly and one is going to go in a chauffeur-driven limo.) Does everyone understand the ground rules? You will have eight minutes to negotiate.

2. Give students eight minutes to negotiate, then discuss their experiences. If you need to, give them two more minutes, but no more. They will learn from the experience even if they don't finish.

   ### DISCUSSION

   - What did you notice about trying to negotiate an agreement?
   - What was easy for your group?
   - What was hard for your group?
   - Did you remember to look at demands and ReallyNeeds? Did that help?
   - How did it feel when you came to an agreement?
   - For groups that didn't come to an agreement, how did that feel?

   Note: *Arrange for groups that didn't finish negotiating an agreement to complete their negotiation at another time.*

LEVEL: A/B/C
(5 MINUTES)

Evaluation/Review of Key Points

1. Ask volunteers to say something that they learned about themselves today.

2. Summarize the key points in this lesson:

   - Negotiation is a way people can solve their conflicts themselves.

   - There are formal and informal versions of the negotiation process.

- Both negotiation processes are based on distinguishing demands from ReallyNeeds and finding solutions that meet the important ReallyNeeds of both or all parties.

- Certain behaviors are helpful in negotiation: not making demands and looking for ReallyNeeds, listening and not interrupting, being respectful and not using escalating behaviors such as name calling or putting down.

LEVEL: A/B/C
(5 MINUTES)

Closing (Optional)

If you so desire, choose a Closing Activity from Appendix B.

Additional Activity

LEVEL: A/B/C
(TIME WILL VARY)

Conflict Journal Activity

Note: *This is a good homework assignment.*

Have students look for examples of informal negotiation. They should describe these, then see how they compare with the formal win-win negotiation described on the handout. Are there ways that people follow those steps even when the negotiation is informal?

Win-Win Negotiation

1. Identify your Demands and ReallyNeeds.

2. Present your Demands and ReallyNeeds to the other person, and listen to the Demands and ReallyNeeds of the other person.

3. Brainstorm possible solutions.

4. Eliminate solutions that are unacceptable.

5. Choose a solution that will meet everyone's important ReallyNeeds.

6. Make a plan to take action.

20 More on Negotiation

LESSON IN BRIEF   Students use a negotiation process based on separating demands from ReallyNeeds and developing solutions that meet the important ReallyNeeds of both or all parties.

NOTES   Win-win negotiation challenges students to use all the conflict resolution skills they have learned thus far. In this lesson, students continue to practice a formal win-win negotiation process. First, they develop negotiation guidelines based on their experience with negotiating, then they role-play a formal negotiation.

OBJECTIVES   Students will be able to:

- identify the steps of win-win negotiation,
- practice negotiation in a role-play,
- name the five negotiation guidelines.

CONFLICT TOOL   Negotiation

PREREQUISITE   Demands and ReallyNeeds (Conflict Skill Lesson 17)

VOCABULARY   *Negotiation*—A collaborative approach to problem solving.

LESSON SEQUENCE

- Gathering (Optional)
- Introduce (or Review) Negotiation
- Discuss Negotiation Guidelines
- Practice Negotiation
- Any Additional Activities You May Choose
- Evaluation/Review of Key Points
- Closing (Optional)

TIME NEEDED   One class period (minimum 40 minutes), depending on the additional activities you choose.

HANDOUTS   *Hints for Good Negotiations; Win-Win Negotiation Role Plays (Level A: Library Liability, Level B: The Curfew Conflict, Level C: Grounded Over Grades); Additional Activity: Vogueville Dress Code Disaster (The Principal, The Teacher, The Parent, The Student)*

Gathering (Optional)

If you so desire, choose a Gathering Activity from Appendix A.

Agenda and Vocabulary Review

Write the agenda on the board and review it with the class. Introduce any vocabulary in the lesson you think will be unfamiliar to your students.

Discuss Negotiation Guidelines

HANDOUTS   *Hints for Good Negotiations*

1. Discuss with students the problems or pitfalls they observed in the vacation negotiation in Lesson 19 (or in other negotiations they have attempted).

    *   Where was there potential for escalating the conflict?
    *   What contributed (or might have contributed) to its escalation?
    *   What behaviors made (or might have made) the disputants angrier?
    *   What helped (or might have helped) the conflict de-escalate?
    *   What behaviors made (or might have made) the disputants less angry?

2. Distribute the *Hints for Good Negotiations* handout and discuss the three suggestions. Do they make sense based on students' experience negotiating? Are there any they would add?

Practice Negotiation

HANDOUTS   *Negotiation Role-Play Cards* (Level A,B, or C)

Note: *This activity was designed as a large group role-play. It may be done by small groups.*

1. Explain to the class that they will be role-playing a negotiation. This role-play is a little different from the ones they have done previously because it involves the whole class. Everyone in the class will play either one role or the other.

2. Divide students into two groups of approximately the same size. Give each student in one group Negotiation Role 1 (either A, B, or C, depending on appropriateness). Give each student in the second group a copy of Negotiation Role 2.

3. Have them proceed with the negotiation as described in the *Win-Win Negotiation* handout from Skill Lesson 19. First, each group gathers to determine its demands and ReallyNeeds. Choose one person in the group to be the recorder and write down what the group identifies.

4. After five minutes, have a representative from each group present their demands and ReallyNeeds to each other in front of the class. The rest of

the class should observe to see what helps this presentation and what hinders it, i.e., what things cause the conflict to escalate or de-escalate, increase or decrease anger, etc.

5. After five minutes, have the class reunite to brainstorm possible solutions to the conflict. Record these on the board. Remind students that the goal of brainstorming is to get as many ideas as possible out, not to judge whether or not they will work. That will come in the next step.

6. After five minutes, end the brainstorm. Have the students return to their original role groups. Explain that they will be going over the possible solutions to evaluate whether or not they meet the ReallyNeeds of one group or the other. There are three ways to evaluate the possible solutions: No Way (draw a line through the idea), Maybe (write a question mark next to the idea), and Possibility (make a check mark by the idea).

7. Go through the list with the class, marking the ideas. Either group may eliminate an idea they dislike, but they must give a reason other than "We don't like it" or "That won't work." They must say why they don't like it or why it won't work. Keep reminding students that the goal is to come up with a solution that will meet important ReallyNeeds of both parties.

8. When the evaluation is finished, have the class reunite. Ask them to look at the Maybes and the Possibilities and see if they can use those to come up with a solution that meets the important ReallyNeeds of both parties.

9. Once a solution is developed, have students return to their original role groups one last time to see if they feel it is a win-win solution.

10. If students are unable to come up with a solution, or if they eliminate all the possibilities during the evaluation period, back up and ask them to reconsider the suggestions they eliminated. Emphasize that the point is to have lots of choices so they can come up with a mutually satisfying (win-win) solution.

DISCUSSION

- What did you notice about this negotiation process?
- What parts of the process were difficult?
- What parts were easy?
- Which steps seem most important or valuable to you?
- What would a more informal negotiation look like?

LEVEL: A/B/C
(5 MINUTES)

Evaluation/Review of Key Points

1. Have volunteers summarize the key points in this lesson.

    *   Negotiation is a way young people can solve their conflicts themselves.

    *   Negotiation should be based on distinguishing Demands from ReallyNeeds and finding solutions that meet the important ReallyNeeds of both or all parties.

    *   Certain behaviors are helpful in negotiation: not making Demands and looking for ReallyNeeds; listening and not interrupting; being respectful and not using escalating behaviors such as name calling or putting down.

LEVEL: A/B/C
(5 MINUTES)

Closing (Optional)

If you so desire, choose a Closing Activity from Appendix B.

Additional Activities

LEVEL: A/B/C
(45 MINUTES)

The Vogueville Dress Code Disaster

HANDOUTS   One set of *Dress Code Disaster Role Cards* for each group of four, with extra copies of the "Student" Role Card

1. Divide students into work groups of four. If you have extra students, make some groups of five. Give each person in the group a Role Card. In groups of five, give the fifth student one of the extra "Student" Role Cards.

2. Have students read their Role Cards and identify their demands and ReallyNeeds. Before they begin to negotiate, warn them that this negotiation is a little tricky because it involves four parties negotiating. Also explain that there are two ground rules. One, they must pretend they have agreed to the negotiation, so if they get stuck they must keep trying. Two, they may reveal any of the information on their Role Card that they wish. However, they may not show the Role Card to the other party.

3. Give students ten to fifteen minutes to negotiate, then discuss.

    DISCUSSION

    *   What did you notice as you did this negotiation?
    *   What made it difficult?
    *   What contributed to escalation in this conflict?
    *   What skills did you use as you negotiated?
    *   What did you do to de-escalate the conflict?
    *   How did having more people affect the negotiation?

LEVEL: A/B/C
(TIME WILL VARY)

Conflict Journal Activity—Create A Role-Play

Note: *This is a good homework assignment.*

Using a conflict from their Conflict Journals, have students write a role-play that involves a negotiable conflict. Or, after students have had additional practice with a role-play like "The Dress Code Disaster," they can create negotiation role-plays that are set outside their immediate world, such as role-plays that take place in show business, the sports world, international business, history, etc.

Hints for Good Negotiations

1. Stay Off the Conflict Escalator

Be respectful.

Avoid words and behaviors that escalate.

2. Talk About ReallyNeeds Instead of Demands

When you hear a demand say: "That sounds like a demand."

Ask: "What do you really need?"

3. Listen

Don't interrupt or act silly.

Use what you know about good listening.

Library Liability

Negotiation Role #1: Sandy

You and Anton are having a conflict because Anton lost a library book. You used the book on a report that you are writing together. You took the book out of the library, but Anton borrowed it from you and didn't return it. Now the library is sending you overdue notices. If you don't return the book, you're going to have to pay for it. You don't have the money to pay for the book. Anton used to be a good friend but now you wonder. You did enjoy working on the report with Anton.

- -

Negotiation Role #2: Anton

Sandy says you lost a library book that Sandy took out of the library for a report you are doing together. You're sure that you returned it before the due date. You feel like Sandy is trying to put the blame on you. You have a history of losing and forgetting things. But this time you are sure it isn't your fault the book is missing. You enjoyed working on the report with Sandy, and the two of you have always been good friends. Is this going to wreck your friendship?

The Curfew Conflict

Negotiation Role #1: Mom

Tom wants to stay out late and hang around with his friends. You say, "No." This has created a great deal of tension in the house, and communication between you and Tom is difficult. You are worried that Tom will get into trouble, which you know can happen even to a good kid who doesn't mean to get into trouble. You also worry about his safety and feel that it is your responsibility as a parent to know where he is. Tom has good grades, and you want them to stay that way. You do trust Tom, but you don't know all his friends and are not sure you trust them. You are not happy with the tension in the house and wish you and Tom were talking things out.

- -

Negotiation Role #2: Tom

You want to stay out late and hang around with your friends without having to tell your Mom where you're going. But your Mom says, "No." You have good grades, and you would continue to keep them up. You would also keep up with your jobs around the house. You feel you've proven that you can be trusted, and you feel your friends can be trusted. You know how to say "no" to something foolish or dangerous. You don't understand why you aren't being allowed this freedom when other kids your age have it. The atmosphere in the house is tense, and you and your Mom aren't communicating very well about anything these days.

Grounded Over Grades

Negotiation Role #1: Kindra

You have been in this school for just a few months, and you're having a hard time making friends. You've been unhappy and had a hard time concentrating on your schoolwork. You just failed your most recent math test, and you can't believe it. You've never failed a test in your life! You feel like you've let yourself down and let your parents down. Your mother is a doctor and your father is a lawyer, and they both believe that you should always get top grades. Your father says you can't go out or use the phone for two weeks. But you've just started getting friendly with a couple of the popular girls at school. How can you have a friendship if you can't go out or talk on the phone? Making friends is more important to you than getting good grades right now.

- -

Negotiation Role #2: Dad

You believe that hard work is the key to success in school and in life. Both you and your wife had to work very hard to get where you are now; she's a doctor and you're a lawyer. Kindra's grades have always been excellent, but since she's been at this new school she hasn't seemed like herself. And now she failed a math test! You want the best for Kindra, and you want her to be able to go to the best college. But she won't get there talking on the phone. You want her to stay home for two weeks and not use the telephone. You don't want to punish her, but she has to keep those grades up.

The Vogueville Dress Code Disaster

"The Principal"

Background At Vogueville Middle School, students are forbidden to wear T-shirts that are "considered by a staff member to be obscene or use questionable language." Students who have worn such T-shirts—usually crude slogans or CD cover designs—have been sent home to change.

One day Carlos Mendez wore a T-shirt that a teacher thought was offensive. She sent Carlos home to change. Carlos was outraged, saying his T-shirt was painted by a famous Mexican muralist. The next day Mr. and Mrs. Mendez called the school to protest, but the principal told them the dress code was clear. The following week, the Mendez family told the principal that they were considering suing the school district, claiming that any dress code was a violation of Carlos' right of free speech.

The Superintendent of Schools feels this is escalating out of control. To de-escalate the conflict she is forming a task force of the principal, a teacher, a parent, and a student representative. The Mendez family says that if the task force can come up with an agreement that satisfies the PTA, they won't sue.

The Principal We've got to keep the dress code as it is. When the kids wear anything they want, the school is disrupted and disorderly. When I came here there was chaos. Test scores were down, teachers were frustrated, and the parents were unhappy. We've worked hard over the past four years to restore order and motivate students to value education. They've told us that they prefer to be in a school environment that is safe, orderly, and productive. The teachers are happier and so are the parents. I won't let this one set of parents destroy all that.

The Vogueville Dress Code Disaster

"The Teacher"

Background At Vogueville Middle School, students are forbidden to wear T-shirts that are "considered by a staff member to be obscene or use questionable language." Students who have worn such T-shirts—usually crude slogans or CD cover designs—have been sent home to change.

One day Carlos Mendez wore a T-shirt that a teacher thought was offensive. She sent Carlos home to change. Carlos was outraged, saying his T-shirt was painted by a famous Mexican muralist. The next day Mr. and Mrs. Mendez called the school to protest, but the principal told them the dress code was clear. The following week, the Mendez family told the principal that they were considering suing the school district, claiming that any dress code was a violation of Carlos' right of free speech.

The Superintendent of Schools feels this is escalating out of control. To de-escalate the conflict she is forming a task force of the principal, a teacher, a parent, and a student representative. The Mendez family says that if the task force can come up with an agreement that satisfies the PTA, they won't sue.

The Teacher
I support the dress code. I like having the students dressed nicely. It shows respect for school. Do they know that the teachers have a dress code too? It's a way all of us, adults and young people, say that something important goes on here. That's not to say that we enforce the dress code well. Personally, I don't find T-shirts disruptive, although they may be annoying and offensive. But other people take offense more easily than I do, and that's their right. Even though I support the dress code, I hate to have a student miss class because of a T-shirt. I can't honestly say that the dress code is more important than being in class.

The Vogueville Dress Code Disaster

"The Parent"

Background At Vogueville Middle School, students are forbidden to wear T-shirts that are "considered by a staff member to be obscene or use questionable language." Students who have worn such T-shirts—usually crude slogans or CD cover designs—have been sent home to change.

One day Carlos Mendez wore a T-shirt that a teacher thought was offensive. She sent Carlos home to change. Carlos was outraged, saying his T-shirt was painted by a famous Mexican muralist. The next day Mr. and Mrs. Mendez called the school to protest, but the principal told them the dress code was clear. The following week, the Mendez family told the principal that they were considering suing the school district, claiming that any dress code was a violation of Carlos' right of free speech.

The Superintendent of Schools feels this is escalating out of control. To de-escalate the conflict she is forming a task force of the principal, a teacher, a parent, and a student representative. The Mendez family says that if the task force can come up with an agreement that satisfies the PTA, they won't sue.

The Parent It seems to me that this dress code is not enforced consistently and is sometimes kind of silly. I mean, my son was sent home for nothing more than wearing a T-shirt with a heavy metal band's name on it. I had to leave work to pick him up. I know other parents who've missed work and even been docked pay because of it. Does that make sense? The kids should be at school, and we should be at work. I'm glad the school has such high standards for school work, but how will the kids learn if they're not in class? What one teacher finds offensive another may not even notice.

The Vogueville Dress Code Disaster

"The Student"

Background At Vogueville Middle School, students are forbidden to wear T-shirts that are "considered by a staff member to be obscene or use questionable language." Students who have worn such T-shirts—usually crude slogans or CD cover designs—have been sent home to change.

One day Carlos Mendez wore a T-shirt that a teacher thought was offensive. She sent Carlos home to change. Carlos was outraged, saying his T-shirt was painted by a famous Mexican muralist. The next day Mr. and Mrs. Mendez called the school to protest, but the principal told them the dress code was clear. The following week, the Mendez family told the principal that they were considering suing the school district, claiming that any dress code was a violation of Carlos' right of free speech.

The Superintendent of Schools feels this is escalating out of control. To de-escalate the conflict she is forming a task force of the principal, a teacher, a parent, and a student representative. The Mendez family says that if the task force can come up with an agreement that satisfies the PTA, they won't sue.

The Student I don't think there should be a dress code. The teachers never give us any credit for being able to do anything. They won't even let us make decisions about what to wear to school. It's really insulting. I'm proud that I go to a good school, and I'm glad the school has gotten over its bad reputation. But what difference does it make what we wear? That doesn't affect what we learn. I know some kids support the dress code. Some of the girls think some of the T-shirts the guys wear are offensive, and I don't think those shirts should be allowed. But now teachers have total control to decide what's offensive, and I don't think that's right.

21 Beginning to Mediate and Arbitrate

LESSON IN BRIEF   Students practice conflict resolution skills by acting as mediators in role-play situations.

NOTES   For many young people, conflict resolution means some kind of third party intervention, usually an adult authority figure who controls the situation and helps the disputants come to an agreement. Two common types of third-party dispute resolution are mediation and arbitration. Although the two terms are often used interchangeably, they are not the same. In mediation, a neutral third party helps the disputants by creating an environment where they can solve their own problem. The mediator doesn't solve the problem for them. In arbitration, the process is much the same, except that an arbitrator does solve the problem for the disputants. This lesson introduces students to third-party dispute resolution, focusing on mediation.

OBJECTIVES   Students will be able to:

- define mediation and arbitration,
- identify the steps in mediation,
- identify the qualities of a peacemaker.

CONFLICT TOOL   Mediation, Arbitration

PREREQUISITES   Win-Win Grid (Conflict Skill Lesson 13); Active Listening (Conflict Skill Lesson 8); Demands and ReallyNeeds (Conflict Skill Lesson 17); Negotiation (Conflict Skill Lesson 19)

VOCABULARY   *Mediation*—Resolving conflicts with the assistance of a neutral third party who does not influence the solution.

Arbitration—Resolving conflicts with the assistance of a neutral third party who directs the solution.

LESSON SEQUENCE
- Gathering (Optional)
- Introduce (or Review) the -Ate Words
- Introduce (or Review) the Qualities of a Mediator or Arbitrator
- Introduce (or Review) the Mediation Process
- Evaluation/Review of Key Points
- Closing (Optional)

TIME NEEDED   One class period (minimum 40 minutes), depending on the additional activities you choose.

HANDOUTS   *The Win-Win Mediation Process, Qualities of a Peacemaker: Mediator or Arbitrator, Model Mediation Script*

MATERIALS   Peacemaker Kit—place the following objects in a box or suitcase: a yardstick, a pair of rubber ears (from a joke shop), a pair of cowboy boots and a pair of ballet slippers (or two distinctly different pairs of shoes), a bag of Hershey's Kisses®, and a roll of masking tape.

LEVEL: A/B/C
(5 MINUTES)

Gathering (Optional)

If you so desire, choose a Gathering Activity from Appendix A.

LEVEL: A/B/C
(3 MINUTES)

Agenda and Vocabulary Review

Write the agenda on the board and review it with the class. Introduce any vocabulary in the lesson that you think will be unfamiliar to your students.

LEVEL: A/B/C
(5 MINUTES)

Introduce (or Review) the -Ate Words

Note: *If this is a review for students, do the quick review activity that follows, then do the mediation role-play.*

1. Write the words "Negotiate," "Mediate," and "Arbitrate" on the board. Ask students to define negotiate. Explain that mediate and arbitrate are two other ways of resolving conflicts.

    •   Mediation is when a neutral third party, called a mediator, helps people resolve their conflict. The mediator does not resolve the conflict for the people, he or she helps them solve the problem themselves.

    •   Arbitration is when a neutral third party, called a arbitrator, helps people resolve their conflict. The arbitrator listens to both sides and helps them talk together but, unlike a mediator, the arbitrator does resolve the conflict for the people.

2. Give students the following examples and ask them to identify negotiation, mediation, and arbitration:

    •   Urvashi, Lea, and Kate were supposed to put up a bulletin board display together, but they couldn't agree on what the theme should be. They finally went to their teacher Mr. Nuñez and asked him to choose the bulletin board theme.

    •   Leroy and Jonas were arguing about what they were doing for their social studies project. After two weeks they realized they hadn't made any progress and they only had a week left to do the project. They sat down together and worked out an agreement.

    •   Ricardo and Diana were playing on the same softball team, but they both wanted to pitch. They were shouting at each other. Finally Linda came up and helped them work out a solution to the problem.

DISCUSSION

- Have you ever used one of these conflict resolution approaches?
- What are some other ways of resolving conflicts that are not on this handout?

LEVEL: A/B/C
(20 MINUTES)

Introduce (or Review) the Qualities of a Mediator or Arbitrator*

MATERIALS Create a Peacemaker Kit by placing the following objects in a box or suitcase: a yardstick, a pair of rubber ears (from a joke shop), a pair of cowboy boots and a pair of ballet slippers (or two distinctly different pairs of shoes), a bag of Hershey's Kisses®, and a roll of masking tape.

1. Ask students what qualities a good mediator or arbitrator should have, or ask: If you were going to talk to a mediator about a conflict you're having, what would you want the mediator to be like? As students come up with suggestions, list them on the board.

2. Show the Peacemaker Kit and explain that it contains some props representing four qualities essential for an effective mediator or arbitrator. (As you discuss each prop in the Peacemakers Kit as described below, note any connections to the class' list.)

3. Tell students the first quality is that a mediator or arbitrator is neutral, fair, and unbiased. Demonstrate by balancing the yardstick horizontally on your forefinger. Explain that the peacemaker is responsible for keeping things balanced and fair and doesn't lean to one side or the other. If he or she does, the balance is lost and the process is upset.

4. Tell students the second quality is that a mediator is a good listener. Demonstrate by showing the rubber ears and explaining that we've already talked about how important listening is in resolving conflicts. When you're helping other people resolve their conflicts it is particularly important to listen well.

5. Tell students that a mediator treats the people in the conflict with respect and tries to understand their P.O.V.s. Show the two pairs of shoes and explain that the mediator needs to try to stand in the shoes of the disputants, no matter how different those shoes are. As a mediator, you might not agree with someone, but you try to understand their feelings and P.O.V. You might not like the shoes they wear, but you need to show the disputants you understand that the shoes they wear are important to them.

---

* From *Peer Mediation: Conflict Resolution in Schools* (Program Guide, pp. 49-51) by Fred Schrumpf, Donna Crawford, and H. Chu Usadel, 1991, Champaign, IL: Research Press. © 1991 by the authors. Adapted by permission.

6. Tell students that a mediator helps disputants work together. Ask for two volunteers to come to the front of the room. Hold up the bag of Hershey's Kisses® and explain the task to the two students:

    Your goal is to earn as many Hershey's Kisses® as you can in 30 seconds. The way you earn Kisses is to get into this position with each other (show an arm wrestling position but do not use the term "arm wrestling"). Each time you touch the back of the other person's hand to the desk, you earn a Hershey's Kiss®. Remember, the goal is to earn as many Kisses as you can in 30 seconds. I'll give you a starting signal and a stop signal.

7. Give the students a starting signal. They will probably compete.

8. After 30 seconds, tell them to stop. Ask: Did you work together or against each other? How could you have worked together? Show how you could complete the task in a cooperative way. What would have been the result of working together?

9. Tell students that a mediator keeps information confidential. Show the masking tape, tear off a piece, and put it over your mouth. Then remove it and explain: One way mediators build trust is by showing that they can keep the problems they hear confidential.

10. Finish the activity by distributing the *Qualities of a Peacemaker* handout and Hershey's Kisses® to the class.

LEVEL: A/B/C
(15 MINUTES)

Introduce (or Review) the Mediation Process

HANDOUTS   *Win-Win Mediation Process*, three copies of the *Model Mediation Script*

> **Note:** *If this is very familiar to your students, proceed to Conflict Skill Lesson 22.*

1. Distribute the *Win-Win Mediation Process* handout. Briefly have students compare the steps in the mediation process with the steps in the Win-Win Negotiation process.

2. Have student volunteers present the Win-Win Mediation Process by acting out the *Model Mediation Script*. The different steps in the Win-Win Mediation Process are indicated in the script, but the actors should not indicate when the various steps are being enacted. That will be part of the discussion that follows.

    DISCUSSION

    *   How did the mediator apply Step One (Opening) in the role-play?
    *   Did the mediator adhere to the Qualities of a Peacemaker?
    *   How did the mediator apply each of the other steps of the Win-Win Mediation Process?

- Do you think that Michael and Sondra came up with a win-win solution?
- Are there other solutions that they might have come up with?

LEVEL: A/B/C
(5 MINUTES)

Evaluation/Review of Key Points

Have volunteers summarize the key points in the lesson.

- Mediation and arbitration involve a neutral third party in the conflict resolution process.
- A mediator does not make a decision for the disputants, while an arbitrator does.
- Mediation and arbitration are collaborative processes and require the willingness of the disputants to work.

LEVEL: A/B/C
(5 MINUTES)

Closing (Optional)

If you so desire, choose a Closing Activity from Appendix B.

Win-Win Mediation Process

1. Opening

2. Gather Information—Facts and Feelings

3. Determine ReallyNeeds

4. Generate Possible Solutions

5. Evaluate Possible Solutions and Choose One

6. Make a Plan

Qualities of a Peacemaker: Mediator or Arbitrator

1. Neutral, Fair, Unbiased

2. A Good Listener

3. Treats Disputants with Respect and Tries to Understand Their P.O.V.

4. Helps Disputants Work Together

5. Keeps Things Confidential

Model Mediation Script[*]

1. Opening

MEDIATOR: Hello, my name is _____, and I am your mediator today. Michael and Sondra, I welcome you both to mediation. Let me explain the ground rules. First, I remain neutral—I do not take sides. Second, everything in the mediation is kept confidential. What is said in mediation is not discussed outside this room. Third, each person takes turns without interruption. There is no name calling or put-downs. Finally, you agree to try your best to reach an agreement. Sondra, do you agree to these rules?

SONDRA: Yes.

MEDIATOR: Michael, do you agree to the rules?

MICHAEL: Yeah.

2. Gather Information—Facts and Feelings

MEDIATOR: Sondra, why don't you go first, and tell me what happened?

SONDRA: Michael and I were arguing in the hallway. I got mad and threw my books at him. Then he shoved me against the lockers and was yelling at me when Mrs. Thomas saw us. She suspended Michael. I never fight with anyone—I just got so frustrated with Michael, I lost control.

MEDIATOR: You say you were frustrated and threw your books at Michael. Mrs. Thomas saw Michael shove you and suspended him. How did you feel when that happened?

---

[*] From *Peer Mediation: Conflict Resolution in Schools* (Program Guide, pp. 49-51) by Fred Schrumpf, Donna Crawford, and H. Chu Usadel, 1991, Champaign, IL: Research Press. © 1991 by the authors. Adapted by permission.

SONDRA: I felt angry at first, then I felt bad that Michael got in trouble because I was the one who started the fight. Now we aren't talking, and nothing I do seems to help.

MEDIATOR: Sondra, you say you're sorry Michael was suspended and you're still frustrated. Michael, tell me your point of view on the problem.

MICHAEL: Sondra is always getting mad at me. We're in this talent contest together and are rehearsing a dance piece. I missed one practice, and she turns it into a war.

SONDRA: It was more than one. You're so irresponsible. You're either late for practice or you don't even bother to come, and you never tell me if you're not coming.

MEDIATOR: Sondra, it's Michael's turn to talk. Please don't interrupt or use putdowns. Michael, you missed a rehearsal, and Sondra got angry. Tell me more about that.

MICHAEL: Sondra takes the talent show much too seriously. She needs to lighten up. She thinks just because we're dance partners I belong to her. She's always bossing me.

MEDIATOR: Michael, are you saying that you want Sondra to be less bossy?

MICHAEL: Yes. This talent show isn't my whole life.

MEDIATOR: Sondra, do you have anything else you want to add?

SONDRA: Michael doesn't take this talent show seriously. I want him to think about how I feel when he stands me up at practice.

MEDIATOR: Sondra, you want Michael to understand your feelings when he doesn't come to practice and doesn't tell you he won't be there.

SONDRA: Yes, that's what I want.

MEDIATOR: Michael, do you have anything to add?

MICHAEL: No.

S T U D E N T   H A N D O U T

3. Determine ReallyNeeds

MEDIATOR:	Sondra, what do you really need?
SONDRA:	Like I said, I want him to come to practice and tell me when he won't be there. But mostly he should come to practice.
MEDIATOR:	Why do you need that?
SONDRA:	I want us to practice so we'll be good in the talent contest. I want to win that $100. And I want us to look good in front of everyone. I don't want us to look like fools.
MEDIATOR:	Michael, what does Sondra ReallyNeed?
MICHAEL:	What do you mean?
MEDIATOR:	What did you hear her say that she ReallyNeeds?
MICHAEL:	Well, she wants us to do a good job in the talent contest. She wants to win $100. She wants me to practice and to let her know if I'm not going to be there or if I'm going to be late.
MEDIATOR:	Michael, what do you ReallyNeed?
MICHAEL:	I want her to lighten up. I'm willing to practice. I mean, I agreed to be in this talent show didn't I?
MEDIATOR:	Is there anything else you ReallyNeed?
MICHAEL:	I want to do a good job. I'd like to win the $100 as much as she does. And I want us to look good too. But I don't want all this pressure.
MEDIATOR:	Sondra, what does Michael ReallyNeed?
SONDRA:	He wants to do well in the talent contest and to win the $100, but he wants for me to not pressure him.
MEDIATOR:	Sondra, is what you're doing now getting you what you ReallyNeed?

SONDRA:	No.
MEDIATOR:	Michael, is what you're doing now getting you what you ReallyNeed?
MICHAEL:	No.

4. Generate Possible Solutions

MEDIATOR:	It sounds like you both want to do well in the talent contest and you are willing to practice your dance routine in order for that to happen. Now, I want you both to think about what you can do to help solve your problems. We'll make a list of possible solutions by brainstorming. The rules for brainstorming are to say any ideas that come to mind, not to judge or discuss the ideas, and to look for as many ideas as possible that might satisfy both of you. Ready? What can you do to solve this problem?
MICHAEL:	I could stop skipping rehearsals.
SONDRA:	And let me know if you can't make it.
MICHAEL:	We could practice before school if we miss a practice.
SONDRA:	I could stop yelling at Michael.
MEDIATOR:	What else could you do to solve the problem?
SONDRA:	We could set up a schedule for rehearsals.
MICHAEL:	I could take the contest more seriously. . . I guess I really didn't act as if it mattered to me.
MEDIATOR:	Can you think of anything else?
SONDRA:	No.
MICHAEL:	No.

5. Evaluate Possible Solutions and Choose One

MEDIATOR: Which of these ideas will probably work best?

MICHAEL: Well, practicing before school would be hard because I already have a hard time getting up that early.

SONDRA: If I don't yell at Michael and stop calling him all the time, he probably would like practice better.

MEDIATOR: Can you do that?

SONDRA: If I get upset about something, I could write Michael a note to explain. . . and then we could talk about the problem instead of arguing. Michael could do the same if he's upset about something.

MEDIATOR: Michael, would this work for you?

MICHAEL: It would be better than yelling.

MEDIATOR: What else are you willing to do?

MICHAEL: Well, with the contest coming up. . . I would be willing to practice after school and on Saturday mornings to make up for the times I've missed.

MEDIATOR: Sondra, are you willing to do that?

SONDRA: That practice schedule would be hard work, but I'll do it. I think we can win if we practice really hard. We also need to let each other know if we need to cancel.

MEDIATOR: How would that work?

MICHAEL: We could either call each other or leave notes in each other's lockers.

MEDIATOR: Sondra, do you agree that would help?

SONDRA: Yes.

MEDIATOR: You both agree to practice after school on a schedule, and on Saturdays. What about time?

SONDRA: How about at 4:00 during the day and at 10:00 on Saturday?

MICHAEL: Okay.

MEDIATOR: You both agree to call or leave a note if you need to cancel practice. You both agree if you have a problem in the future, you will write a note to explain the problem and then try to work it out by talking.

6. Make a Plan

MEDIATOR: (Writes up the agreement, then hands it to Sondra and Michael to sign.) Please look this agreement over to be sure it is correct, then sign it. (Sondra and Michael sign, then the mediator signs. Mediator shakes hands with Sondra then Michael.) Thank you for participating in mediation. Would you two like to shake hands? (Michael and Sondra shake.)

More on Mediation and Arbitration

LESSON IN BRIEF	Students practice conflict resolution skills by acting as mediators in role-play situations.
NOTES	This lesson gives students an opportunity to practice third-party dispute resolution. Having discussed the qualities of a peacemaker and discussed and observed the mediation process, students are now ready to try mediation themselves. Like negotiation, mediation requires that they use all the conflict resolution skills they've learned. The goal of this lesson is to give students practice in pulling together what they've learned. Its goal is not to teach them how to be peer mediators—that would require longer and more in-depth training.
OBJECTIVES	Students will be able to:

- define mediation and arbitration,
- identify the steps in mediation,
- use the mediation process in a role-play.

CONFLICT TOOL	Mediation, Arbitration
PREREQUISITES	Win-Win Grid (Conflict Skill Lesson 13), Active Listening (Conflict Skill Lesson 8), Demands and ReallyNeeds (Conflict Skill Lesson 17), Negotiation (Conflict Skill Lesson 19)
VOCABULARY	*Mediation*—Resolving conflicts with the assistance of a neutral third party who does not influence the solution.
	Arbitration—Resolving conflicts with the assistance of a neutral third party who directs the solution.
LESSON SEQUENCE	

- Gathering (Optional)
- Introduce (or Review) the -Ate Words
- Practice Mediation through Role-Playing
- Any Additional Activities You May Choose
- Evaluation/Review of Key Points
- Closing (Optional)

TIME NEEDED	One class period (minimum 40 minutes), depending on the additional activities you choose.
HANDOUTS	*Mediation Role-Play (Level A: Bicycle Bickering, Level B: Honor Roll Rivals, Level C: Bad Attitude Blues), Qualities of a Peacemaker* (Skill Lesson 21), *Win-Win Mediation Process* (Skill Lesson 21).

Gathering (Optional)

If you so desire, choose a Gathering Activity from Appendix A.

Agenda and Vocabulary Review

Write the agenda on the board and review it with the class. Introduce any vocabulary in the lesson you think will be unfamiliar to your students.

Review of the -Ate Words (Optional)

HANDOUTS   If you did not distribute them in the previous lesson, you will need the *Qualities of a Peacemaker* and *Win-Win Mediation Process* handouts.

1. Write the words "Negotiate," "Mediate," and "Arbitrate" on the board. Ask students to define negotiate. Explain that mediate and arbitrate are two other ways of resolving conflicts.

    *   Mediation is when a neutral third party, called a mediator, helps people resolve their conflict. The mediator does not resolve the conflict for the people, he or she helps them solve the problem themselves.

    *   Arbitration is when a neutral third party, called an arbitrator, helps people resolve their conflict. The arbitrator listens to both sides and helps them talk together, but unlike the mediator, the arbitrator does resolve the conflict for the people.

2. If you did not do this in the previous lesson, distribute the *Qualities of a Mediator* handout. Review the qualities and ask students why each quality is important.

3. If you did not do this in the previous lesson, distribute the *Win-Win Mediation Process* handout. Review the steps with the class.

Practice Mediation Through Role-Playing

HANDOUTS   *Mediation Role-Play Cards* (Level A, B, or C); *Win-Win Mediation Process*

1. Explain to the class that they will be practicing the Win-Win Mediation Process by role-playing. The role-plays will be in groups of four with four roles:

    *   Mediator (follows the *Win-Win Mediation Process* handout)
    *   Disputant 1 (uses the first role card from the appropriate level)
    *   Disputant 2 (uses the second card from the appropriate level)
    *   Observer (watches and listens to determine what specific behaviors on the part of the mediator help the disputants solve their problem)

2. Divide students into groups. If necessary, you may have some groups of five, with two observers instead of one. Have students choose roles, or if necessary, you may assign roles to group members. Once students are in groups and understand their tasks, begin the role-play.

3. As students role-play, move from group to group to observe where students have difficulty. Leave about ten minutes for the discussion.

4. When students have finished, process the role-play by having the students report to the class. Begin by having all the mediators report what resolution their disputants came up with. Next, have each disputant describe their experience in the mediation. Finally, have the observers report what specific behaviors they observed that helped the disputants solve their problem.

DISCUSSION

- What did you learn doing this role-play that you didn't know before?
- Did anything surprise you as you participated in the mediation process?
- What were difficult things about the process for you?
- What would happen if the disputants kept interrupting each other and getting mad at each other, refusing to follow the ground rules?
- What could you do if the disputants have no idea how to solve their problem?

Evaluation/Review of Key Points

Have volunteers summarize the key points in the lesson.

- Mediation and arbitration involve a neutral third party in the conflict resolution process.
- A mediator does not make a decision for the disputants, while an arbitrator does.
- Mediation and arbitration are collaborative processes and require the willingness of the disputants to work.

Closing (Optional)

If you so desire, choose a Closing Activity from Appendix B.

Additional Activities

Journal Activities

Students can practice mediation by choosing a conflict from their journals and writing a mediation script or role-play based on it. They should take care to change the names of the disputants and some of the details of the conflict to protect the privacy of the people involved.

Have students look for examples of arbitration and record them in their journals. Encourage them to examine the arbitration and describe how they feel it went, e.g., was the arbitrator neutral? Did he or she facilitate problem-solving? Was the solution a Win-Win?

Staying neutral may be an important quality in a mediator and arbitrator, but it isn't always easy. Have students experiment with trying to remain neutral during a difficult situation. Ask them to describe in their journals what it was like trying to remain neutral, how it was difficult, and what they did to help themselves stay neutral.

Bicycle Bickering

Situation: Pat lent Chris his/her bicycle. While Chris was using the bike, the chain broke. Chris crashed the bike, and now it has a bent front wheel. Now they disagree about who should pay to have the bike fixed.

Pat: You feel that Chris should pay to have the bike fixed. Chris says the chain was rusty, but it wasn't that bad. You think Chris was just careless about riding it. Your family can't afford to buy a new bike or to get this one fixed.

Background: You and Chris have been friends for years, but this is not the first time Chris wrecked something of yours. Chris always treats your stuff carelessly. You sometimes feel that if Chris really liked you, Chris would treat your things more respectfully.

- -

Situation: Pat lent Chris his/her bicycle. While Chris was using the bike, the chain broke. Chris crashed the bike, and now it has a bent front wheel. Now they disagree about who should pay to have the bike fixed.

Chris: You feel that you shouldn't have to pay to fix the bike. The chain was really rusty, and you don't think it's your responsibility. You think Pat hasn't taken proper care of the bike, and now Pat is more worried about repairing the bike than the fact that you might have been really hurt.

Background: You and Pat have been friends for years, and you feel bad about the bike, but it's not the end of the world. Pat always acts like his/her stuff is really precious. It's not that big a deal to get the bike fixed, and it's just not your responsibility. You sometimes feel that Pat cares more about his/her things than your friendship.

Honor Roll Rivals

Situation: Pat and Chris were ready to fight in the hallway between class.

Pat: Chris sits near you in the lunchroom and keeps looking at you and whispering to friends. You know they're talking about you. Chris has even thrown food at you when no teachers were looking. Today you accidentally dumped a slice of pizza in Chris' lap when you walked by.

Background: You and Chris used to be good friends, but for the past year Chris acts like he/she is better than you because you don't make the honor roll and Chris does. You've tried hard to make the honor roll, but you haven't quite made it yet. This is really frustrating to you.

- -

Situation: Pat and Chris were ready to fight in the hallway between class.

Chris: Pat has such a chip on his/ her shoulder. It's like you're not allowed to have new friends—besides, these are people you have more in common with. But Pat always puts your new friends down. You know it was not an accident that the slice of pizza dropped in your lap. You want your pants dry cleaned at Pat's expense.

Background: You and Pat used to be good friends, but for the past year Pat acts like he/she resents you because you make the honor roll and Pat doesn't. You've made new friends, but you still like Pat.

Bad Attitude Blues

Situation: Chris knocked Pat into a locker yesterday. Now they are threatening each other and are ready to fight.

Pat: You are a new student in school. For the past month, Chris has been saying stuff about you and giving you dirty looks. Yesterday Chris pushed you into a locker. Chris says it was an accident, but you don't believe that.

Background: You miss your old friends, and you want to make some new ones at this school, but Chris seems to have it in for you. Chris has a bad attitude.

- -

Situation: Chris knocked Pat into a locker yesterday. Now they are threatening each other and are ready to fight.

Chris: You are angry at Pat because Pat came into the school as a new student and put down the school and your friends. If that's going to be Pat's attitude, there is going to be trouble.

Background: You are the informal leader of a large group of students. You have the influence to have the new student accepted or rejected by the rest of the students.

Extending the Concepts of Part Two: Additional Activities

CONFLICT TOOL	# Exploring/Understanding Conflict
	Classifying Conflict
ACTIVITY IN BRIEF	Students classify conflicts by looking at their various aspects and examine the differences and similarities between conflict at the interpersonal, community, national, and international levels.
HANDOUTS	*Versus vs. Versus, Conflict Sort Cards* (you will need one set of cards for each group of four)

1. Review the definition of conflict students have worked with so far: "A dispute or disagreement between two or more people." Explain that people divide conflicts into different types or categories. These categories may be based on what causes the conflict, what goes on in the conflict, or who is involved. For example, you might have conflict categories based on where the conflicts take place: home conflicts, school conflicts, work conflicts, neighborhood conflicts, etc. Ask for examples of conflict categories. Conflict categories help people deal with the conflict.

2. Distribute the *Versus vs. Versus* handout. Explain that it describes one way of categorizing conflicts. Go over the handout and discuss each type of conflict. The definition of conflict they have used so far only covers conflicts between people. How would they change the definition to incorporate the conflict categories described here?

3. Divide students into working groups of three or four and give each group a packet of *Conflict Sort Cards*. Have students sort the cards by placing them in one of the five categories. (Some conflicts may fit in more than one category.) Before they begin, warn them that there may be some conflicts about where cards belong. Explain that part of the learning in this activity comes from the discussions they have as a result of making a decision. They should try to resolve the conflicts and come to a consensus. If they are not able to, that will be part of the learning, too.

DISCUSSION

- How did your group sort the conflicts?
- Were there cards that didn't belong to one category alone?
- Were there cards that didn't belong to any category?
- How do you feel about the different categories of conflict?
- How would different categories affect how you handle conflicts?
- Which types of conflicts are most difficult for you?
- Did you have any difficulties or disagreements about sorting the cards?
- How did you handle those disagreements?

4. Write the following classification scheme on the board. As you do, explain that it is another way of classifying conflicts based on who is involved:

Adult vs. Adult

Young Person vs. Young Person

Adult vs. Young Person

Young Person vs. Institution

Young Person vs. Group

Adult vs. Institution

Discuss each category, making sure students understand what they mean. Have each group re-sort the conflict sort cards using these new categories.

DISCUSSION

- How did your group sort the conflicts?
- Were there cards that didn't belong to one category alone?
- Were there cards that didn't belong to any category?
- How could sorting conflicts in this way help you deal with the conflict?
- How would different categories affect how you handle conflicts?
- Which types of conflicts are most difficult for you?
- Did you have any difficulties or disagreements about sorting the cards?
- How did you handle those disagreements?

5. If you have time and think your students have a good grasp on the idea of conflict categories, you may want to try having each group develop its own way of classifying conflicts. Then they should sort the *Conflict Sort Cards* according to that classification scheme. (Whatever classification scheme the students come up with, it will not work for every conflict. They may include a category called "Miscellaneous.")

DISCUSSION

- What categories did your group devise? What process did you use to come up with those?
- Were there cards that didn't belong to one category alone?
- Were there cards that didn't belong to any category?
- How could sorting conflicts in this way help you deal with the conflict?
- How would different categories affect how you handle conflicts?
- Did you have any difficulties or disagreements about sorting the cards?
- How did you handle those disagreements?

LEVEL: A/B/C

Versus vs. Versus[*]

"Versus" means "against." The abbreviation or short form of "versus" is "vs."

We often use the word "versus" to show that people are in a conflict.

Why would a word that means "against" be used to show that people are in a conflict?

YOU VS. YOU

A conflict inside of you is called an "Internal Conflict."

PERSON VS. PERSON

A conflict between two or more people is called an "Interpersonal Conflict."

GROUP VS. GROUP

A conflict between groups of people is called an "Intergroup Conflict."

NATION VS. NATION

A conflict between countries is called an "International Conflict."

---

[*] From William J. Kreidler, *Elementary Perspectives: Teaching Concepts of Peace and Conflict* (Cambridge, MA: Educators for Social Responsibility, 1990), p. 109.

Conflict Sort Cards

Marla says that Nancy ripped her sweater when she borrowed it. Nancy says that it was ripped when she got it.

Martin asked Rich if he wants to hang out with the guys on Saturday night. Rich can't decide whether to go or not. Some of Martin's friends are pretty tough guys.

The leader of the Serbian forces in the Balkans says that he won't make peace with the Croatians. He says that the leader of the Croatians cannot be trusted.

The boys say that the girls can't play softball during freetime after lunch. The girls say they have a right to play if they want to.

Some of the boys think that the girls should be able to play softball during freetime after lunch. Some of the boys disagree.

The U.S. wants Japan to stop "dumping" electronic goods in the U.S. at prices lower than similar U.S. made goods. It's putting American workers out of work. Japan says it is just practicing "free trade."

Mrs. Jones and her neighbors are getting worried because so many Cambodian refugees are moving into the neighborhood. They think property values will go down and crime will go up.

The school administrators and the faculty senate want to implement a dress code banning "inappropriate" student attire. The Student Council voted against such a dress code.

Mr. Smith is a shop owner who tells a Spanish speaking customer that he won't wait on her until she learns English. The English speaking customers in the store applaud when he says this. The customer leaves confused.

Aiesha has a chance to go to Kenya with a church group, but her parents won't let her go because there is a war on and they feel it's too dangerous.

Tanesha hears a song that she thinks is really offensive to women, but all her friends, both girls and boys, seem to like it, so she doesn't say anything.

Tom's Dad says things about Mexicans that are really racist and insulting. A good friend of Tom's is Mexican, and Tom is ashamed to have him over when his Dad is home.

There are a couple of kids in Dana's homeroom who give the new immigrants from Mexico and Asia a hard time. They mimic their English and tease them as soon as they walk through the door. Dana's teacher has told them to stop, but when his back is turned they keep it up.

Every nation has different laws about fishing. Some countries allow big "drift nets" to catch tuna, but these nets also trap a lot of birds and dolphins. Some people in the U.S. want to boycott goods from countries that allow drift nets.

A group of neighbors does not want a new shopping center across the street from where they live. It will bring in too much traffic and put some local shops out of business. The developers insist that the shopping center will be good for the community.

One boy picks on Mario whenever he walks by. The guys standing near him always laugh. Mario's friends all say, "Don't take that from him. Beat him up!"

Conflict Category Webs*

ACTIVITY IN BRIEF   Students use webbing as a way to examine aspects of conflict at various levels.

Have students work in groups of three or four to create a web chart based on conflict categories. Each group can brainstorm some types of conflict, then create web charts identifying different aspects of each type of conflict. They can also create interlocking webs that explore specific aspects of the conflict. For example:

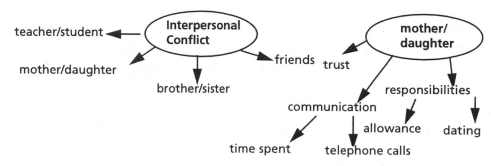

CONFLICT TOOL

Demands and ReallyNeeds

Positive ReallyNeeds

ACTIVITY IN BRIEF   Students practice phrasing ReallyNeeds in ways that are open-ended and will lead to a variety of solutions.

1. Explain that sometimes it's difficult to frame ReallyNeeds in positive terms. Young people often get stuck saying things like: "Inez Really-Needs her stuff not to be bothered by her sister" instead of "Inez ReallyNeeds her stuff to be safe and undisturbed." The former is framed in way that promotes a particular solution, while the latter is more open ended, allowing young people to come up with a variety of solutions.

2. Have students practice reframing the following:
    *   Jerome ReallyNeeds his Dad not to get mad at him.
    *   Angelina ReallyNeeds not to hurt her friend.
    *   Chang ReallyNeeds not to break up with his girlfriend.
    *   Florie Ana ReallyNeeds there not to be racial prejudice in her school.
    *   Arnie ReallyNeeds there to be no fighting or violence in his school.
    *   Geneva ReallyNeeds not to have to move away from her friends.
    *   Frederic ReallyNeeds not to be beaten up after school.
    *   Ito ReallyNeeds not to be teased about his English.

---

* This activity is based on a suggestion by Janet Patti.

CONFLICT TOOL

Mediation, Negotiation, Arbitration

Which Is It? Mediation, Arbitration, Negotiation?

ACTIVITY IN BRIEF

Students reinforce the distinctions between mediation, arbitration, and negotiation and examine how these three approaches might be used at the interpersonal, community, national, and international levels.

Have students classify the following as Mediation, Arbitration, or Negotiation:

- The workers in a large factory are members of a labor union. There are different factions in the union, and they cannot agree about what demands to make in the upcoming contract discussions with the management of the factory. Finally, the union leadership calls a meeting with representatives of the different factions so that they can work out their differences and present a united front during contract discussions.

- Andy and Sheila are second graders arguing over who gets to play with a truck. Their teacher comes over and tells them that since Sheila had the truck first she can play with it for ten minutes. Then she must give it to Andy.

- Two boys on the basketball team are constantly arguing and putting each other down. Several times it has interfered with a game. One day after practice, the coach sat them down and had them talk out the problems they had with each other. It turned out that these problems went back several years, but once the boys talked about it, they were able to work out an agreement.

- After several years of civil war, the warring parties in the Balkans sat down with neutral representatives from the United Nations. The U.N. representatives suggested a process the parties could use to resolve their disputes with each other.

- Kiesha and Mona had a fight and they hadn't spoken to each other for over a week. They'd been friends since the third grade and each really missed the other. Finally, Kiesha called Mona and said, "Let's try to work this out. I miss my good friend."

- Representatives of the factory workers and representatives of management have been talking for days, trying to work out a new contract. So far they haven't made any progress, but they keep trying.

- Representatives of the factory workers and representatives of management have been talking for days, trying to work out a new contract. So far they haven't made any progress. Finally they decide they need help. They arrange for a neutral third party to help them come to a resolution, and both sides agree that they will abide by whatever that neutral third party tells them to do.

Annie Arbitrator

ACTIVITY IN BRIEF Students practice the various skills needeed to successfully arbitrate conflicts.

Note: *This makes a good homework assignment.*

1. Explain that Annie Arbitrator is a fictional newspaper columnist along the lines of Ann Landers or Dear Abby.

2. Have students write two letters to her, describing a conflict. The first letter should give the P.O.V. of one disputant, the second should give the P.O.V. of the other disputant.

3. Have students trade letters with another student and write a response from Annie Arbitrator in which she offers a solution or solutions to the conflict.

Part Three:
Dealing With Differences

Introduction to Dealing with Differences

When we talk with young people of middle school age, they often express great concern about conflicts that are rooted in issues of diversity, i.e., conflicts in which race, ethnicity, culture, sex, and individual difference play an important role. They express feelings of helplessness about these types of conflicts, as if human differences can form barriers that are too great to be surmounted.

We know from our experience working with young people and the adults in their lives that this need not be true. Middle school students can deal with diversity-based conflicts as effectively as they deal with any others. They just need insight into these conflicts, tools to deal with them, and an opportunity to practice these new skills. Like all conflict resolution in the middle school, diversity-based conflicts can be best dealt with by emphasizing prevention.

The lessons in this unit are based on several significant research findings about diversity, diversity-based conflict, and prevention. First, people of any age are less likely to be prejudiced against those who are different if they are understanding and appreciative of their own culture and background. Second, they are less likely to be prejudiced if they are in an environment that values diversity. Third, they are less likely to be prejudiced if they have a cognitive understanding of such concepts as stereotyping, discrimination, and scapegoating. Finally, our own experience tells us that they will be better equipped to meet prejudice and diversity-related conflicts if they have conflict resolution skills and have practiced those skills in diversity-related scenarios.

The overall organizing scheme for our approach to diversity is based on the work of Patti DeRosa and Ulric Johnson of Cross Cultural Consultation.* They describe the awareness of diversity as "The Five Cs." They are:

COLOR An objective description of those aspects of the self or group that usually are not changeable, such as skin color, sex, sexual orientation, physical size.

CULTURE The values, beliefs, symbols, behaviors, ways of living, and shared history of a group of people. Culture is an interpretation of color, class, character, and context. For example, skin color is an objective description, while race is a cultural construct. Weight is an objective description, but overweight is culturally defined. Sex is an objective description, while gender roles are culturally defined.

CLASS Refers to power relations and examines the individual/group identity relative to power, authority, hierarchy, status, and the degree of access to, control over, or ownership of resources.

CHARACTER The unique aspects of each individual person, including personal preferences, idiosyncrasies, and personality traits. People who share similar color, culture, class, and context still possess aspects of the self that are unique to them alone.

---

* Patti DeRosa and Ulric Johnson's work has been adapted with their permission. Cross Cultural Consultation (288 South Main St. #177, Randolph, MA 02368) is an organization that provides training and assistance on cultural diversity to human service organizations, schools, community groups, and corporations.

CONTEXT The reality in which the individuals/groups currently exist, based on time, location, environment, and socio-political, economic, and historical conditions. Color, culture, class, and character cannot be seen in isolation from context and cannot be fully understood outside of the context that shapes their meaning.

In this unit, we have reformulated the Five Cs into the Diversity Deck, with four suits and wild cards. The suits are Color, Culture, Clout (Class), and Character. The wild cards provide the Context.

These concepts are woven through the five lessons in this unit:

Skill Lesson 23	Appreciating Diversity
Skill Lesson 24	Diversity and Conflict
Skill Lesson 25	Understanding Culture
Skill Lesson 26	Understanding Clout
Skill Lesson 27 & 28	Understanding and Dealing with Stereotyping, Prejudice, Discrimination, and Scapegoating

Guidelines for Discussions

Because talking about diversity can be sensitive and threatening for young people, it's important to prominently display the guidelines for discussion presented earlier. Keep reminding students to adhere to them.

1. Keep the room free of put-downs.

2. Respect other people's contributions.

3. Respect confidentiality.

4. Everyone has the right to pass; no one will be forced to talk.

5. Don't be afraid of feelings.

6. Remember your "Privacy Circles," those areas of your life you do not want to talk about. (See appendix H for the "Privacy Circles" activity that helps students identify topics that are too personal to discuss in class.)

7. Keep asking, "What am I learning right now?"

Our experience has shown that with guidance, middle school students can learn to delight in diversity, as well has handle the sometimes daunting conflicts associated with difference. This can be a challenging unit to teach, because the process of learning to understand prejudice and overcome it is often difficult. But it is also rewarding. As one pilot-test teacher commented: "This unit took all my skill as a teacher. I have a racially mixed class and the kids were really engaged in the discussions. There was one day in particular when it was all worthwhile. That was the day I saw light bulbs going on over the kids' heads all over the classroom."

23 Appreciating Diversity

LESSON IN BRIEF	Students explore the concept of diversity using the Diversity Deck, i.e., attributes and characteristics of diversity.
NOTES	Research tells us that if we want students to appreciate people different from themselves, they are more likely to do this if they are in an environment that generally appreciates diversity. Since middle school students, like adults, tend first to think of the negative aspects of diversity, this lesson focuses on the positive aspects. The first goal of the lesson is to give students permission to talk about diversity. The second is to give them a way of thinking about diversity in their own lives through using a tool called the Diversity Deck.
OBJECTIVES	Students will be able to

- define diversity,
- describe the "Five Suits of Cards" in the Diversity Deck,
- identify their own cards in the Diversity Deck,
- identify positive things about diversity.

CONFLICT TOOL	Diversity Deck
VOCABULARY	*Diversity*—The differences between human beings in attributes or characteristics.
	Culture—The common ways of living shared by members of a group.
	Clout—The degree of power, influence, and status an individual or group has.
LESSON SEQUENCE	

- Gathering (Optional)
- Agenda and Vocabulary Review
- Define Diversity and Introduce the Unit
- Present Mini-Lecture/Discussion on Diversity
- Practice Using the Diversity Deck
- Evaluation/Review of Key Points
- Closing (Optional)

TIME NEEDED	One class period (minimum 40 minutes)
HANDOUTS	*The Diversity Deck*
MATERIALS	3 inch x 5 inch cards

LEVEL: A/B/C
(5 MINUTES)

Gathering (Optional)

If you so desire, choose a Gathering Activity from Appendix A.

LEVEL: A/B/C
(3 MINUTES)

Agenda and Vocabulary Review

Write the agenda on the board and review it with the class. Introduce any vocabulary in the lesson you think will be unfamiliar to your students.

LEVEL: A/B/C
(5 MINUTES)

Define Diversity and Introduce the Unit

1. Ask the class what they think of when they hear the word "diversity." Or ask how humans are different from each other. Record responses on the board.

2. Explain that "diversity" means the differences among humans in their attributes or characteristics. These differences may be inborn, like skin color or sex, or acquired, like education and interests. (You may need to emphasize that "differences among people" does not mean, in this case, "disagreements among people.")

LEVEL: A/B/C
(10 MINUTES)

Present Mini-Lecture/Discussion on Diversity

HANDOUTS   *The Diversity Deck*

1. Distribute *The Diversity Deck* handout and present the following mini-lecture to students:

    You've identified many ways that people are different from each other. One way to think about these differences is to compare them to a card game. Human diversity is like being dealt cards from a deck with four different suits plus some wild cards. We're born with some of the cards; some we acquire as we grow older. Regular decks of cards have four suits: clubs, diamonds, spades, and hearts. The diversity deck also has four suits.

    The first suit is the *Color* card. This suit represents all the things that you're born with but can't change. Some examples are skin color, sex, age, sexual orientation, ethnic background.

    The second suit is the *Culture* suit. Culture means the group or groups you and your family most identify with. These cards represent the life-styles of that group—things like food, clothing styles, recreation. It also refers to the shared history, beliefs, and values of the group.

    The third suit is *Clout*. This means the economic status, power, and influence you have.

    The fourth suit is *Character*. The character cards are your individual talents and interests, likes and dislikes, and personal beliefs and values.

    Finally, there are the Wild Cards, which are called *Context* cards. They're the ones that determine when, where, and with whom you live.

2. Read the following story to the class and ask them to identify the key cards that Ada Coleman has been dealt from the Diversity Deck.

Ada Coleman is going out to celebrate tonight. She and a few friends are going to a modest neighborhood restaurant in honor of Ada's new job. She's just been named assistant to the editor of *Gloss,* a magazine for African-American women. Ada can't believe she has the job—it's the kind of job she dreamed about ever since she was in the seventh grade. Ada grew up in a large family in Detroit without much money. But she was always good at writing, and she got top grades in grammar and spelling. Some people said that poor black girls couldn't get jobs in glamorous fields like magazines. But Ada's parents always encouraged her to think big and assured her that they'd find a way for her to go to college. Ada went to state college with a scholarship. Now, with this new job, she won't be making much money, but she feels like she's on her way in the career she loves.

DISCUSSION

- What Color Cards was Ada dealt from the Diversity Deck?
- What Culture Cards was she dealt?
- What Clout Cards was she dealt?
- What Character Cards was she dealt?
- What Wild Cards determined the Context Ada was in?
- Suppose everything else about Ada was the same, but her Wild Cards put her in Georgia in 1850 instead of Detroit in 1995. How might her story have been different?

LEVEL: A/B/C
(10 MINUTES)

Practice Using the Diversity Deck

1. Introduce the group activity by explaining that the *Diversity Deck* cards put us into groups with other people, and the groups reflect one or some of the cards we have, but not all.

2. Ask students to physically move to one side of the room or the other, depending on which group they are part of.

Say: Those of you who are male, move to this side of the room. Those of you who are female, move to that side of the room.

DISCUSSION

- What suit is this characteristic from?
- How did you get that card? Were you born with it, did you choose it, were you given it?
- Have one person in the group name his or her favorite subject in school. Does everyone in the group have the same favorite subject?

3. Continue with the following, followed by a brief discussion after each (feel free to change them or add your own):

African-American/Not African-American or Asian-American/Not Asian-American:

- What suit is this characteristic from?
- How did you get that card? Were you born with it, did you choose it, were you given it?
- Have one person in the group name his or her favorite food. Does everyone in the group have the same favorite food?

Like to eat broccoli/don't like broccoli:

- What suit is this characteristic from?
- How did you get that card? Were you born with it, did you choose it, were you given it?
- Have one person in the group name his or her favorite musical group. Does everyone in the group have the same favorite musical group?

4. Continue with the following:

Like to watch _____ on TV/Don't like to watch _____

Have brown eyes/Don't have brown eyes

Like dressing up/Prefer to go casual

Attend religious services/Don't attend religious services

Speak more than one language/Speak only one language

Microlab on the Diversity Deck

LEVEL: A/B/C
(15 MINUTES)

1. Divide students into microlab groups of three or four. Give each student two minutes to address the following:

- How have the cards from the Diversity Deck influenced your life?
- How have you been influenced by the diversity of others?
- In what ways is diversity a positive or useful thing?

2. Be sure to signal each time two minutes has elapsed.

DISCUSSION

- What did you learn from this activity?
- What feelings came up as you talked about your Diversity Deck?

Evaluation/Review of Key Points

LEVEL: A/B/C
(3 MINUTES)

1. Have volunteers say what they think went well today and what might have been different.

2. Summarize the key points of the lesson:

- We are all dealt cards from the Diversity Deck.
- The cards can be categorized: Color, Culture, Clout, Character, and Wild Cards.
- Some of the cards we are born with, some we choose, some we acquire as we grow older.

Closing (Optional)

If you so desire, choose a Closing Activity from Appendix B.

THE DIVERSITY DECK

Human diversity is like being dealt cards from a deck with four different suits and some Wild Cards. Some of the cards we're born with, some we acquire as we grow older.

Color Suit

These cards represent the characteristics with which you're born. You usually cannot change them:

Skin Color

Ethnicity

Sex

Physical Size

Culture Suit

These cards represent the characteristics of the group with which you identify:

Food

Language

History

Beliefs and Values

Wild Cards

These cards represent the context that you live in. All the other cards are affected by these cards:

Place

Time

The People Around You

Clout Suit

These cards represent the amount of power, influence, and status you have:

Economic Status

Social Status

Power and Authority

Character Suit

These cards represent your individual personality traits:

Talents, Abilities, and Skills

Goals

Preferences and Dislikes

Personal Beliefs and Values

24 Diversity and Conflict

LESSON IN BRIEF	Students explore some of the ways diversity can affect conflict by re-examining the concepts of the P.O.V. Glasses and the Conflict Escalator.
NOTES	Having established that diversity is positive and enriching, this lesson begins the process of helping students look at the ways in which diversity can lead to conflicts.

Two conflict activity types from earlier in this curriculum guide are very useful here. The P.O.V. Glasses are obviously very influenced by such diversity-related factors as culture, gender, ethnicity, and so on. Since students already have a thorough grounding in the importance of P.O.V., this helps them better understand the influence of diversity on conflict. The focus of this lesson is on the three ways that diversity can contribute to the escalation of conflict—ammunition, misunderstanding, and prejudice. The lesson also helps students gain a deeper understanding of diversity-related conflicts by drawing on an activity type with which they are very familiar. Many of the issues raised in this lesson, such as cultural misunderstanding and prejudice, are dealt with in more depth in the following lessons.

OBJECTIVES

Students will be able to:

- describe the three ways diversity influences the Conflict Escalator,
- classify conflicts by Diversity Escalators,
- suggest strategies for de-escalating and resolving diversity-related conflicts.

CONFLICT TOOL

Conflict Escalator

PREREQUISITE

Conflict Escalator (Conflict Skill Lesson 3)

VOCABULARY

Prejudice—A negative judgment or opinion formed without knowledge of the facts.

Assumptions—Conclusions based on limited knowledge of the facts.

LESSON SEQUENCE

- Gathering (Optional)
- Agenda and Vocabulary Review
- Introduce Conflict and Diversity
- Discuss Diversity and the Conflict Escalator
- Sort Conflict By Diversity Type
- Any Additional Activities You May Choose
- Evaluation/Review of Key Points
- Closing (Optional)

TIME NEEDED One class period (minimum 40 minutes), depending on the additional activities you choose.

HANDOUTS *Diversity and the Conflict Escalator, Diversity Conflict Sort Cards*

LEVEL: A/B/C
(5 MINUTES)

Gathering (Optional)

If you so desire, choose a Gathering Activity from Appendix A.

LEVEL: A/B/C
(3 MINUTES)

Agenda and Vocabulary Review

Write the agenda on the board and review it with the class. Introduce any vocabulary that you think will be unfamiliar to your students.

LEVEL: A/B/C
(5 MINUTES)

Introduce Conflict and Diversity

1. Ask students: We've discussed some of the benefits and positive aspects of diversity. What are some of the problems that diversity can create? Acknowledge the contributions that are made.

2. Explain: Diversity can be enriching, but it can also lead to problems between people. Like all conflicts, diversity-related conflicts can be constructive or destructive, depending on how we respond to them. Today we're going to look at how diversity affects one of the conflict concepts we learned earlier, the Conflict Escalator.

LEVEL: A/B/C
(10 MINUTES)

Discuss Diversity on the Conflict Escalator

HANDOUTS *Diversity and the Conflict Escalator*

1. Distribute the *Diversity on the Conflict Escalator* handout and discuss it with the class, using the following mini-lecture as a guide.

   There are three ways issues of diversity can affect how conflicts escalate. They are ammunition, misunderstanding, and prejudice.

   ## AMMUNITION

   The conflict starts up the escalator. It's often an ordinary conflict, not rooted in diversity. As it escalates, issues of diversity are dragged in as ammunition, usually in the form of name-calling. If the person who is the target of the ammunition feels insulted or attacked, the conflict will escalate.

   ### EXAMPLE

   Roberto and Steven are two boys playing with a big squirt gun. Steven thinks it is his turn to shoot the gun, but Roberto won't give it up. They bicker for a while, and, as the conflict escalates, Steven says, "You won't give me the gun. You are really gay, Roberto."

   - Can you think of any other examples of ammunition on the conflict escalator?
   - What might be some ways to deal with ammunition in a conflict?

MISUNDERSTANDING

In this case, the conflict begins and escalates because of a misunderstanding that is rooted in cultural difference. The parties don't understand the actions of the other because they don't understand the other's culture. As a result, they make assumptions and misinterpret the behavior of the other, and the conflict escalates.

EXAMPLE

Sondra, who is African-American, has just become friends with Sung Quat, a Cambodian classmate. As Sondra gets off the bus one morning, she sees Sung Quat across the school yard. She shouts and waves to her, but to her surprise, Sung Quat folds her arms and turns her back. Sondra is hurt, thinking she has been rejected by her new best friend.

- What do you think was the misunderstanding in this conflict?
- What is Sondra's P.O.V.?
- What do you think Sung Quat's P.O.V. might be?

What Sondra doesn't realize is that in Cambodian culture she just humiliated her friend by causing everyone in the school yard to look at Song Quat.

- Can you think of any other examples of people being led up the conflict escalator because of a cultural misunderstanding?
- What are some ways to deal with or prevent a conflict based on misunderstanding?

PREJUDICE

In this case, the conflict begins and escalates because one or both parties have prejudices against the other. These prejudices are in their conflict baggage and lead them to make assumptions and behave based on their prejudice. These assumptions and behaviors contribute to the escalation of the conflict.

EXAMPLE

Jason and Marcus are using the computer—the only one in the class. They are playing a math game. Alicia comes up and asks if she can play the game too. "I'm really good at it," she says. "I play it at home with my Dad." Both boys wave her away. "This is for boys only," says Jason. "Yeah," says Marcus. "Girls are no good at computers."

- Can you think of any other examples of prejudice contributing to people going up the conflict escalator?
- What might be some ways to handle prejudice in a conflict?
- What might be some ways not to handle prejudice in a conflict?
- What might make it escalate further?

These three things may happen singularly or in combination. For example, a conflict rooted in prejudice may, as it escalates, include ammunition in the form of name-calling.

LEVEL: B/C

2. Make the following points, in addition to the previous lesson:

One conflict escalator may also lead to another. For example, a conflict that begins as a misunderstanding can lead to the disputants developing real prejudices.

Finally, the three ways diversity affects conflict are related because of the context they are in. You remember the Context Wild Cards in the Diversity Deck? If you are in a context where there is a general prejudice against fat people, then "fat" becomes a hurtful word to use as ammunition. If there weren't prejudice against fat people, "fat" would just be a descriptive word and couldn't be used as ammunition.

- Can you think of examples where one conflict-escalating behavior led to another?
- What role do the Context Wild Cards play in these escalators?

LEVEL: A/B/C
(15 MINUTES)

Sort Conflicts by Diversity Type

HANDOUTS *Diversity Conflict Sort Cards* (you will need one set for each group of three or four students)

1. Divide students into groups of three or four. Give each group a set of the *Diversity Conflict Sort Cards.*

2. Have students classify the conflicts as Ammunition, Misunderstanding, or Prejudice. If they think some of the conflicts are a combination (and many of them are), they should say what escalators they see and what the combination is.

DISCUSSION

- Which of the conflicts were just Ammunition?
- Which were just Misunderstanding? Prejudice?
- Which were a combination of escalators?

3. Have each group choose one of the conflicts and develop a way to de-escalate and resolve the situation. Give the groups five minutes to develop their plans, then have them share the results with the class.

LEVEL: A/B/C
(2 MINUTES)

Evaluation/Review of Key Points

Evaluation: Have volunteers summarize the key points in the lesson.

- Diversity can be enriching, but it can also lead to conflict.
- Diversity can influence conflict escalation in three ways: Ammunition, Misunderstanding, and Prejudice.

LEVEL: A/B/C
(5 MINUTES)

Closing (Optional)

If you so desire, choose a Closing Activity from Appendix B.

Additional Activities

LEVEL: A/B/C
(TIME WILL VARY)

Conflict Journal Activity

Have students go over the conflicts in their journals to look for examples of Diversity Escalators. Have them describe the conflict and the role diversity played in the escalation of the conflict. Then have them brainstorm some possible de-escalation strategies.

LEVEL: A/B/C
(TIME WILL VARY)

Concerns About Diversity Conflicts

Note: *This makes a good homework assignment.*

Conflicts that are rooted in diversity are among the most troubling for middle school students to deal with and understand. The P.O.V. Glasses and the Conflict Escalator can help with this, but students still may have many feelings about these conflicts. It can be helpful to give them a forum for expressing some of these feelings and concerns.

One suggestion for this is to have students write a paragraph or two on the theme "Why diversity leads to conflict," or "Why I think diversity conflicts are a problem for our school." Encourage students to be specific about the kind of diversity they are discussing and to name some of the feelings these conflicts evoke in them.

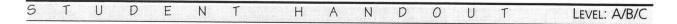

Diversity and the Conflict Escalator

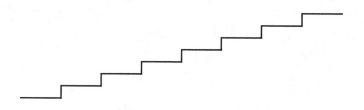

Three ways diversity affects how conflict escalates:

AMMUNITION

- Trying to hurt the other person by attacking the cards in their Diversity Deck: Color, Culture, Clout, or Character.

- Some examples of ammunition are: Name-calling, Character Assassination, Global Statements

MISUNDERSTANDING

- Conflict results from misunderstanding the other person's actions or motives because you don't understand their culture.

PREJUDICE

- Conflict comes from making negative judgments about people because of the cards in their Diversity Deck, that is, because of the groups of which they are a member.

Diversity Conflict Sort Cards

Ahn and Paolo were working on a report for health class. Somehow the computer file with their report was deleted from the disk. Now they are arguing over whose fault it is. "Stupid Cambodian," says Paolo. "I should have known you wouldn't know anything about computers. You probably grew up in a rice paddy!"

Angel and Jesus were looking for a place to eat in the cafeteria. They started to sit at one table where there were two other boys sitting. One of the boys said sarcastically, "Oh, great, look who's joining us." The other boy said, "It's the heavenly duo!" The first boy said, "Their parents must think their kids are God or something."

Shirlee and Raquel were planning a slumber party. As they made up a list of whom they wanted to invite, Raquel suggested inviting Annie. "Forget it," said Shirlee. "I don't want that nerd at my party. She'd probably bring a book and read all the time." "Well it's supposed to be *our* party, and I want her to come. I like her. She's nice," said Raquel. "She's a nerd. And stuck up because she's always on the honor roll," said Shirlee. "I want people at the party who are fun, not super-intellectuals."

Danny Kwong was kept after class because the teacher, Mrs. Rockland, thought he might be responsible for a pencil tapping epidemic at the beginning of class. Danny claimed he had nothing to do with it. He kept his head down and avoided looking Mrs. Rockland in the eye. His parents had always told him that it was disrespectful to look an authority figure in the eye. "He denies it, but I'm not sure I trust him," thought Mrs. Rockland. "Chinese kids are usually so well behaved, but he won't look me in the eye when I'm talking to him. He seems like he has something to hide."

Carole's grandmother, who lived with Carole's family, died over the weekend. When she came to school, Carole told her friend Kindra about it. As she talked to Kindra, Carole started to cry. Kindra put her arm around Carole to comfort her. Some kids walking down the hall saw her and called out, "Hey look at the gay girls!" Kindra shouted back, "What's the matter? Don't you have any respect?" One of the kids said, "You want to make something of it, gay girl?"

Urvashi has stopped speaking to her friend Kate, and Kate doesn't know why. Just yesterday at lunch the girls had been talking about what they wanted to be when they grew up, and Urvashi said she'd like to have her own dress shop. Kate said, "Why don't you run a 7-11? That's what most Indians do." Urvashi said, "Because I want a dress shop." They didn't talk anymore about it, but Urvashi has been avoiding Kate ever since. "Fine," Kate thinks. "If she doesn't want to be friends, who needs her?"

Brian's younger brother who's in elementary school just showed up at the softball diamond and asked if he could play. "Forget it," said Brian. "This isn't for little kids. Get lost."

Kevin lives with his grandmother, who always told him not to eat Mexican food because it was probably cooked in a dirty kitchen. One day Kevin was over at Oscar Mendez' house, and Oscar's family insisted he stay for dinner. Kevin hardly touched his meal. The next day, Oscar confronted him in the hall. "You insulted my mother by not eating her food!" he said.

Christine and Nancy are arguing about which bus stop to wait at. "I hate having to walk to the one on Indiana Ave." says Christine. "It's two blocks away." "Well I hate waiting at the one on Chisholm St.," says Nancy. "Those girls from the Technical High School wait there and they scare me. They're so tough. You just don't know what girls like that are going to do."

The convenience store near the Healy Middle School has a sign on the door that says, "Only three middle school students at a time will be allowed in this store. You cannot be trusted in large groups." A group of students from the student council are filing a complaint with the town anti-discrimination task force.

25 Understanding Culture

LESSON IN BRIEF	Students explore the meaning of culture and its relationship to conflict by playing a cross-cultural simulation game.
NOTES	The cultures to which we belong and with which we identify influence every aspect of our lives. Young people often understand culture at an intuitive level, but have never really discussed it openly. In this lesson, students have an opportunity to explore different aspects of culture and examine how cultural differences can lead to conflicts. The cross-cultural game is a safe way for students to look at aspects of culture and cross-cultural communication that may lead to conflict. There are real-life parallels to this game, and we encourage you and your students to make these connections.
OBJECTIVES	Students will be able to:

- define culture;
- identify key elements of a culture;
- describe how cultural differences can affect conflict.

CONFLICT TOOL	Cross-cultural Simulation, Conflict Escalator
VOCABULARY	*Culture*—The common ways of living shared by members of a group.

Cross Cultural—Between two or more cultures. |
| **LESSON SEQUENCE** | |

- Gathering (Optional)
- Define Culture
- Play the Reba-Ambler (Cross-cultural) Game
- Any Additional Activities You May Choose
- Evaluation/Review of Key Points
- Closing (Optional)

TIME NEEDED	One class period (minimum 40 minutes), depending on the additional activities you use.
HANDOUTS	*You Are a Reba, You Are an Ambler*

LEVEL: A/B/C
(5 MINUTES)

Gathering (Optional)

If you so desire, choose a Gathering Activity from Appendix A.

LEVEL: A/B/C
(3 MINUTES)

Agenda and Vocabulary Review

Write the agenda on the board and review it with the class. Introduce any vocabulary in the lesson that you think will be unfamiliar to your students.

LEVEL: A/B/C
(10 MINUTES)

Define Culture

1. Explain the meaning of culture and subculture:

   The definition of "culture" that we will be using in this lesson is the one we used for the Diversity Deck: the collection of common ways of living shared by a group. Because the United States is such a diverse country, we all belong to many cultures. If we live in the U.S., then we are part of U.S. culture. We may also belong to the culture of our ethnic group. Everyone in this room, including myself, is part of a specific culture—the middle school culture. There may be one or two main cultures or cultural groups that we identify with, as well as many subcultures.

2. Pose the following situation to students:

   A group of Martians has landed in front of our school. They are peaceful and friendly and intensely curious about life on earth. They know that there are many cultures on earth, and they have come into the building to find out about the culture of our middle school. What would they see going on in the building, and what would that tell them about middle school culture?

3. Have students work in pairs for two minutes to share ideas. Then bring the class together to brainstorm. Record student contributions on the board, under the heading, "Elements of Middle School Culture." If students need some help getting started, use some of the questions suggested below.

   DISCUSSION

   - What do people in the middle school eat?
   - How and where do they eat?
   - What do they do every 40 minutes or so?
   - What do they do once they move to the next room?
   - What kinds of clothes do people in middle school wear?
   - What does the clothing tell you about them?
   - What work do the adults in the middle school do?
   - What work do the young people do?
   - Are there differences between what girls do in middle school and what boys do?

- Looking at this list, what does it tell you about culture generally?
- What aspects of our lives does culture affect? (Every aspect.)

LEVEL: A/B/C
(25 MINUTES)

Play the Reba-Ambler (Cross Cultural) Game*

HANDOUTS   *You Are a Reba, You Are an Ambler* (You will need enough Reba hand-outs for half the class and enough Ambler handouts for the rest of the class.)

1. Write the words "Reba" and "Ambler" on the board. Explain that students are going to have an opportunity to experience living in a different culture for a short time. They will either be members of the Reba culture or the Ambler culture. First they will learn about their own culture, then they will meet the other culture.

2. Distribute Reba handouts to half the class and Ambler handouts to the rest of the class.

   Note: *There are important gender differences in the Ambler culture. Therefore, try to evenly divide the boys between the two cultures. If you do not have enough boys, use an appropriate substitute, such as purple armbands. In this case, sentences about Ambler men would refer to Ambler people clothed in purple.*

3. Have students read their handouts, then meet within their culture groups for five minutes to discuss their culture. Write the following questions on the board for them to discuss among themselves:
   - What does your culture like to do?
   - How do you interact or relate to yourselves? To others?
   - How do you speak? What is your body language like?
   - If you had a cultural motto, what would it be?

4. When both groups feel they know their culture, present the following scenario:

   You have been at Reba-Ambler School all day. Classes are over for the day, and it is now a social hour. There is only one room available for the social hour. You are now together in this room. This is your time to mingle and get to know each other. As you mingle, remember the characteristics of your culture. Keep track of your own points.

5. Give students three to five minutes to mingle. You are likely to see physical actions mirror cultural behaviors. The Amblers will probably stay still while the Rebas move quickly from their side of the room and flood the Ambler side.

6. Have everyone return to their seats. Ask each culture to describe the other (one at a time). As the Rebas describe the Amblers, write the descriptive words on the board. Regarding Amblers you are likely to hear: stand-offish, stuck up, rude, snobs, etc. Then ask the Amblers to describe the Rebas, and write the descriptive words on the board. Rebas are likely to be described as: pushy, in

---

* This activity is adapted, with permission, from "Brief Encounters," *Simulation Game by Thiagi,* (Bloomington, IN: Workshops by Thiagi, 1993), pp. 39-45.

your face, too friendly, annoying, etc.

7. Once the lists are complete, have representatives from each culture read their sheets aloud.

DISCUSSION
- What did you notice about how the cultures saw each other, and how they were described on the handouts? (The handouts were positive or neutral in tone, the other culture described them in negative terms.)
- Why did the descriptions come out so negatively?
- What assumptions did each culture make about the other?
- How could these have led to conflict starting or escalating?
- How could they have learned about each other and avoided misunderstandings?
- What things do you need to think about when you are talking to someone from a different culture?

LEVEL: A/B/C
(3 MINUTES)

Evaluation/Review of Key Points

1. Have volunteers say something they learned about culture from today's lesson.

2. Summarize the key points in this lesson:
   - We all live in many subcultures.
   - Conflicts can arise out of misunderstandings about other cultures.
   - We can decrease misunderstandings.

LEVEL: A/B/C
(5 MINUTES)

Closing (Optional)

If you so desire, choose a Closing Activity from Appendix B.

Additional Activities

LEVEL: A/B/C
(TIME WILL VARY)

Conflict Journal Activities

Have students describe a time that they saw or were part of a conflict where cultural differences played an important role. What cultures were involved? How did they affect the conflict? What feelings came up in the conflict? How did the conflict end?

A variation on this is to have students either look at conflicts they've already recorded, or record new conflicts that they think occurred because of cultural differences. What role do cultural differences play in causing the conflict to begin or escalate? How do the people in the conflict interpret the differences? What assumptions do they make about the other people?

You Are a Reba

About the Reba Culture

Rebas are very friendly.

Rebas are outgoing. They love to talk with aliens.

Rebas like to talk to as many aliens as possible. They don't talk for long. A Reba likes to say: "I talked to many aliens. Now they feel welcome."

Rebas like to shake hands. It makes them feel they've made contact. If an alien doesn't offer to shake hands, the Reba will grab it.

Rebas put their faces right in the face of the alien they're talking with.

Rebas are informal. Rebas think it is polite to call everyone by their first names.

Boys and girls behave in the same way, except Reba boys like to talk with alien girls best. And Reba girls like to talk with alien boys best.

LEVEL: A/B/C

You Are an Ambler

About the Ambler Culture

Amblers stick to themselves. They enjoy being with other Amblers.

Amblers never start a conversation with a stranger. They do speak when spoken to. When they speak, they cross their arms.

Amblers are very polite. They say "How do you do?" and "sir" and "madam." Too much touching is considered rude.

Among Amblers, boys are the weaker gender. They are protected by Ambler girls.

Ambler boys avoid eye contact with alien girls, and they don't talk directly to alien girls. They talk through their protectors.

Ambler boys can talk to alien boys, if the alien boys talk first. They can maintain eye contact with alien boys.

26 Understanding Clout

LESSON IN BRIEF Students explore the effect of "clout"—power, influence, and economic status—on conflict by playing a simulation game.

NOTES While middle school students are very aware of and interested in the dynamics of power in conflict, the concept of "clout" can be a little more slippery. In this lesson, clout is defined in a simplified form as a combination of power, influence, and economic status, or PIES. The goal of this lesson is to increase student awareness of clout and its role in conflict and to enable students to discuss clout in terms that are meaningful to them.

> **Note:** *In pilot-testing this curriculum we found that this lesson was much less meaningful to sixth graders than to seventh and eighth graders. If you have a group of sixth graders, and you feel this material is either too sophisticated or not interesting to them, feel free to skip this lesson.*

OBJECTIVES Students will be able to:

- define three aspects of clout: power, influence, and economic status;
- describe their experience in a simulation game;
- discuss how clout influences conflict.

CONFLICT TOOL PIES Chart

VOCABULARY *Clout*—The combination of an individual's power, influence, and economic status. Clout is highly dependent on the Context of an individual.

LESSON SEQUENCE
- Gathering (Optional)
- Define "Clout"
- Play the Clout Card Game
- Any Additional Activities You May Choose
- Evaluation/Review of Key Points
- Closing (Optional)

TIME NEEDED One class period (minimum 40 minutes), depending on the additional activities you choose.

MATERIALS A deck of playing cards with the face cards and aces removed.

LEVEL: A/B/C
(5 MINUTES)

Gathering (Optional)

If you so desire, choose a Gathering Activity from Appendix A.

LEVEL: A/B/C
(3 MINUTES)

Agenda and Vocabulary Review

Write the agenda on the board and review it with the class. Introduce any vocabulary in the lesson you think will be unfamiliar to your students.

LEVEL: A/B/C
(5 MINUTES)

Define Clout

1. Draw a pie chart on the board that looks like this:

The Clout Pie

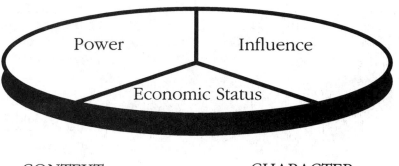

CONTEXT   CHARACTER

2. Present the following mini-lecture:

> You may remember that *Clout* is one of the suits in the Diversity Deck. *Clout* consists of three elements: power, influence, and economic status. They vary from person to person in their importance.
>
> *Power* means how much ability you have to get the things you need to survive and thrive—food, clothing, shelter, work, protection, education, and other resources. Power is also how much other people recognize that ability.
>
> *Influence* is how much other people respect you and will do or help you do what you want.
>
> *Economic Status* refers to how much money you have and the things that go along with that money. It can also mean how much money people think you have.
>
> Clout is very dependent on the Wild Cards that provide one's *Context*. It is also dependent on the other cards of the Diversity Deck: Color, Cul-

ture, and Character.

For example, most middle school students don't have much Clout. They don't have a lot of power in the larger world, they don't have much influence, and they are usually dependent on their families for their economic status. But if you change the context from the larger world to the middle school, young people among their peers may have quite a lot of Clout—especially power and influence.

LEVEL: A/R/C
(30 MINUTES)

Play the Clout Card Game

MATERIALS A deck of playing cards with the face cards and aces removed.

Note: *Students may have strong feelings about this activity. Leave enough time for them to discuss the activity and process their feelings.*

1. Tell students that they will be playing a game that explores issues of Clout: power and status. Show the deck of cards and explain that you have removed the face cards and the aces. Only cards numbered two through ten remain.

2. Continue to explain the directions for the game as follows:

   Each of you will receive a card, face down. You are not to look at your cards until I explicitly tell you to, which will not be until the game is over. If anyone accidentally sees their card, they should ask for a new one. When I give the signal, take your card and lift it to your forehead, without looking at it, and hold it face out. (Demonstrate this.) Everyone else will be able to see your number, but you will not.

   We'll be using only numbered cards, and the numbers indicate the relative status you have. A person with a high card (an eight, nine, or ten) has high status or is popular. A person with a low card (a two, three, or four) has low status or is unpopular.

3. When students understand the meaning of cards, explain the situation.

   Once you have your cards to your foreheads, I'm going to ask you to imagine that you are about to get on a bus for a field trip and are figuring out with whom you want to sit. Remember, don't look at your own card, but do treat other people as a two, or three, or five, or nine, or ten, or whatever card they have on their forehead. Also, don't tell other people what their card is, and don't look in their glasses to try and see your card. Part of the fun is not knowing.

4. Distribute the cards, face down. Then give a signal and have students bring the cards to their foreheads without looking at them. Have students stand and mill about, negotiating with whom they wish to sit. Observe how they treat different numbered people. Allow three to five minutes for this, then call, "Freeze! DON'T LOOK AT YOUR CARDS YET!"

5. Ask students to line up around the room, without looking at their cards, in order from ten to two, based on what number they think they have. Designate which end of the room is ten, and which end is two.

6. When students have finished lining up, ask students to guess, without looking at their cards, the number they have. After all the students have guessed their number, tell them they may look at their number.

7. After students have seen what number they had, collect the cards and have students return to their seats.

DISCUSSION

- First address the high numbers. How did you know you were a high number? How did people treat you? What were subtle and not-so-subtle behaviors and clues to your status?

- Now address the low numbers. How did you know you were a low number? How did people treat you? What were subtle and not-so-subtle behaviors and clues to your status?

- Now address the middle numbers. How did you know you were a middle number? How did people treat you? What were subtle and not-so-subtle behaviors and clues to your status?

- How did it feel when you realized you had a high number?

- How did it feel when you realized you had a middle number?

- How did it feel when you realized you had a low number?

- Did any of you high number people try to associate with low number people? What happened?

- Did any of you low number people try to associate with high number people? What happened?

- What's the difference between a high number person trying to associate with a low number person, and a low number person trying to associate with a high number person?

- Did you middle number people try to associate with either high or low number people? What happened?

- High number people, why did you treat the low number people the way you did? (If someone says, "You told us to," remind them that the directions said, "You are about to get on a bus for a field trip and are figuring out with whom you want to sit. Remember, don't look at your own card, but do treat other people as a two, or three, or five, or nine, or ten, or whatever card they have on their forehead." In other words you did not say specifically how they were to treat the other numbers.)

- Did anyone want to or try to get rid of the distinctions between numbers? What stopped you?

- What places and situations do you see how high Clout people treat lower Clout people?

- What are some real-life examples of high numbers? Low numbers? Middle numbers?

- What are some real-life examples of people trying to eliminate or reduce distinctions between high Clout and low Clout people?

LEVEL: A/B/C
(3 MINUTES)

Evaluation/Review of Key Points

1. Have volunteers say something they will remember from this lesson.

2. Summarize the key points of the lesson:

   - Clout is a combination of power, influence, and economic status.
   - Clout is tempered by culture, color, and character.
   - Clout changes depending on where you are (your context).
   - We learn ways of behaving toward people with different Clout, just as we did in the Clout Card Game, but we can change those ways.

LEVEL: A/B/C
(5 MINUTES)

Closing (Optional)

If you so desire, choose a Closing Activity from Appendix B.

Additional Activity

LEVEL: A/B/C
(TIME WILL VARY)

Conflict Journal Activity

Have students look for examples of Clout in conflicts they see in school, community, and the world. Ask them to analyze these examples of Clout using the PIES chart and to comment on how it affects the conflict's beginning and escalation.

Understanding Stereotyping, Prejudice, Discrimination, and Scapegoating

---

LESSON IN BRIEF   Students learn terms related to stereotyping and prejudice through brainstorming and case studies.

NOTES   Research tells us that young people are more likely to resist prejudice if they have a way of talking about it, i.e., if they understand such terms as stereotyping, prejudice, discrimination, and scapegoating. Common sense tells us that they will also be more likely to intervene in conflicts related to prejudice and discrimination if they have some examples of how this can be done. This lesson focuses on helping students acquire and understand the vocabulary of prejudice by building their own experience with these concepts. It goes on to help students examine effective and ineffective ways to handle prejudice-related conflicts, using skills they have already acquired.

OBJECTIVES   Students will be able to:

- define stereotyping, prejudice, and discrimination;
- give examples of each;
- describe how each is potentially dangerous and can contribute to conflict.

CONFLICT TOOL   Understanding Stereotyping, Prejudice, Discrimination, and Scapegoating

PREREQUISITES   Conflict Styles (Conflict Skill Lesson 12)

VOCABULARY   *Stereotype*—A mental image of a group based on opinion without regard to individual differences.

Prejudice—A negative judgement or opinion formed about a group without knowledge of the facts.

Assumptions—Conclusions based on limited knowledge of the facts.

Discrimination—Treating people in a less favorable way because they are members of a particular group. Discrimination is prejudice in action.

Scapegoating—Holding one person or group responsible for all the community's problems. Isolating or rejecting a person or group.

LESSON SEQUENCE
- Gathering (Optional)
- Agenda and Vocabulary Review
- Introduce Stereotyping with "All Kids..."
- Microlab on Stereotyping
- Define Stereotyping, Prejudice, Discrimination, and Scapegoating

- Any Additional Activities You May Choose
- Evaluation/Review of Key Points
- Closing (Optional)

TIME NEEDED

One class period (minimum 40 minutes), depending on the additional activities you use.

HANDOUTS

Understanding Prejudice: Some Definitions

MATERIALS

Magazines, newspapers, and other advertising media

LEVEL: A/B/C
(5 MINUTES)

Gathering (Optional)

If you so desire, choose a Gathering Activity from Appendix A.

LEVEL: A/B/C
(3 MINUTES)

Agenda and Vocabulary Review

Write the agenda on the board and review it with the class. Introduce any vocabulary in the lesson you think will be unfamiliar to your students. (Do not define stereotype, prejudice, discrimination, and scapegoating. They will be covered during this lesson.)

LEVEL: A/B/C
(15 MINUTES)

Introduce Stereotyping with "All Kids…"

1. Explain that today's lesson focuses on stereotyping and prejudice. Note that as young people, everyone in the class has been a victim of some kind of stereotyping.

2. Write on the board the sentence stub "All kids…" (Or, if you are working with level B or C students, "All teenagers…") Ask students to brainstorm all the ways they have heard people complete that sentence, such as: "All kids are noisy," "All kids break things," "All kids are ignorant," etc. Write their responses on the board.

3. Continue the brainstorm as long as energy is high. When it slows down, ask for last contributions and wrap it up.

   ### DISCUSSION

   - Who do you hear say these things about young people?
   - Which of these would you call positive?
   - Which of these would you call negative?
   - Are they true for all young people?
   - Are they true for some young people?
   - How does it feel to have people assume you're one way just because you're a young person?

4. When the discussion of the brainstorm is complete, explain that all of these are examples of stereotypes.

   - What might be a definition of stereotype?

LEVEL: A/B/C
(10 MINUTES)

Microlab on Stereotyping

1. Divide students into microlab groups of three or four. Give each student two minutes to address the following:

   - How could these stereotypes harm young people?
   - Tell about a time when you were hurt by a stereotype.
   - What feelings did you have?

   Remember to signal each time two minutes is up.

   ### DISCUSSION

   - What did you notice as you did this activity?
   - What feelings did these stereotyping incidents bring up?

LEVEL: A/B/C
(10 MINUTES)

Define Stereotype, Prejudice, Discrimination, and Scapegoating

HANDOUTS   *Understanding Prejudice: Some Definitions*

1. Distribute the *Understanding Prejudice: Some Definitions* handout and present the following mini-lecture/discussion:

   A *stereotype,* as we just saw, is a mental image of a group based on opinion without regard to individual differences. A stereotype says that all the members of a group are the same. One problem with stereotypes is that while some members of the group, maybe even most members of the group, are like the stereotype in some ways, no member of the group is like the stereotype in all ways. As you said, some young people fit some of the stereotypes you named, but no one fits them all. Unfortunately, stereotypes easily lead to prejudice.

   Prejudice is a negative judgement or opinion formed about a group without knowledge of the facts. It is based on stereotypes. A prejudiced person assumes that all the members of a group will act a certain way. Prejudice is the first step to discrimination.

   Discrimination means treating people in a less favorable way simply because they are members of a particular group. Discrimination is prejudice in action. Discrimination may mean leaving people out of things (like clubs or organizations), not allowing them to have things they need (like education or housing), or simply treating other people better than the members of the group being discriminated against.

   Scapegoating is holding one person or group responsible for all the community's problems. It also means isolating or rejecting a person or group. When a person scapegoats, he often projects his own weaknesses or faults onto others. Scapegoating is usually done against people who cannot fight back.

2. Tell the students:

Suppose I said to you now that wearing Reeboks® shows uncommonly good taste and superiority of mind. Reebok people get to go to lunch. Everyone else has to miss lunch. Reebok people also get extra cake at lunch. And they get to leave school early. And they get to go to a concert tonight. Free. Non-Reebok people are not supposed to associate with Reebok people.

DISCUSSION

- What would this be an example of?
- Who is discriminated against in this example?
- How are non-Reebok people being discriminated against?
- Does it make any sense to discriminate against non-Reebok people?
- How might it hurt the Reebok people to not be able to associate with non-Reebok people?

LEVEL: A/B/C
(5 MINUTES)

Evaluation/Review of Key Points

1. Have volunteers identify one thing they learned from today's lesson.

2. Summarize key points from the lesson:

- Review the definitions of stereotyping, prejudice, discrimination, and scapegoating.
- Stereotyping can lead to prejudice, which can lead to discrimination, which can lead to scapegoating.

LEVEL: A/B/C
(5 MINUTES)

Closing (Optional)

If you so desire, choose a Closing Activity from Appendix B.

Additional Activities

LEVEL: A/B/C
(TIME WILL VARY)

Conflict Journal Activity

Have students record examples of conflicts that involve stereotyping, prejudice, or discrimination. How did these influence the conflict? How was the conflict resolved?

LEVEL: A/B/C
(TIME WILL VARY)

Find the Stereotypes

MATERIALS Magazines, newspapers, and other advertising media

Note: *This makes a good homework assignment.*

Have students look for examples of stereotyping in magazine, newspaper, television, and radio advertisements. Have them describe the advertisements, explain how they promote stereotypes, and point out which groups are stereotyped.

Understanding Prejudice:
Some Definitions

Stereotype—A mental image of a group based on opinion without regard to individual differences.

Prejudice—A negative judgement or opinion formed about a group without knowledge of the facts.

Discrimination—Treating people in a less favorable way because they are members of a particular group. Discrimination is prejudice in action.

Scapegoating—Holding one person or group responsible for all the community's problems. Isolating or rejecting a person or group.

Dealing with Stereotyping, Prejudice, Discrimination, and Scapegoating

LESSON IN BRIEF	Students identify strategies for dealing with conflicts that are rooted in stereotyping and prejudice.
NOTES	Once students have acquired the vocabulary of prejudice, they are ready to discuss how to handle prejudice-related conflicts. In this lesson, students examine effective and ineffective ways to handle prejudice-related conflicts, using skills they acquired earlier in this course of study. A theme to emphasize during this lesson is that positive and constructive action can be taken to deal with these conflicts.
OBJECTIVES	Students will be able to:

Students will be able to:

- define stereotyping, prejudice, and discrimination;
- describe how each is potentially dangerous and can contribute to conflict;
- identify strategies for dealing with prejudice-related conflicts.

CONFLICT TOOL	Understanding Stereotyping, Prejudice, Discrimination, and Scapegoating
PREREQUISITE	Conflict Styles (Conflict Skill Lesson 12)
VOCABULARY	*Stereotype*—A mental image of a group based on opinion without regard to individual differences.

Prejudice—A negative judgement or opinion formed about a group without knowledge of the facts.

Assumptions—Conclusions based on limited knowledge of the facts.

Discrimination—Treating people in a less favorable way because they are members of a particular group. Discrimination is prejudice in action.

Scapegoating—Holding one person or group responsible for all the community's problems. Isolating or rejecting a person or group.

LESSON SEQUENCE	• Gathering (Optional)
	• Agenda and Vocabulary Review
	• Discuss How Stereotyping and Prejudice Are Harmful
	• Identify Strategies for Prejudice-related Conflicts
	• Evaluation/Review of Key Points
	• Closing (Optional)
TIME NEEDED	One class period (minimum 40 minutes), depending on the additional activities you use.
HANDOUTS	*Prejudice Situation Cards, We All Lose!, Interrupting Prejudice Case Studies, Strategies for Interrupting Prejudice*

LEVEL: A/B/C
(5 MINUTES)

Gathering (Optional)

If you so desire, choose a Gathering Activity from Appendix A.

LEVEL: A/B/C
(3 MINUTES)

Agenda and Vocabulary Review

Write the agenda on the board and review it with the class. Introduce any vocabulary in the lesson that you think will be unfamiliar to your students.

LEVEL: A/B/C
(20 MINUTES)

Discuss How Stereotyping, Prejudice, Discrimination, and Scapegoating Are Harmful*

HANDOUTS   *We All Lose!* (one copy for each group), one set of *Prejudice Situation Cards* for each group of three to four students

1. Divide students into groups of three or four. Give each group a copy of the *We All Lose!* handout and a set of *Prejudice Situation Cards*.

2. Have a student in the group draw one of the cards and read it to the group. The group then fills in the first box on the handout, identifying the act involved and how it harms the people in the situation.

3. When the group is satisfied with its responses to the first situation, a second student draws another card and the process is repeated. The group keeps drawing cards until the handout is filled in completely.

4. Begin the discussion by having each group share with the class its responses to one of the situations.

DISCUSSION

- What are some of the ways people in these situations "lost" as a result of stereotyping, prejudice, discrimination, or scapegoating?

- What are some ways the people who did the stereotyping, prejudice, discrimination, or scapegoating "lost"?

- What kinds of conflicts do these situations represent? How would you classify them?

- What is the role of stereotyping, prejudice, discrimination, or scapegoating in the conflicts—is it the cause of the conflict? An escalator?

- Can you think of other examples where people have lost out because of stereotyping, prejudice, discrimination, or scapegoating—either as victims or perpetrators?

- How do you think the people in these situations learned stereotypes or prejudices?

- Have you ever been the victim of stereotyping, prejudice, discrimination, or scapegoating?

---

* From Nancy Schniedewind and Ellen Davidson, *Open Minds to Equality.* © (Boston: Allyn and Bacon, 1983). Adapted with permission.

Identify Strategies for Prejudice-related Conflicts

Handouts *Interrupting Prejudice Case Studies* (two case studies for each group of three or four), *Strategies for Interrupting Prejudice* (one for each group of three or four)

1. Review the six styles for handling conflicts that were introduced in Skill Lesson 5. If needed, redistribute the *Six Ways of Handling Conflicts* handout from that lesson. Explain that all of these ways can be used to deal with prejudice- and stereotype-related conflicts.

2. Divide students into groups of three or four and give each group a copy of the *Strategies for Interrupting Prejudice* handout. Explain that each group will receive two different case studies that tell of how someone dealt with or "interrupted" prejudice in a conflict. Some of the people were effective, some were not. The group will have about five minutes to read the case, then discuss the questions on the handout and decide what they think. (You may allow more time for this activity if you choose.)

3. Distribute two case studies to each group. Some groups will have the same case studies as others. You will want to consider the standards of your community in choosing which case studies to use. Allow about five minutes for each case study. As the groups work, give them time warnings. After five minutes, they should move on to the second case study, unless you are able to give them more time.

4. When the groups have finished, have each group share with the class one of the case studies they discussed.

Discussion

- What were the most ineffective ways of dealing with these conflicts?
- What values were at work in these conflicts?
- What role did values play in the conflicts?
- Did any of the people in these cases use conflict productively? How?
- Have you ever been in similar situations? What did you do?

LEVEL: A/B/C
(5 MINUTES)

Evaluation/Review of Key Points

1. Have volunteers respond to the following question. If you were going to describe this class to a friend who was not here, what is one thing you would say about it?

2. Summarize key points from the lesson:

    *   Stereotyping can lead to prejudice, which can lead to discrimination, which can lead to scapegoating.

    *   Stereotyping, prejudice, discrimination, and scapegoating harm all the people involved.

    *   Conflict resolution skills can help in handling prejudice-related conflicts.

LEVEL: A/B/C
(5 MINUTES)

Closing (Optional)

If you so desire, choose a Closing Activity from Appendix B.

Prejudice Situation Cards

1. Steven was hit in the eye with a softball, and to everyone's surprise, he started to cry. The other guys then started to snicker. Jorge felt bad for him, but laughed along with the other guys.

2. Some Latino students asked Shirley to join their group to do a math project. She thought that because their English wasn't good they couldn't be very smart. She joined another group. Their group got an A. Shirley's didn't.

3. Gabe was a great dancer. One day the phys. ed. teacher suggested that Gabe might want to take up ballet. Gabe liked the idea, but the more he thought about it, the more he was afraid that the other guys would make fun of him. He dropped the idea, along with lots of good exercise and a possible career.

4. Denise fell on the sidewalk. Her ankle really hurt. A black woman stopped to help her up. "I'm a doctor," she said. "Sit on this bench and let me look at that." Denise didn't trust the woman and said, "No thanks. I'm fine." She limped away.

5. Joan's family doesn't have much money and lives in a different neighborhood from Lu Ellen's. When Joan invited Lu Ellen to a birthday party, Lu assumed the house would be messy and dirty. She didn't go, and everyone told her later how nice the house was, and how good the food was.

6. Tyrell missed the bus and needed a ride to school. Ms. Gomez, who is 82, offered him a ride. Tyrell refused, thinking she'd drive off the road. He killed his feet walking the four miles to school, was late, and it started to rain.

7. Arnie's younger sister keeps calling her friend a "wild Indian." She shoots him again and again with a toy gun. Arnie is bothered by this name-calling, but he doesn't say anything.

8. Karen is having trouble in math class. She keeps going for extra help, but her grades are not improving. The teacher tells her it's okay because girls don't do well at math.

We All Lose!

Card Number _____

Stereotype or Prejudice _____

Harm caused by stereotype or prejudice to each person in the situation:

_____

_____

_____

Card Number _____

Stereotype or Prejudice _____

Harm caused by stereotype or prejudice to each person in the situation:

_____

_____

_____

Card Number _____

Stereotype or Prejudice _____

Harm caused by stereotype or prejudice to each person in the situation:

_____

_____

_____

Interrupting Prejudice
Case Studies

Case 1 A group of five middle school boys and girls were concerned about racial conflicts in the school. One of them had heard about a group of athletes that comes to middle schools and talks with students about prejudice and racism. They wanted to bring this group to their school. They met with the assistant principal and a guidance counselor and got their help in arranging an assembly. They raised money for the speakers by having a bake sale and by asking some business people to help them. The speakers came and spoke to the students, and everyone was inspired by them.

Case 2 Martin, who is an eighth grader, saw a group of three elementary students picking on a retarded man in his neighborhood. The man was getting upset, and this made the children tease him all the more. It made Martin angry to see this. "Hey you kids, knock it off, or I'm going to come after you myself." The children saw who was yelling and ran off.

Case 3 Eileen hangs out with some girls who are very popular. They often tease and laugh at Charlene, a girl in their class who doesn't have much money. Eileen hates the way they pick on Charlene, but goes along with it because she really wants this group of girls to like her.

Case 4 Liu is new to the country and doesn't speak much English. She has been teased by a group of boys in school. Now, whenever she sees these boys coming, she walks away quickly. She tries never to be where they are.

Case 5 Jon is at his relative's house on Sunday afternoon. He's sitting with all the men in his family, watching the football game. One of his uncles starts to say racist things about some of the players on the team. Jon is uncomfortable, but doesn't know what to do. His father isn't saying anything either. Jon thinks, "If I don't say anything he'll stop. I'll just let it go. It's his house."

Case 6 In homeroom some of the students are talking about gay men and making jokes. Mark's face gets very red, and suddenly he blurts out, "My uncle's gay, and he's a great guy. You guys don't know what you're talking about so just shut up!" Someone says, "Okay, Mark, relax!" The teacher comes in and the kids take their seats. Later, another student comes up to Mark and says, "I have a gay uncle, too. And I really like him. I was glad you told those kids to shut up."

Case 7 Ruth, who is African-American, is constantly in conflict with Isabel, a Latina girl in her grade. Ruth feels that Isabel is always putting her down and making racist comments about her. Isabel makes the comments in Spanish, so Ruth isn't sure. Ruth likes to go to the Youth Center, but doesn't feel comfortable when Isabel is there. She is tired of these conflicts, so she approaches Isabel one day. "Look," she says. "We really get on each other's nerves. So I'll make a deal with you. I'll stay out of your way for the whole school day if you stay out of the Youth Center." Isabel agrees to the deal.

Case 8 One day Mario's friend Dan started making jokes about Italians, saying they were stupid and dirty. Mario, who is Italian, didn't say anything. But as he walked home from Dan's house he thought to himself, "I'm going to say something. I just need to calm down and figure out how I want to say it. Then I'm going to call him tonight."

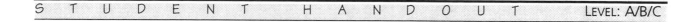

Case 9 Because of surgery she had on her leg, Casel walks with a brace and a cane. Before the surgery she couldn't walk at all. Now she goes to a new school where a group of boys taunt her every day on her way to her sixth period class. She's tried ignoring them, but they keep doing it. One day she sees one of the boys in the library, sitting by himself. She goes up to him and says, "Why do you and your friends pick on me? I never did anything to you." The boy mumbles an apology. "Will you stop?" Casel asks. The boy agrees, then leaves.

Case 10 The students in one middle school stick pretty much with their own racial and ethnic group. They don't mix much, and when they do, it's often because they're in conflict. But one of the teachers has organized a project to paint a mural on the side of the school. Eight students have been chosen to design and paint the mural. They are students from all different racial and ethnic backgrounds, and they have to make decisions together and work together. As a result of working on the project, they get to be friends and start hanging out together.

Strategies for Interrupting Prejudice

Case Study Number _____

What conflict styles did you see in this situation?

_____Aggressive   _____Give In

_____Collaborate   _____Avoid or Delay

_____Compromise   _____Get Help

If you were the person in this situation, would you feel satisfied with the way it turned out?

In what ways was this response effective?

In what ways was it ineffective?

Identify three other possible responses:

Case Study Number _____

What conflict styles did you see in this situation?

_____Aggressive   _____Give In

_____Collaborate   _____Avoid or Delay

_____Compromise   _____Get Help

If you were the person in this situation, would you feel satisfied with the way it turned out?

In what ways was this response effective?

In what ways was it ineffective?

Identify three other possible responses:

Extending the Concepts of Part Three: Additional Activities

CONFLICT TOOL

Diversity Deck, Point of View

Diversity and the P.O.V. Glasses

ACTIVITY IN BRIEF Students practice using the tool of the P.O.V. Glasses to understand conflicts rooted in racial and ethnic differences.

HANDOUT *Diversity and the P.O.V. Glasses*

1. Review with students the concept of the P.O.V. Glasses, that is, the lenses through which we view the world. The lenses are tinted by our experiences, goals, feelings, values, and needs.

2. Write the words "Experiences," "Goals," "Feelings," "Values," and "Needs" on the board. Have students describe how Diversity Deck cards influence each of these.

3. Distribute the *Diversity and the P.O.V. Glasses* handout. Discuss the handout, particularly how the different Diversity Deck cards can contribute to tinting the lenses. During the discussion, be sure to emphasize that some cards affect the P.O.V. Glasses more than others, depending on the individual.

   DISCUSSION
   - What Primary Tints are most influential in your P.O.V. Glasses?
   - Do you think this is true for most people?
   - How could different Primary Tints lead to conflict between people?

Diversity and the P.O.V. Glasses

Identify ways that cards from the Diversity Deck could help tint the
P.O.V. Glasses...

Experiences: **Values and**
                                                   Beliefs:

Goals:

Feelings: **Needs:**

Indicate the ones you believe become Primary Tints.

Diversity Bag Reports

ACTIVITY IN BRIEF   Students review and explore in greater depth the "Diversity Deck" by applying it to their own backgrounds.

Note: *This makes a good homework assignment.*

1. Have students make Bag Reports that represent the various Diversity Deck Cards they have "been dealt." Each student takes a paper bag and puts into it five to ten different objects that represent some aspect of his or her Diversity Deck. There should be at least one object representing each suit, i.e., something representing Color, Culture, Clout, and Character. The fifth item should represent a Wild Card. If there are additional items, they can be representative of any of the suits. On the bottom of the bag, students should write their names.

2. Collect all the bag reports and then redistribute them, so that everyone has a bag that is not his or her own. Caution them not to look at the name on the bottom of the bag. Give everyone five minutes to examine the contents of the bag he or she is holding. Then have each student summarize what they have learned about the person from the contents of the bag. The goal is not to guess who the person is, but rather to describe what their Diversity Deck is like. When everyone has finished, students should look on the bottom of the bag and return the bag to its owner.

The Diversity School

ACTIVITY IN BRIEF   Students apply principles of appreciating diversity to a school setting.

MATERIALS   3 x 5 inch cards

1. Ask students to imagine what a school would be like that valued diversity, i.e., a school where differences were seen as positive and useful and opportunities for learning.
   - What activities would be going on?
   - How would people talk to each other?
   - What would teachers be doing?
   - What would students be doing?

2. Distribute 3 x 5 cards and have students anonymously write one specific characteristic of the diversity school. For example, students could work on projects and share them with the class. Or, teachers could ask students for their ideas about running the school.

3. When students have finished, collect the cards, then redistribute them and have each student read his or her card aloud. When the whole class has finished, discuss as suggested below.

4. Have some volunteers take the cards and make a series of posters for the classroom that will remind students of the qualities they identified

for the Diversity School. Post these around the room—or the school.

DISCUSSION

- Would you add anything to the ideas expressed on the cards?
- What makes it difficult to appreciate diversity?
- In what ways does our middle school appreciate diversity?
- In what ways does our school not appreciate diversity?
- Of the things suggested on the cards, what could we begin to do to create a school that appreciates diversity?

CONFLICT TOOL

Understanding Culture

Microlab on Cultural Background

ACTIVITY IN BRIEF   Students share several aspects of their cultural background in a microlab format.

1. Divide students into microlab groups of three or four. Give each student two minutes to tell something about his or her background, addressing the following (be sure to signal each time two minutes has elapsed):
   - Where were your grandparents and/or parents born?
   - What is your cultural background?
   - What is an important value that your family has that they have communicated to you?

2. Bring the class back together for a discussion on the following questions:
   - What did you notice about diversity as you did this activity?
   - How did it feel to talk about your culture cards in particular?

3. Ask volunteers to share what their cultural group is and the value that is important to them. Write the name of cultural groups and the values described on the board or on chart paper. When a cultural group or value is repeated, place a check next to the phrase to see how often a particular value comes up.

DISCUSSION

- To what degree are there similarities in the values listed?
- How can we account for some of the differences in family values listed?
- How do you suppose these family values came about?
- What do these values tell us about particular ethnic or cultural groups?

Living Cross Culturally/The Culture of Burping

ACTIVITY IN BRIEF Students explore aspects of culture by examining how a particular behavior—in this case, burping—can be interpreted differently in different cultures.

HANDOUTS *Eurp! Burp! The Culture of Burping*

1. Explain to students that we all live in many different cultures, and the "rules" for what's acceptable vary from culture to culture. An example of how "rules" may vary is the acceptability of burping. Burping in public is generally considered rude and impolite. If it happens, the person who burps is expected to say, "Excuse me."

2. Distribute the *Eurp! Burp! The Culture of Burping* handout. Give students a few minutes to fill it out. Then discuss.

   Note: *When you do this activity, you will likely have to endure a short epidemic of burping, followed by laughter. It will go away, so we suggest simply reminding students to say, "Excuse me," and going on with the lesson.*

DISCUSSION

- What happens when you burp in your family? (Have several students respond to get a feel for the variety of burping rules.)
- How is it different with your friends?
- What would be different about burping during a speech? In church?
- What would be your reaction in each of these situations?
- What's different about each of these situations?
- How did you learn the rules for burping or not burping?
- How do people react when a baby burps compared to when you burp?
- Why the difference?
- What different rules or meaning might there be regarding burping in other cultures? Other times?
- How could these different rules about burping lead to conflict?
- How do people adapt their behavior from culture to culture? Why?

Eurp! Burp!
The Culture of Burping

We all live in several different cultures, and we learn slightly different rules of behavior in each one. Take burping for example.

Everyone burps occasionally. In mainstream U.S. culture, burping in public is considered rude, and if you burp you are expected to say, "Excuse me."

But these rules vary slightly from subculture to subculture.

1. What happens if you burp when you're with your family?

2. What happens if you burp when you're with your friends?

3. What happens if you burp when you're in the middle of a speech?

4. What happens if you burp in the middle of class?

5. What happens if a baby burps?

Discuss Aspects or Elements of Culture

ACTIVITY IN BRIEF   Students explore various elements and aspects that make up "culture."

HANDOUTS   *Elements of Culture*

1. Distribute the *Elements of Culture* handout and discuss with students.

    ### DISCUSSION

    *   What are the differences between the two lists? (List A is a practical structure for the more internal elements in List B.)
    *   Which list should come first? Why? (List B comes first, then is expressed through the activities in list A.)
    *   What kinds of conflicts could result from the different cultural elements on list B?

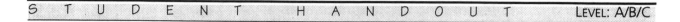

Elements of Culture

List A	List B
Shelter	Values
Clothing	Customs
Food	Gender Roles
Arts and Crafts	Biases
Music and Dance	Standards of Beauty
Work	Family Structure
Religious Structures	Beliefs
Government	Nonverbal Communication
Language	View of the World
Protection	Expectations
Ways of Educating	Child Rearing Practices

CONFLICT TOOL

The Clout P.I.E.

Clout and Conflict Role-Plays

ACTIVITY IN BRIEF   Students examine ways that clout influences conflict and conflict resolution.

1. Choose role-plays from earlier skill lessons for students to do in class.

2. Each role-player should have a status card taped to his or her forehead (see Playing the Clout Card Game, p. 255). As students role-play, have them react to the status of the other person. For example, a nine in conflict with a three might say, "I can't be bothered with this." Students in the audience should watch to see how status differences affect the conflict. An interesting variation is to have the role-players switch status cards, but not roles, halfway through the exercise.

3. At first, give the role-players very different status levels, so that, for example, a ten is in conflict with a two. As you repeat the activity, make the cards' numbers closer together.

    DISCUSSION
    *   How did the Clout cards affect the conflict?
    *   Did it affect how the conflict was resolved?
    *   What kinds of things did the high status person do in the conflict?
    *   Did or could the low status person do those things?
    *   How did changing the status change the role-play?
    *   What experiences have you had in conflicts with people who were of very different status than you?

More Practice with the Clout PIES

ACTIVITY IN BRIEF   Students explore the concept of clout using case studies of middle school students.

HANDOUT   *The Clout PIES of Four Middle School Students*

1. Divide students into work groups of three or four. Distribute *The Clout PIES of Four Middle School Students* handout. Have students read the handout and decide as a group the following (write these questions on the board):
    *   Of the four people on the handout, who has the most Clout?
    *   What are the elements of each person's Clout?
    *   How does Context affect each person's Clout?
    *   How does Character affect their Clout?
    *   What do we know about their Culture? How does it affect their Clout?
    *   What do we know about their Color? How does it affect their Clout?

    (Tell students to remember that Color cards in the Diversity Deck are more than skin color.)

2. Bring the class together to discuss their conclusions. Emphasize the following points:
   - Clout is not dependent on having large pieces of all three sections of the PIE.
   - Clout varies depending on the context of the PIES.
   - Clout depends in part on other people's perception of your PIES.

DISCUSSION
   - Who did you think had the most Clout?
   - What influenced their Clout?
   - What would it be like to be in a conflict with Andres? With Sophia?

The Clout PIES
of Four Middle School Students

The Clout Pie:

Power   Influence

Economic Status

CONTEXT   CHARACTER

Gina An eighth grade student who is on the honor roll. She has a small circle of friends who say things like, "She won't let you down," "She keeps secrets," "You can depend on her." Other students don't know her or her family well, but they know she gets good grades in school. Gina's family doesn't have a lot of money, but she has never gone hungry either. The students who don't know her say things like, "She's smart," and "She's quiet."

Andres A seventh grade student who wants very much to be accepted by a group of eighth grade boys. Because his family has a lot of money, he often treats boys in this group to snacks and lends them money when they need it. Lately, though, he's been wondering how successful he's been. He always has to call the boys to go do things; they rarely call him. One of the boys had a party last weekend, and Andres didn't find out about it until Monday. He feels lonely.

Paul An eighth grade softball star. Paul is smart, good-looking, and his family has a lot of money. Most of the other Asian students in his school have reputations for being smart, but Paul is best known for being an athlete. He doesn't have much use for people who aren't athletes, and he some-times leads his buddies in teasing and scapegoating weaker students. He seems to especially dislike other Asian students.

Sophia A sixth grade student who moved to this country from Greece two and a half years ago. Her father died when she was young, and her mother struggles to feed and clothe three children on her pay as a factory worker. Sophia is known as a jolly person—she's often with a group of students, laughing and having a good time. If she makes a mistake in her English or if her clothes are old, she jokes about it. She likes organizing things and is often elected by other students to do special tasks.

CONFLICT RESOLUTION IN THE MIDDLE SCHOOL   **285**

CONFLICT TOOL

Understanding Stereotyping, Prejudice, Discrimination, and Scapegoating

Make a Collage*

ACTIVITY IN BRIEF   Students explore how discrimination works out in practice.

MATERIALS   Magazines, glue sticks or paste, large sheets of newsprint, markers in various colors

1. Divide the class into five groups. Explain that the project is for each group to make a collage that illustrates something about stereotyping. You will give each group materials. They may use those materials and *no others*. Each group will be graded based on the same criteria: an effective visual statement of what stereotyping is and how it can be harmful.

2. Distribute materials to the groups as follows:

   Group 1: A sheet of newsprint, a glue stick or paste, many magazines, three markers in different colors.

   Group 2: A sheet of newsprint, a glue stick or paste, many magazines, one marker.

   Group 3: A sheet of newsprint, a glue stick or paste, four magazines, one marker.

   Group 4: A sheet of newsprint, a glue stick or paste, one magazine.

   Group 5: A sheet of newsprint, one magazine.

3. Give each group 20 minutes or so to complete their collages. During that time, note how the groups work together and the comments students make. If students complain about how the materials were distributed, be very matter-of-fact. Say something like, "That's the way life is. Sorry, but there are no changes."

4. After 20 minutes, have the groups share their collages with the class.

   ### DISCUSSION
   * How did you feel while doing the project?
   * How did you feel when you looked at other groups?
   * In what ways was your project easy? Hard? Frustrating? Fun?
   * Why do you think I set up the project this way?
   * Are there other situations in school where some people start out with greater advantages than others?

---

* From Nancy Schniedewind and Ellen Davidson, *Open Minds to Equality.* © 1983 Allyn and Bacon. Adapted by permission.

- Are there other situations in the world where some people have more advantages and others are discriminated against?

Viewing "Names Can Really Hurt Us"

ACTIVITY IN BRIEF   To discuss how a program of diversity appreciation and prejudice reduction affected a group of middle school students.

MATERIALS   Video "Names *Can* Really Hurt Us"[*]

1. View the video. "Names *Can* Really Hurt Us" is a video that shows how an intensive diversity awareness and prejudice reduction program was used with a group of New York City middle school students. During a two-week period these students moved from an intellectual understanding of prejudice to a first-hand sharing of the pain of prejudice in their lives. They began to feel empowered to help reduce prejudice, increase tolerance, and create harmony.

2. After viewing the tape, ask students to find a partner and spend three minutes each recalling images in the film that stood out for them and why those images were so powerful.

3. Bring the class together and discuss as suggested below.

DISCUSSION
- What images did you find most powerful?
- What gave those images their power?
- What strategies for countering prejudice did you see in the video?

---

[*] "Names *Can* Really Hurt Us" is available through the Anti-Defamation League (1-800-343-5540).

Part Four: Infusing Conflict Resolution into the Standard Curriculum

29 *Overview of Infusion**

No two people are exactly alike. All of human interaction involves dealing with differences, and thus dealing with conflict. This concept underlies the infusion of conflict resolution into the curriculum—into any and all subject areas.

Why infuse conflict resolution into the standard curriculum?

- Learning about the dynamics of conflict and the skills of conflict resolution gives students insight into the human interactions that make up the subject matter in many fields of inquiry.

- The curriculum topics themselves become more interesting and more personally relevant to students.

- Infusing conflict resolution into curricula gives students a chance to practice and reinforce key conflict resolution concepts and skills.

- Infusion offers students the opportunity to learn conflict resolution skills via a third party, such as a historical figure or a fictional character. For students in early adolescence, this can be a comfortable access route for learning interpersonal skills.

- Integrating conflict resolution into standard subject matter challenges students to apply what they have learned in other contexts.

- Infusing conflict resolution sends a message that conflict resolution is an important part of school since it is not being segregated to one corner of the curriculum or school day.

What curriculum subjects and topics can be used?

Conflict resolution can be infused into many topics in many subjects areas including English/language arts, social studies, history, current events, geography, math, and science.

The goal in infusing conflict resolution into your curriculum is to deepen the curriculum, not to water it down. Effective infusion lessons are not short activities tacked on the end of a skill area. They can be long-term themes and projects, or concepts woven throughout your courses. Either way,

---

* ESR thanks Rachel Poliner for contributing this chapter.

infusion can enlarge students' understanding of conflict resolution as well as subject material.

Start by reviewing your curriculum goals and themes. Conflict resolution will not help students learn basic skills like spelling or multiplication. But it will help them understand anything that involves making decisions or solving problems. For example, although it won't help students with grammar, it will help them understand characters in literature—their motivations, their choices, their struggles. And in math, while conflict resolution concepts won't help students learn to do computations, it will help them learn *when* to do computations, how problems are chosen, who defines them, and much more.

Identify which of your curriculum goals and themes have to do with communication, understanding different perspectives, making decisions, solving problems, or other conflict resolution-related tools. The topics that relate to those goals and themes will provide rich opportunities for infusing conflict resolution.

What are some methods of infusing conflict resolution into other subject areas?

There are three major infusion methods:

(1) Use conflict resolution *concepts* in lessons. For example, you can use the conflict escalator or a win-win grid in a history lesson.

(2) Incorporate conflict resolution *skills,* such as problem solving, into lessons. This gives students a chance to practice their conflict resolution skills in new and varied contexts.

(3) Use the *instructional strategies* that promote the six themes of the Peaceable Classroom: cooperation, communication, affective education, appreciation of diversity, responsible decision making, and conflict resolution. For example, you can use microlabs or brainstorming in a science lesson. A short list of instructional strategies can be found in appendix D.

When can connections be made between conflict resolution and my curriculum?

Infusing conflict resolution into the curriculum can be done before, during or after teaching the basic skills lessons of *Conflict Resolution in the Middle School.*

- Teaching a skill first lets you focus specifically on the interpersonal skills of your students. Once they have learned and practiced the skills, you can infuse the skills into subject matter, helping students make wider connections.

- For some students and for certain skills it may be helpful to teach the skills in the context of subject matter first, and later relate them to students' own lives. For example, middle school students often find identifying the emotions of fictional characters to be less threatening than identifying and discussing their own emotions. If they can start with emotions in fiction, they may be able to ease into reflecting and talking about their own feelings.

- You can also let your curriculum determine when you infuse conflict resolution topics. Let's say your curriculum includes a semester focus on the civil rights movement. Teach the unit with the materials and approaches that you have found successful. There will be frequent opportunities to point out connections to conflict resolution such as anger management, demands versus ReallyNeeds, conflict styles, and understanding prejudice and discrimination.

Debriefing an infusion activity

By infusing conflict resolution into the curriculum, students' understanding of *both the subject area and conflict resolution* can be deepened. The questions that you create for class discussions, small group work, and journal writing will help them to accomplish this. Effective debriefing questions are an important component of effective infusion. Here are some sample questions that relate to literature.

- When do you think the conflict started? When did the characters get on the escalator?

- What were some of the early escalating behaviors? Did you observe any bulldozing or global statements?

- Identify some of the communication potholes in the conversation between the characters. What could they have said that would have been less escalating?

- Name the conflict styles used by the main characters in the last passage that we read. What are the phrases and actions that show you their styles?

You can develop questions to ask your students as you observe what connections your students are able to make between the subject area and conflict resolution. Below is a list of some of the connections that can be made between conflict resolution and other subjects:

Language Arts: classifying and observing conflicts, identifying emotions and their effects, improving ways of communicating, becoming aware of many points of view, empathizing with characters' struggles with stereotyping, prejudice and discrimination.

History and social studies: understanding actions and conflict styles of historical figures; more deeply observing and interpreting current events, social movements, and the development of war and peace; relating interpersonal conflict to intergroup conflict.

Mathematics: understanding that people (who have their own points of view) choose what problems to solve, what skills to use in the process, that different skills will deliver different results, and that people make different decisions even when they have the same results.

Science: learning that science affects community conflicts, that social conflicts affect science, and that a person's point of view affects how he or she approaches a scientific problem.

CONFLICT TOOL

Identifying Conflicts/Conflict Sort

Conflict Bag Report:*

A bag report is a type of oral report. Students take a plain brown bag. On the front they write the title and author of the book they are reporting on. They may also draw a picture. Inside the bag they place five objects, each representing a conflict in the book. (Most books will have more than five conflicts. Students are free to choose the five they wish.) On the back of the bag they write the names of the characters involved in each conflict. They also write their own names on the bag. To present their Bag Reports, students remove each object from the bag and describe the conflict that object represents and which character is involved. If you would like there to be more writing with this type of report, students can write a paragraph for each object explaining the conflict and why they chose that object.

Conflict Sort—Option One

This first type of Conflict Sort activity is the most sophisticated. It can be done individually or in groups. Have students identify all the conflicts they can from the book they are reading and then write each conflict (with a page reference) on a 3" x 5" card. They need only write a sentence or two describing the conflict and who is involved. When they have finished identifying conflicts, they should classify them according to a classification scheme that they develop.

Conflict Sort—Option Two

This type of conflict sort is simpler. Students begin by devising a classification scheme for conflicts. They then make a chart and list three conflicts from the book that fit the designated categories.

FOR EXAMPLE

From the book *Bridge to Terabithia* by Katherine Paterson (New York: Thomas Crowell, 1977):

GOALS	RESOURCES	VALUES
Jess wanted to be an artist but no one else wanted him to.	Janice Avery took May Belle's Twinkies.	Leslie was disgusted with the girls for telling Janice's secret.

---

* The author learned about Bag Reports from Barbara Scotto, Driscoll School, Brookline, MA

CONFLICT TOOL

Conflict Escalator

Conflict Escalator with Specific Conflicts

Students identify a conflict in the book then map it on the escalator by writing a behavior in the conflict on each step. Students should be sure to identify the feelings that escalate with each step and to list the contents of the baggage the characters are carrying with them.

For example:

In *The Bully of Barkham Street* by Mary Stolz (New York: HarperCollins, 1963) there is a conflict on pages 114-116 that can be mapped as follows:

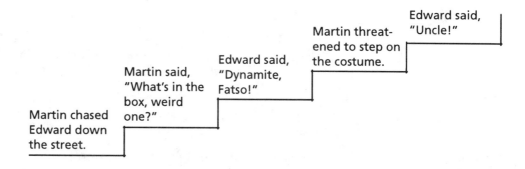

Conflict Escalator with All or Most of a Book

Conflict escalators can be used to map all of a book or significant portions of it. Used this way, students note on the escalator the major events leading to conflicts in the book. They are less focused on two or three characters and more concerned with the main characters involved in major conflicts in the book.

CONFLCIT TOOL

Anger Thermometer/Other Feelings

Feelings Charts

Have the class brainstorm a list of feeling words. Next, have students choose ten of the feelings words and make a chart. For each word they should write a definition. They should cite (with page references) an incident from the book when a character felt that emotion.

Where On the Anger Thermometer (Or Continuum)?

Have students identify ten incidents from the book that involve some degree of anger. They should describe each incident, then draw an Anger Thermometer (or Continuum for more advanced students) next to that description, identifying the degree of anger in that incident.

Feeling Word Continuum

The Anger Sort activity in Conflict Skill Lesson 5 is, in addition to a discussion starter, a vocabulary-building activity. Challenge students to come up with their own versions of the Anger Sort using other emotions. Have them begin by choosing a theme emotion such as love, fear, or jealousy. They should find five to ten words that express various degrees of that feeling. Next they write the words on 3" x 5" cards (one word to a card) and place them on a continuum of least to most intense. When they have completed their decks of feeling words, they can trade with other students to have them try to arrange the words from least to most.

How Feelings Feel

Have students collect from various books words, phrases, or sentences that show unusual ways feelings are described or expressed. These might be from scenes (not always including conflicts) where characters are trying to express feelings or even identify feelings to themselves. They might also be where the author is describing how a character is feeling. Encourage students to collect examples that go beyond, "She felt sad when she saw the dead squirrel."

CONFLICT TOOL

De-Escalating Conflict—CAPS

If It Were Me I'd De-Escalate It This Way...

Have students identify a conflict in the book and describe or write about how it has escalated. Next have them identify as one of the characters and complete the statement, "If I were in this conflict, I'd de-escalate it this way..." They should go on to describe what they would do to de-escalate the conflict: the behaviors they would use, what they would say, what they would do or not do, and how they think the other character would react.

Examples of De-Escalation

CAPS is only one way to de-escalate conflicts. Have students look for examples of de-escalation in many books. They can write up each example saying who's involved in the conflict, what the conflict was about, and how it was de-escalated. For each example, they should write a word or phrase that summarizes the de-escalation approach. Examples include talking it out, clearing up misunderstandings, apologizing, etc. If they see patterns or common approaches in the examples they collect, they can classify them together on the chart.

Conflict Stories with First Lines and Last Lines

This writing exercise is a fun way for students to practice de-escalating conflicts. Give students the first line of a story that clearly indicates a conflict. Also give them the last line that clearly indicates the conflict is resolved. Have them write the story that will connect the first sentence with the last and will show how the characters de-escalated and resolved their conflict.

SAMPLE STORY LINES

First Line: "Some friend you turned out to be," Marina said to Claire. "Just stay out of my life!"

Last Line: Marina smiled at Claire. "I'm really glad we worked this out."

First Line: "I was counting on you to back me up," Roberto shouted at James. "You totally let me down!"

Last Line: "You're a good friend James," Roberto said. "And a *dependable* friend."

First Line: "I'm sorry Captain," said Star Cadet Williams. "I cannot obey that order. It would put too many lives in danger."

Last Line: "Thank you Captain," said Star Cadet Williams. "It means a lot to me to have you say that."

First Line: "Forsooth my lad," said the old man. "Ye cannot really believe that's the best course of action!"

Last Line: "Aye, a feast like this is a splendid way to celebrate our success. And a special toast to you my lad!"

CONFLICT TOOL

Win-Win Grid, Problem Solving, Conflict Management Styles

Suggesting Endings

Have students stop reading a book once a key conflict is established and have them brainstorm the possible endings to the book or solutions to the conflict. These need not be realistic endings—encourage students to use their imaginations. Emphasize that the point is not to "guess the ending" but rather to come up with as many alternate endings as possible.

Using the Win-Win Grid

A variation on the above activity is to have students stop reading a book once a key conflict is established and develop possible endings using the

Win-Win Grid. They should come up with at least one solution for each square on the grid, although they may come up with more. As part of using the Grid, have them identify what the characters in the conflict want. Again, emphasize that the point is not to "guess the ending" but rather to come up with as many alternate endings as possible.

Identifying Conflict Styles

Have students make a chart of the different conflict resolution styles they worked with in Conflict Skill Lesson 12. Next, have them find examples of those styles from either one book or several books. For each style on the chart they should describe the style used in a particular book, including who used the style, in what conflict, and the result.

Conflict Stories with First Line and Last Line

The writing exercise suggested for De-Escalating Conflict can also be used for this theme. Give students the first and last line of the story. Ask them to show how the characters used a particular conflict resolution style to get to a Win-Win ending. As part of the story they should identify the P.O.V.s of the characters and state what the characters want.

CONFLICT TOOL

Listening

Listening for Detail

Read aloud a selected passage from a book that describes a conflict and how it escalates. The first time you do this activity use a fairly short and simple passage. Then repeat the activity using longer and more complex excerpts to add to the challenge. When you have finished reading, ask students to re-call the details of the conflict, including identifying any escalating behavior they may have heard described. Also ask students what they think led up to this conflict and what they think might happen next. This is a good activity to pique students' interest in a book they are about to read.

Paraphrase Practice

Play "You Say, I Say" while having a book discussion. Divide students into groups of four and explain that they will be discussing a book they have all read. Explain how the discussion will proceed: The first student makes a statement about the book under discussion, such as, "I like the way the characters learned to talk to each other about their differences." The second student also comments on the book, but cannot do so until he or she paraphrases what the first student says, such as, "You say you liked the way the characters learned to talk about their differences; I say I didn't like it when they called each other names." The third student also comments on the book, but must first paraphrase what student number two said, and so on. This activity works best when you give students a focus for their discussion, such as reactions to how the characters grew and changed, reactions to how the characters handled conflicts, how students would have handled the conflicts if they had been the main character, etc.

CONFLICT TOOL

Point of View

Identify the P.O.V. of the Characters

There are several ways to do this activity. One is to have students read the first chapter or two of a book and identify the main characters. Have them then summarize what they know about each character's P.O.V. on the central problem in the book thus far. Ask them to keep these summaries. Follow up with a description of how each character's P.O.V. changed in the course of the book and what led to those changes. This is an excellent activity for helping students explore how characters grow and change as a result of conflicts and other experiences.

FOR EXAMPLE

From *Bridge to Terabithia* by Katherine Patersen:[*]

The P.O.V. of various characters on Jess' artistic ability:

Jess: Loves being able to draw; it's a release for him; a joyful thing.

Jess' Father: Thinks drawing is for girls; it's useless; a waste of time.

Miss Edmonds: Jess should be encouraged; he has a wonderful talent.

The Other Teachers: It's a waste of good paper.

Another variation is to have students identify the major P.O.V.s of characters in a book and how they affect the plot and the main characters.

FOR EXAMPLE

In *The Foxman* by Gary Paulsen,[**] the main character hears tales from his male relatives about the greatness and glory of war. Then he makes friends with the mysterious Foxman, a severely disfigured old man who lives alone in the woods. There he hears another P.O.V. about war that emphasizes its horrible and destructive aspects. Ultimately, both these P.O.V.s influence his own.

Fractured Fairy Tales

Read students *The True Story of the Three Pigs* by Jon Scieszka,[***] a very funny book that tells the story of the Three Pigs from the P.O.V. of the wolf. Discuss how the story differs from the original, how changing the P.O.V. changes the

---

[*] Katherine Paterson, *Bridge to Terabithia* (New York: Thomas Crowell, 1977).

[**] Gary Paulsen, *The Foxman* (Nashville: T. Nelson, 1977).

[***] Jon Scieszka, *The True Story of the Three Little Pigs: by A. Wolf* (New York: Viking Kestrel, 1989).

story, what makes the story funny, etc. Then have students rewrite familiar fairy tales from the P.O.V. of the villain or of a minor character. Encourage them to have fun with this, although the stories need not be humorous.

CONFLICT TOOL

Demands and ReallyNeeds

Demands and ReallyNeeds Handout

Use the Demands and ReallyNeeds handout that follows to help students explore in more depth the characters' P.O.V. Follow up by having students develop solutions for the conflict in the book that are based on the characters' ReallyNeeds.

Demands and ReallyNeeds Comics

Students can summarize the Demands and ReallyNeeds of the characters in a book by creating a cartoon or comic strip that show the characters' Demands in talk balloons and their ReallyNeeds in thought balloons.

CONFLICT TOOL

Negotiation, Mediation, Arbitration

Negotiating Between Characters in Books

Have students identify two disputing parties in a book. Then have them write up a description of each character and the conflict they share. These descriptions become role-play cards. Students role-play the characters and, as the two disputants, try to come up with a solution to their conflict. They can use everything they know about listening, de-escalating, Demands and ReallyNeeds, and so on in trying to reach a Win-Win resolution. This solution need not have anything to do with the one in the book (if there is a solution).

Mediating Between Characters in Books

This activity is just like the one above, except there is a third party involved—the mediator. Using the mediation process from Skill Lesson 21, the mediator tries to help the disputing characters come to a Win-Win solution. It is important for the role-play that the characters agree to try to come to a solution and that the players know they should try to come up with a solution. They may be angry and they may act out, but they can't refuse to cooperate at all or the mediation won't work. (Students who have done Skill Lesson 21 will know this, but they should be reminded.)

Examples of Third Party Intervention

Have students look for examples of third party interventions in books they have read. Are the interventions mediation or arbitration? Are they successful or do they escalate the conflict?

Etc.—Writing Activities for Conflict Resolution

Writing Role-Plays

Have students create role-plays that can be used in skill lessons or for follow up and review.

School Paper

If your school has a school paper, students can write articles describing various conflict resolution concepts and how young people could use them. They might also start a "Dear Abby" type of advice column, giving suggestions on how to handle conflict situations.

Demands and ReallyNeeds
In Fiction

Book Title: _____

Author: _____

Describe a conflict in the book. _____

_____

_____

Who are the characters in conflict? _____

_____

_____

What Demands are the characters making? _____

_____

_____

List two or three ReallyNeeds for each character. Underline the ones you think are most important. _____

_____

_____

What is the outcome of the conflict in the book? Do you think it is a good solution?

_____

_____

_____

What would be a solution that would meet the important ReallyNeeds of the characters?

_____

_____

_____

31 Social Studies

Note: *The suggestions that follow combine history and current events. We assume that students study history using both text and trade books (fiction and non-fiction) and current events.*

Identifying Conflicts, Conflict Sort

Conflict Timeline

Have students create a timeline for the classroom that identifies conflicts and conflict-related events. Encourage them to go beyond wars and peace treaties and include such social conflicts as the civil rights movement, labor history, peaceful negotiations, etc. Keep this timeline up all year so that students can add to it as they identify more conflicts.

Conflicts in Historical Fiction

Have students identify the conflicts in a fictional book set in a period of history they are studying. What kinds of conflicts do the characters have? How are they similar to or different from the conflicts students experience in their own lives? How does the time the characters live in influence the conflicts they have?

Conflicts in the News

Have students identify ten conflicts in the newspaper over a one week period. Have them write a sentence or two describing the conflict on a 3" x 5" card. At the end of the week, have them examine their conflicts and develop a way of classifying the conflicts.

Looking for Conflict Types

A variation of the above activity is to assign each student two types of conflict, such as civil wars and domestic disputes. Then have them read the newspaper (or watch T.V. news) for a week, looking for examples of those types of conflict.

Positive Uses of Conflict

There are two ways to do this activity. One is informal. In the course of class discussions point out when conflicts have had positive results or have been used in a constructive way. A more formal version of the activity is to have students research ways in which conflict has been used constructively in history.

CONFLICT TOOL

Conflict Escalator

History On the Escalator

Plotting historical conflicts on the escalator can help students understand how large conflicts started and developed—and how they might have been resolved. Historical conflicts on the escalator usually take place over a much longer span of time than the interpersonal conflicts students have been mapping on escalators, so they may need some help getting the knack of identifying key incidents in history that contributed to a particular conflict. One way to expand this activity is to have students write a paragraph for each step on the escalator, explaining why the particular incident contributed to the escalation of the conflict.

Current Events On the Escalator

Current events can often be plotted or mapped on the conflict escalator. This is a useful way of helping students understand the cause and effect that leads to conflicts escalating or de-escalating. The escalator can also be used to help students compare interpersonal conflicts with other types of conflicts. What causes international conflicts to escalate? Are they the same or different from interpersonal conflicts? What kind of baggage is carried to these larger conflicts? What kinds of emotions are present at each step?

CONFLICT TOOL

Anger and Other Feelings

Feelings On the Historical Conflict Escalator

Have students plot on the escalator a conflict from a work of historical fiction. Have them identify the feelings at each step of the conflict. Ask students to describe how the historical events of the time influenced both the conflict and the feelings the characters had about the conflict.

Feelings in the News

Have students clip a newspaper story that describes a conflict and mount the clipping on a piece of paper. The paper should be large enough to leave a generous margin. Students should circle key aspects of the conflict described in the story and draw a line from the circle to the margin. In the margin they should write the feelings that the disputants are probably having at that point in the conflict.

CONFLICT TOOL

De-Escalating Conflict—CAPS

Historical De-Escalations

Have students research and report on how an historical conflict was de-escalated. This is a good activity to combine with one of the activities above—

the "Conflict Timeline" for example, or "History on the Escalator." Have students identify the specific actions that were taken to de-escalate the conflict.

If I Were In Charge

Students choose a conflict from the news and describe how they would de-escalate the conflict. They may use the CAPS approach to de-escalation or develop a plan of their own. In either case, they should describe the specific actions they would take and discuss what they predict would be the consequences of those actions in de-escalating the conflict.

CONFLICT TOOL

Win-Win Grid, Problem Solving, Conflict Management Styles

Conflict Resolution Continuum

Make a chart of the Conflict Resolution Styles introduced in Conflict Skill Lesson 12 and hang it on the wall. Whenever a conflict comes up in class, either historic or a current event, have students identify where on the chart they think the resolution efforts belong. Keep track of which conflict resolution approaches are used most often. Are there any conflict resolution styles the students would add?

Peacemaking in the Paper

Just as there are always conflicts in the news, so are there attempts to make peace between disputing parties. Have students follow one of these peacemaking attempts in the newspaper and report on how it is progressing. They need not choose an international conflict; there are also local disputes, civil wars, labor problems, diversity related community disputes. Students should report on what conflict resolution styles they see being used, whether there are Win-Win or Win-Lose results, and what the long-term results seem to be.

Using the Win-Win Grid

Use the Win-Win grid to help students develop solutions to either historical or current conflict situations. Have them place what actually happened in the appropriate box on the grid. Then have them invent possible solutions for the other boxes in the grid. Discuss what would have had to happen for those solutions to be the actual outcome.

CONFLICT TOOL

Listening

Historical Active Listening

Have students work in Micro Labs and, using some of the activities from the Point Of View section that follows, have two students role-play the P.O.V. and two students be the listeners. Then the students trade roles.

Listening for Who, What, When, Where, Why

If students are not familiar with the Five Ws approach to news writing (Who, What, When, Where, Why), explain it. The Five Ws are also useful information to have about conflicts. Then read a story from the newspaper that describes a current conflict. Read only the first paragraph or two—just enough for Who, What, When, Where, Why to be established. Then have the class identify the Five Ws of the conflict. This is a quick and fun exercise that can be repeated many times. The more you do it, the better students get at hearing the Five Ws. You can also vary what you ask them to listen for. Try having them identify the feelings they hear or some of the details.

CONFLICT TOOL   # Point of View

P.O.V. on Historical Conflict

Have students identify the P.O.V.s in historical conflicts. This may be the P.O.V.s of individuals or the P.O.V.s of groups. Have them identify, along with the P.O.V., what they know about the needs, goals, experiences, values, and feelings that color the P.O.V. lenses of the parties involved.

P.O.V. in the Newspaper

Have students choose a newspaper article that tells about a conflict. Have them identify and write a description of the P.O.V. of everyone mentioned in the article. How have the differing P.O.V.s led to conflict or contributed to the conflict escalating?

CONFLICT TOOL   # Demands and ReallyNeeds

Demands and ReallyNeeds in History[*]

Have students identify the Demands and ReallyNeeds in historical conflicts. It helps to make a simple chart as in this example from Colonial America:

	THE BRITISH	AMERICAN COLONISTS
Demand	They must pay taxes	We won't pay taxes
ReallyNeeds	Payment for protection from Indians, French	More representation in government
	To get out of debt	Money to benefit colonies
	To reaffirm power over the colonies	To make own decisions To be respected by Britain

[*] This activity is adapted with permission from *Getting to the Heart of It* (Watertown, MA: Tom Snyder Productions, 1993) Computer software.

Demands and ReallyNeeds in Current Events

Have students do the "P.O.V. in the Newspaper" activity. When they have finished identifying the P.O.V.s in the conflict, have them go over it again to determine if they can identify any Demands and ReallyNeeds in the story. It may be difficult to determine from the story what the ReallyNeeds are. If this is so, students can conjecture based on the best available evidence.

CONFLICT TOOL

Negotiation, Mediation, Arbitration

Negotiation/Mediation/Arbitration in History

Using the *Conflict Timeline* activity have students mark and write descriptions of how some of the conflicts were resolved using either negotiation, mediation, or arbitration. Discuss: What did these resolutions lead to? Were they successful? Were they long-lasting? What can we learn about "Good Resolutions" from looking at these historical examples?

Negotiate/Mediate/Arbitrate Historical Conflicts

Using the *Demands and ReallyNeeds in History* activity have students complete their charts of Demands and ReallyNeeds. Then have them role-play to develop resolutions that will meet the Demands and ReallyNeeds of the disputants.

Negotiation/Mediation/Arbitration in Current Events

Have students read the newspaper for a week to identify instances of negotiation, mediation, or arbitration. Some of the questions students can address are: What kinds of approaches were used for what kinds of conflicts? Were they successful? Do you think they will meet the important ReallyNeeds of the disputants? Which approaches are used the most? Do you see more Win-Win, Win-Lose, or Lose-Lose resolutions? Why do you think that is?

Introduction to Infusing Conflict Resolution into Math and Science*

While the connections between conflict resolution and both English and social studies are fairly straightforward to most teachers, mathematics and science connections are often not as obvious. Therefore, the math and science infusion chapters that follow contain complete and fully-detailed lesson plans.

Why infuse conflict resolution into math and science?

Many of the curriculum standards for math and science developed in recent years by professional associations and by state Departments of Education emphasize the need for teaching more than computational skills and basic concepts. Many of the new frameworks call for teaching math and science as human endeavors. Infusing conflict resolution into those subject areas can help you to fulfill the new standards.

For example, the National Council of Teachers of Mathematics' Standards call for more:
- communicating about quantitative reasoning;
- relating math skills to other subjects and to real world problems;
- using statistical methods to describe, analyze and make decisions;
- interpreting different mathematical representations;
- and pursuing open-ended problems.

The National Research Council's National Science Education Standards include:
- understanding the relationship of science, technology, and society;
- learning about populations, resources, and environments;
- gaining deeper understanding of topics and skills related to health;
- developing an appreciation for the historical and current contributions made to science by individuals in different cultures.

The chapters that follow demonstrate how to infuse conflict resolution tools and themes into mathematics and science lessons, ultimately helping you to achieve these curriculum standards.

Some teachers may be unfamiliar with the type of math activities included in the math chapter. For more background information see *The Power of Numbers* by Fred E. Gross, Patrick Morton, and Rachel A. Poliner (Cambridge, MA: Educators for Social Responsibility, 1993). As you do the lessons in the mathematics chapter, keep in mind that there is rarely only one right answer. Students and teachers can accept different answers as long as the answers can be supported with evidence and reasoning. This is where some of the deepest connections can be made between conflict resolution and mathematics—this is where students can learn that even in math there are many valid points of view.

* ESR thanks Rachel Poliner for contributing this chapter.

32 Mathematics

What Counts as Conflict and Violence? *

LESSON IN BRIEF This activity involves an article entitled, "Justice Department Contradicts FBI on Crime Rate" (p. 315) and a handout for students (p. 316). The activity will help students learn that people calculate the crime rate based on different definitions of crime and violence. The activity also encourages students to come to their own definitions of crime.

CONFLICT TOOLS Identifying Conflicts, Point of View

OBJECTIVES Students will learn that:
- people can collect completely different data to answer the same question;
- people make choices about the mathematical techniques they use;
- people can draw different conclusions even when they look at the same data.

HANDOUTS *Justice Department Contradicts FBI on Crime Rate* and worksheet

1. Distribute the article "Justice Department Contradicts FBI on Crime Rate," and have the students read it.

2. Distribute the worksheet and have students work in small groups to answer the questions.

3. Discuss responses with the whole class.

NOTES For question 1, students may want to measure crime in several ways. They may suggest using a technique similar to the FBI and thus count crimes reported to several law enforcement agencies. They may suggest taking a sample of a few urban, suburban, and rural areas, and then estimate what these numbers would expand to for the whole country. Or students may have other ideas for how to measure the country's crime rate. In any case, allow your students time to explore the opposing views in this article.

In question 4, crime rate measures the overall rate at which crimes occur during the course of a year.

For question 8, students are likely to have different points of view. Have them support their opinions with information from the article.

---

* This activity is from *The Power of Numbers: A Teacher's Guide to Mathematics in a Social Studies Context*, by Fred Gross, Patrick Morton, and Rachel Poliner © 1993 Educators for Social Responsibility. Adapted for this curriculum by Rachel Poliner.

In question 9, the responses may vary. One answer is: An increase in the rate could just reflect an increase in the number of crimes being reported. Also, if more agencies are included in the poll, then there is the possibility of the rate increasing.

Justice Department Contradicts FBI on Crime Rate

by Jeff Nesbit

WASHINGTON—Crime in the United States last year fell to its lowest level in 13 years, the Justice Department reported yesterday.

An estimated 34.9 million crimes were committed in 1985, down from more than 35.5 million in 1984 and a peak of 41.4 million in 1981, the Bureau of Justice Statistics said in its annual Uniform Crime Survey.

Those findings contrasted sharply with the FBI's annual Uniform Crime Report issued in late July, which showed an increase of nearly 5 percent in crimes reported in 1985.

The two reports attempt to measure the same thing—whether crime is on the rise or falling off from year to year—but take entirely different approaches.

The widely circulated FBI report is based on crime reports provided by nearly 16,000 local law enforcement agencies.

The Bureau of Justice Statistics interviews more than 100,000 people twice a year to see how their lives have been touched by crime during the course of the year and, from the results, projects the number of crimes committed in the country.

The FBI's 1985 crime report said that about 12.5 million crimes were known to police that year, compared to the nearly 34.9 million crimes the Bureau of Justice Statistics said were actually committed last year.

The FBI doesn't count crime. Two-thirds of the crimes in this country are never reported, said a Bureau of Justice Statistics official who asked to remain anonymous. "The FBI gets their numbers from 16,000 law enforcement agencies. How can you trust those figures?"

A preliminary FBI crime report that will be issued later this month "will show that crime has gone up 10 to 15 percent" during the first six months of 1986, a crime index trend that is not reflected in the Bureau of Justice Statistics own report, this official said.

"The two reports are very different," he said. "We estimate the total number of crimes committed....Ours is a better report."

The FBI crime report has come under attack in the past because it doesn't gauge unreported crimes, and, critics say, law enforcement agencies sometimes under- or over-report crimes in their region for political reasons.

The FBI has tentatively begun to make some major changes in the program but it will be "years and years" before they are reflected in the report, said Harper Wilson, an FBI spokesman for the uniform crime reporting division.

The latest Bureau of Justice Statistics' National Crime Survey, which has been conducted every year since 1973, found that since 1981 the number of violent crimes has dropped 12 percent, personal thefts have fallen 15 percent and household crimes (burglary and auto theft) have declined 18 percent. In the last year alone, the study showed, violent crime was down 3.3 percent, personal thefts 2.3 percent and household crimes 1.1 percent.

In Boston, police recorded a total of 68,998 crimes in 1985 up 7.3 percent over the previous year.

The greatest jump came in the number of manslaughters, which doubled, from 8 to 16. Other violent crime also saw significant increases: rape rose 15 percent to 538, aggravated assault 13 percent to 5,076, and murder over 7 percent to 88. Robbery increased nearly 13 percent to 6,278; larceny nearly 11 percent to 27,026; motor vehicle theft nearly 4 percent to 18,474; and burglary by less than 1 percent to 11,539.

"Justice Department Contradicts FBI on Crime Rate" Worksheet

The article "Justice Department Contradicts FBI on Crime Rate" contains some interesting information about the interpretation of statistics. Read the article carefully and consider how each government agency came up with its conclusions. Answer the following questions.

1. How would you measure crime for one year?

2. What did the Justice Department conclude about the 1985 crime rate?

3. What did the FBI's annual crime report say about the crime rate?

4. What does the crime rate measure?

5. Compare the methods that the FBI and the Bureau of Justice Statistics use to find the crime rate.

6. Who found a higher crime rate? Is there a significant difference between the two rates?

7. The FBI crime report has been criticized. Why?

8. Which method, the FBI's or the Justice Department's, do you think represents actual crime more realistically? Why?

9. The FBI reports a 5 percent increase in the crime rate during 1985. Is an actual increase in crime the only factor that could explain this rate increase? If not, what other factors could contribute to the rate increase?

10. List three questions directed at both groups of researchers that would help you better understand their studies.

The Average Arbitrator*

LESSON IN BRIEF Data is often organized through mathematical procedures that simplify, summarize, and represent the data. Averages, of course, identify the central tendencies. This lesson shows that the various ways of determining averages—the mean, median, and mode—result in different summaries and representations. Be sure to review the concept and techniques for calculating each type of average before students do "The Average Arbitrator" activity.

CONFLICT TOOL Arbitration, Point of View

OBJECTIVES Students will learn that:
- different mathematical methods can lead to different interpretations,
- an individual's point of view affects his or her approach to a mathematical problem,
- we can think critically about mathematical techniques.

MATERIALS One calculator for each student

HANDOUTS *The Average Arbitrator*

1. Divide students into groups and give them the handout and calculators.

2. Review the role of an arbitrator. An arbitrator is a third party who listens to all sides of a dispute and then decides what the solution will be. Before the arbitration begins, the disputants must agree to abide by the arbitrator's decision. Explain that in this activity each student will be an arbitrator.

3. In this exercise students will see that numbers in the extreme will make the mean average very different from the median or mode. The answer to question 1 is that $28,846.15 is the mean average of the salaries of all employees. The answer to question 2 is that $18,000 is the mode average of the salaries of all employees or the mode average of the salaries of the workers only. Ask the students why each character would use different techniques. Are they both valid mathematically? Do they seem valid or fair in other ways?

4. If students wish they had more data, such as what the company down the street pays, or whether sales are up or down, encourage them to invent their own scenarios—they just have to keep track of the assumptions they are inventing. When students have made their decisions, have them present their arguments to their classmates. Student decisions may vary as there are sound rationales for several different decisions.

---

* This activity is adapted from *The Power of Numbers: A Teacher's Guide to Mathematics in a Social Studies Context,* by Fred Gross, Patrick Morton, and Rachel Poliner © 1993 Educators for Social Responsibility. Adapted for this curriculum by Rachel Poliner. See *The Power of Numbers* for a full exploration of averages, frequency distributions, and their role in decision making.

The Average Arbitrator

You are the arbitrator with the responsibility of helping the management and union of a manufacturing corporation come to an agreement on salary increases.

The union represents 59 workers and is looking for a raise in salary, but is meeting resistance from the board of directors. The chair of the board states that the average yearly salary for employees within the corporation is $28,846.15. Therefore, the board has proposed a $1,000.00 salary increase for the workers for the next fiscal year. On the other hand, the union leader states that the average yearly salary of employees is $18,000.00 and the union would like a salary increase of $7,000.00 per worker for the next fiscal year.

POSITION AND NUMBER IN EACH POSITION	YEARLY SALARY PER INDIVIDUAL	TOTAL SALARY PER POSITION
1 President	$ 200,000.00	$ 200,000.00
3 Vice Presidents	100,000.00	300,000.00
5 Managers	50,000.00	250,000.00
10 Supervisors	30,000.00	300,000.00
11 Workers	28,000.00	308,000.00
20 Workers	20,000.00	400,000.00
22 Workers	18,000.00	396,000.00
6 Workers	16,000.00	96,000.00
		$2,250,000.00

The union leaders and management representatives have rejected each others' arguments and cannot agree on a proposal. Therefore, as the arbitrator, you must decide on the salary increase. But first, you must answer some questions.

1. Which averaging method was used by the chair of the board?

2. Which averaging method was used by the head of the union?

3. What other statistical information might help you make your decision?

4. Now make your decision and explain it in writing, including your rationales and calculations.

A Graphic Point of View*

LESSON IN BRIEF
In the previous activities students learned that a person's perspective influences the data that they collect and the conclusions that they draw from it. This activity reinforces that concept and shows how data, in turn, influences us.

CONFLICT TOOL
Point of View

NOTES
The math education standards promote increasing students' abilities to read, interpret, and create graphs and other visual displays of data. This is a more open-ended task than some students may be accustomed to, so be patient and let them struggle a bit if necessary. The task isn't difficult once students realize that there isn't just one "right" answer. (Before doing this activity, students should already be familiar with simple line graphs.)

OBJECTIVES
Students will learn:
- that visual displays of data represent the point of view of the person who designed them,
- that people dictate how data is portrayed,
- to think critically about points of view—their own and those of other people,
- to read graphs more thoroughly and carefully.

HANDOUTS
A Graphic Point of View

1. Give students the handout, *A Graphic Point of View.* Ask them to look at Graph A first. Read the title aloud, "Percentage of adults who were high school graduates." Ask them to read the graph and create simple sentences based on the graph's information. Write several of their sentences in one area of the chalk board. There are many possible sentences, such as, "The percentage of high school graduates has increased a lot," or "The percentage of high school graduates more than doubled from 1940-1980." Sentences can include specific quantitative data or not.

2. Ask students to read Graph B. Do not read the title aloud. Ask them to create simple sentences about the data in this graph and write several of their sentences in a different area of the board. Again, there are many such sentences. Let students create sentences until they realize that the graphs represent the same data.

3. Discuss the different visual representations of the data:
   • What mathematical choices did the creator of the graph make? (Answer: In Graph A, she stopped the vertical axis at 80% and spread out the percentages, while squeezing the timeline. In Graph B, she spread out the timeline and squeezed the percentages, which included the whole span of 0-100%, into less space. These techniques are called

---

* The activity was created by Rachel Poliner.

scaling and cropping.)

- Are both of these representations valid?
- What were your first impressions when you looked at each of them?
- If someone used Graph A in a speech or a news story, what might his goals be?
- If someone used Graph B in a speech or a news story, what might her goals be?
- Describe how you felt when you realized the graphs represented the same data. Did it change your point of view?

4. Ask students to create other representations of the same data that look different from either Graph A or Graph B. The new graphs could be in line graph format or other graphing formats, such as bar or circle graphs. Be prepared to help students identify the strengths and weaknesses of each format.

S T U D E N T   H A N D O U T

A Graphic Point of View

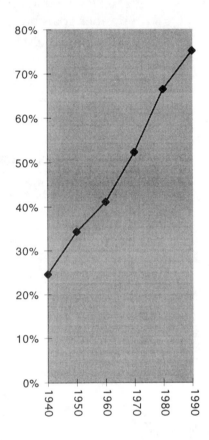

Graph A

Percentage of adults who were high school graduates. (Data from US Census Bureau.)

Graph B

Percentage of adults who were high school graduates. (Data from US Census Bureau.)

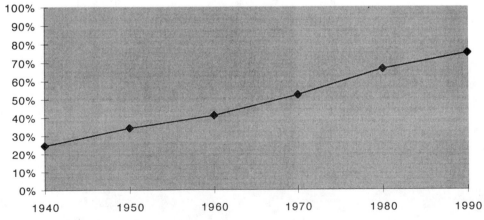

Resources

Gross, Fred E., Patrick Morton, and Rachel A. Poliner. *The Power of Numbers: A Teacher's Guide to Mathematics in a Social Studies Context*. Cambridge, MA: Educators for Social Responsibility, 1993.

The Power of Numbers is made up of two large areas of study: opinion polls and census data. Two of the activities above are from the curriculum's polling project, "Counting on Opinions." If students are able to conduct all of the activities, exercises and projects in Counting on Opinions, you will have the chance to infuse numerous conflict resolution topics into the polling context. There are additional concepts covered including identifying bias (point of view) in language and sampling techniques, expressing point of view with graphs and data, and drawing opposing conclusions from data. Additionally, the on-going polling projects that students create and conduct will provide in-depth opportunities to encourage students' interpersonal conflict resolution skills of communicating, listening, and cooperating. *The Power of Numbers* is available from Educators for Social Responsibility, 1-800-370-2515.

Erickson, Tim, et al. *Get It Together: Math Problems for Groups Grades 4-12*. Berkeley, CA: Regents of the University of California, 1989.

Get It Together includes more than 100 activities, all structured cooperatively and in a jigsaw format. The problems cover a wide range of math skills: measurement, sets, arithmetic, geometry, algebra, and more. The topics addressed include food, geography, mysteries, and other puzzling data. The book also offers advice to teachers on how to introduce, facilitate, and assess cooperative learning. Write to EQUALS, Lawrence Hall of Science, University of California, Berkeley, CA 94720.

Mistrick, Kevin J. and Robert C. Thul. *Math for a Change*. Chicago: Mathematics Teacher's Association of Chicago and Vicinity, 1993.

Math for a Change consists of 38 case studies of social issues infused with algebra, geometry, and high math skills. Issues such as poverty, AIDS, hunger, employment, and many others offer opportunities to consider points of view, power dynamics, questions of fairness, and numbers conflicts.

33 Science

The Lorax: Connecting Environmental Science to Community Conflicts and Decision Making[*]

LESSON IN BRIEF   This is a sequence of activities. First, students will learn to identify natural resources, differentiate between renewable and non-renewable resources, and consider the implications of the use of these resources. Next, students will consider conflicts over natural resources brought up in *The Lorax* by Dr. Seuss. They will read the story and discuss the use of resources and people's responsibility for environmental problems. Then they will read an article from *People Magazine* called "A Boy Sides With Dr. Seuss's Lorax, And Puts A Town At Loggerheads." Finally, they will play the roles involved in a town council meeting trying to address the conflict.

CONFLICT TOOLS   Point of View, Conflict Styles (The -Ate Words), Active Listening (P.E.A.R.), Communication Potholes, the Conflict Escalator, Negotiation, Demands and ReallyNeeds

The Lorax, Part 1: Identifying Natural Resources

NOTE   While this part of the lesson is not directly related to conflict resolution, it gives students the necessary background for the subsequent activities.

OBJECTIVES   Students will:
- trace everyday objects back to their origins,
- discover that everything comes from the earth,
- define what a natural resource is,
- distinguish renewable from non-renewable resources,
- reflect on the implications of natural resource use.

VOCABULARY   *Natural resources, recyclable, non-recyclable, renewable resources, non-renewable resources*

MATERIALS   Colored markers or pencils

Dictionaries

Encyclopedias

---

[*]   This activity is reprinted from *Trash Conflicts: A Science and Social Studies Curriculum on the Ethics of Disposal,* by Amy Ballin, with Jeffrey Benson and Lucile Burt (Cambridge, MA: Educators for Social Responsibility, 1993).

1. Write the term "natural resources" on the board. As a class, come up with a definition and examples. This definition can be revised as the lesson continues. Write the list of examples on the board. (Examples: oil, iron, tin, cotton, trees, aluminum.)

2. Once the list is on the board, ask students to identify which resources are renewable, meaning that we can replace them by growing or making more, and which are non-renewable, meaning that there is a limited supply which cannot be replaced. (Examples: oil is a non-renewable resource; a tree is a renewable resource.)

3. Have students make lists of what they are wearing and then try to trace each item back to its natural resource. (Examples: Leather shoes come from animal skin. Vinyl shoes are made from plastic, which is manufactured from petroleum, which is drilled from the earth.) Students can use dictionaries and encyclopedias to search for this information.

4. Once students understand the concept of natural resources, have the class return to the original definition and decide if they are satisfied. They should revise their definition as they see fit.

5. Have students make a list of things they used from the time they got up this morning until now. This includes getting up, showering, dressing, eating, and getting to school. It will help for them to remember all of their activities first and then figure out what they used for each one. (Example: Brushing teeth involves a toothbrush, toothpaste, water, and a glass).

6. When students have completed their lists, have them trace three of the items that they used back to their natural resources and, for each, decide if the product comes from a renewable or non-renewable resource. Students can help each other and use dictionaries and encyclopedias for this section.

7. When students have completed tracing their three items, they can each choose one to share with the class. (If there are certain items students can't trace, these might be done for homework. See step 9 below.)

8. Hold a class discussion to take a final look at the definition of natural resources. Consider these questions:
   - Are you satisfied with the definition? If not, how would you change it?
   - Can you think of any item that can't be traced back to the earth? (There aren't any.)
   - What problems could arise from the use of non-renewable resources?
   - Choose one renewable and one non-renewable resource (such as trees and oil); what would happen if these resources were used up?
   - What are some ways non-renewable resources can be conserved?

9. If further practice seems like a good idea, or if students are excited about the research, ask students to trace one or two other items back to their origins as homework. These items may be additional ones from their lists, those that they couldn't trace during class or simply something they are curious about—perhaps their favorite objects.

Have the students display their findings on a poster or bulletin board. Non-renewable resources can be written in one color, renewable ones in another. Or, working in groups of three or four, students can consolidate the information on the poster by diagramming products from their common resources in a branching tree formation such as the one below. (This would take an additional class session.)

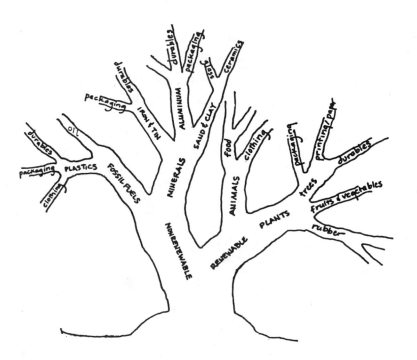

The Lorax, Part 2: Thinking About The Lorax

OBJECTIVES

Students will:
- explore the environmental effects of manufacturing,
- learn about the role of consumers in production,
- examine how controversy grows out of environmental concerns,
- recognize the complexity of decision-making about natural resources,
- identify what influences an individual's point of view in a community conflict,
- use communication skills and avoid S.T.A.R.E.S in the context of a community conflict,
- use negotiation skills such as looking for demands and ReallyNeeds.

NOTES

The issues in this activity can be addressed at various levels of complexity. See "Supplementary Information" following step 2 for suggestions.

CONFLICT TOOL

Point of View, Conflict Styles (The -Ate Words), Active Listening (P.E.A.R.), Communication Potholes, the Conflict Escalator, Negotiation, Demands and ReallyNeeds

PREREQUISITE

Identifying Natural Resources (*The Lorax*, Part 1)

VOCABULARY

Clear-cutting, natural resource, monoculture, selective cutting

MATERIALS

Copies of *The Lorax* by Dr. Seuss, or one copy to be read aloud, or "The Lorax" video available from either the EPA or video stores

Copies of the handout, *A Boy Sides with Dr. Seuss's Lorax...* (or a summary of it)

Copies of *Roles* on handout, cut and separated

Video camera (optional)

1. Read *The Lorax* aloud in class, view the video, or assign the book to be read for homework. Certain students may feel they are too old for Dr. Seuss. Therefore, before reading, ask the class if any of them have read *The Lorax*. What do they remember? Suggest that they think of the ways a younger child would react to the book as they themselves read it in class.

2. Discuss the story using the questions below or others that you create.

    - Why did the Once-ler cut down the Truffula trees?

    - Why do the Bar-ba-loots, Swomee Swans, and Humming-fish have to leave?

    - What kinds of problems does the Thneed factory cause for the environment?

    - What could the Once-ler have done to minimize his factory's effect on the environment?

- A Thneed is defined as a "Fine-Something-That-All-People-Need." What are some "thneeds" that we think we need?

- Do you think that Dr. Seuss has represented all of the members of logging industry?

- What are the various ways each character has responsibility for the destruction of the environment in the story? (How are the people who bought "thneeds" responsible?) Is any character free of responsibility?

- What do you think the Lorax's message "UNLESS" means?

SUPPLEMENTARY INFORMATION FOR TEACHERS

There are a number of issues that could make the scenario depicted in *The Lorax* more complicated. We offer two of them here as a supplement to be refered to as desired, with related suggested questions for students. These issues are the use of natural resources for medicinal purposes, and the intentional growing and harvesting of trees.

A. The use of natural resources for medicinal purposes: a case study of Taxol

What if a thneed was not just an extra something that every one wants? What if a thneed could cure cancer? Recently it was discovered that the bark of a 100-year-old Yew tree (Latin name Taxol) found in the Pacific Northwest is effective in treating certain kinds of cancer. The problem for many environmentalists is that it takes six 100-year-old Yew trees to treat one cancer patient. It is likely that at least 200,000 patients a year would seek the drug. Environmentalists are concerned that the spotted owl, who lives in the Yew, will become extinct along with many other species, not to mention the potential loss of the Yew tree itself.

So far, Taxol (the name given to the new drug after the Latin name of the tree) has only been used on cancer patients for whom other treatments have failed. About a quarter to a third of the people who have tried the drug have responded favorably. Tumors have gotten smaller, and some have disappeared for months. No one has been cured by Taxol yet, but it has enabled patients to live longer and with less discomfort.

- Do you feel there is any difference between cutting down trees to make toys, furniture or other items, and cutting them to make medicines for life threatening diseases? Why do you feel this way?

- What would you and/or the Lorax think about killing trees to provide a medicinal cure for a sickness that kills 10 people per year? What about 10,000 people per year?

- What if the trees were discovered to have bark that could be made into a pain-reliever ? Acne cover-up? Would you feel differently if the trees were an endangered species?

Fortunately, we do not have to answer the questions specifically about Taxol. A drug company has found ways to extract the necessary ingredients to make Taxol from the needles of the Yew tree, so the trees will not have to be killed to manufacture the anti-cancer drug. But that may not be true of other natural resources found to have medicinal value.

B. Can logging be done intentionally and responsibly?

How accurate is Dr. Seuss's portrayal of the logging industry? In *The Lorax*, it seems that loggers find forests and cut down all the trees. Actually, there are several practices that vary among logging companies. Some companies own land and cut down trees that they have grown specifically for harvesting. Then they replant, usually with one kind of tree. This creates a "monoculture," which limits the diversity of animals that could live in that environment.

Sometimes, even if companies own land for growing and harvesting, consumer demand is so great that companies must find more trees to cut beyond those on their own land. For this purpose they frequently turn to the national forests. The processes used to harvest these trees are "clear-cutting" of large areas, clear-cutting of many small areas, or "selective cutting." Clear-cutting of large areas is an efficient means to obtain a large number of trees. However, it can destroy animal populations dependent on that particular type of forest. Clear-cutting many small areas may be less efficient but is also less destructive to local animal populations. Selective cutting, once thought of as the most environmentally sound method, is now thought to require the most energy consumption for the number of trees obtained; it also causes extra damage to the forests due to the moving of equipment and people in the process of obtaining the selected trees.

- Should companies be able to do what they want on land that they own? Is intentionally growing trees for harvesting the best way to provide trees for wood products?

- What method did the Once-ler use to cut the trees? What other methods could the Once-ler have used to harvest the Truffula trees?

3. Read or summarize the handout *A Boy Sides With Dr. Seuss...* in class, or assign the article for homework. After reading the article, discuss the controversy using the following questions, or do the role play described below.

DISCUSSION QUESTIONS

- Where do most families in Laytonville work? Why are they so strongly affected by *The Lorax?*
- Why did one mother say her child had to choose between "Dr. Seuss and Daddy"?
- What do you think the town should do to bring the various factions together?

- Does Dr. Seuss seem to be saying that loggers are bad, or do you agree with his statement that he is not saying that?
- Do you think the book should be banned? Why or why not?

4. After reading the story and the article, students can create a meeting of a town council that allows for all sides to be heard and then try to come to an agreement. The *Roles* handout outlines some roles that could be used, as well as questions to help students define each person's attitude. If you prefer, assign roles without using the handout. Encourage students to figure out their characters' concerns and argument tactics for themselves.

   This activity can be done by assigning groups of three students to each role. The roles and corresponding questions should be cut up and separated so that each group sees only those questions that pertain to them. Each group formulates a position based on the questions provided and other ideas students may have. The groups can then appoint one group member to play the role at the meeting, or three meetings can be held so that all students have the opportunity to play their roles. The teacher may want to add additional characters depending on class size. New characters could be more neutral on the issue.

   If a video camera is available, students may want to dress up and have their performance videotaped.

   The following questions can be used for a discussion after the role play:

   - Was a decision about *The Lorax* made? If not, why not? If yes, what was the decision, and how was it made?
   - Was each speaker truly heard by other "citizens"?
   - What was difficult or easy about playing your role?
   - What did you like or not like about playing your role?
   - Is there anything you wish you had done or said differently in playing your role?

5. Optional follow-up activity: Have students, working in small groups, make lists of all the things they use in the classroom that come from trees. In the same small groups, or as a whole class, ask students to decide whether all the items made from trees are necessary. Could anything be eliminated or substituted? How would the substitution affect the environment? the school budget? the classroom setting? (Example: Consider replacing wooden desks with plastic ones.)

A Boy Sides with Dr. Seuss's Lorax, and Puts a Town at Loggerheads

The trouble began the day Sammy Bailey came home from school last spring. The Laytonville, Calif., second grader had just finished reading *The Lorax* by Dr. Seuss, the sad tale of a fuzzy little creature who loses his forest home when the greedy Once-lers cut down all the Truffula trees. A troubled and thoughtful Sammy had taken the story's lesson to heart. "If you cut down a tree," he told his father, Bill Bailey, "then it's just like someone coming in and taking away your home."

Another parent might have been touched by his child's sensitivity; Bailey was not. The owner of a logging supplies mail-order business, he was incensed by what he saw as a flagrant attack on the livelihood of Laytonville, a tiny (pop.1,096), single-industry lumber town 150 miles north of San Francisco. Rounding up support from other outraged parents, Bailey, 46, and .his wife, Judith, 42, asked the local school board in September to remove *The Lorax* from the second-grade required-reading list. "Teachers....mock the timber industry, and some of our kids are being brainwashed," screamed Bailey's full-page ad in the local weekly. "We've got to stop this crap right now!"

The skirmish quickly mushroomed into a cause celebre when some teachers and other townsfolk, viewing the Baileys' campaign as a threat to academic freedom, responded with equal passion. The issue came to a head early this month as 150 parents, teachers and kids gathered for a boisterous showdown with the school-board in the lunchroom of the Laytonville Elementary School. After some 30 pro-Lorax speakers and one pro-logger argued their case, the board voted to keep the 1971 children's classic on the reading list, at least for now. But board members also scheduled a meeting next month to determine whether that whole list should be preserved--or shelved.

The only certainty is that the dust has not yet settled in Laytonville, where a feud has long been simmering between loggers and conservationists. Last year a group of Earth First! environmentalists set up a blockade for three days outside town, preventing the timbermen from cutting down old-growth trees and destroying the habitat of the rare spotted owl. "The spotted owl is dependent on those trees for survival," says Sierra Club representative Bill Arthur. "As goes the owl, so goes the health of the forest."

Now, with *The Lorax* and its conservationist message bringing the battle into the classroom, Laytonville's loggers are feeling besieged. "Our industry is under attack," says Art Harwood, 36, manager of a sawmill that employs 300 people in the neighboring Branscomb. Now, he says, "(the environmentalists) are trying to hang the ozone and the rain forest on us, and it's easy to take that Lorax and use it against us too." The father of two children, Harwood says the Seuss book isn't the only problem at the town's schools; he cites an assembly at which students were taught environmental theme songs with lyrics such as "These are trees that live so long, it's really a shame to cut them down." He is also disturbed that sawmill representatives weren't invited to Career day last April at Laytonville High. Judith Bailey's complaint is more personal. "I don't mind the Lorax being taught to a child at an age when they don't have such a black-and-white view of good and bad," she says. "But it's stressful on the child when he has to choose between Dr. Seuss and Daddy."

As for Theodore Geisel, 85, better known as Dr. Seuss, he says he wrote the book not about logging but about the cause of conservation in general. The La Jolla, Calif., author of 47 rhyming works, including *The Grinch Who Stole Christmas* and *The Cat in the Hat*, says *The Lorax* "is about people who raise hell in the environment and leave nothing behind. I'm not saying logging people are bad. I live in a wooden house and sit in a wooden chair."

Meanwhile, to 9-year-old Sammy Bailey, the issues of academic freedom, logging and the fate of the spotted owl no longer seem paramount.

Though he is aware that his parents have been labeled book banners, he is more concerned now about his third grade studies, the care of his pet rabbit, Silver, and his chores as water boy for the local high school football team. Sammy won't say any more about *The Lorax*, but class-mate Jenni Cothern, 8, thinks she understands what Dr. Seuss had in mind. "The lesson was," she says, "'Don't chop all the trees at one time 'cause the animals will have no place to live.'" Or as the Lorax counsels, "Plant a new Truffula. Treat it with care. Give it clean water. And feed it fresh air."

—Ron Arias, Liz McNeil in Laytonville

Roles

Town Councilors (5):

The role of the council is to make sure each speaker is heard and to try to reach an agreement about banning or not banning the book *The Lorax* in schools. During the meeting, the members of the council are in charge of calling on people to speak. While the other participants are preparing, the councilors should come up with questions that they want to ask each of the participants listed below. After all views have been expressed, the councilors leave the room to confer and then return to present their final decision.

The other participants include the owner of a logging company, a local citizen (not a logger) who supports academic freedom, a teacher, a Sierra Club member, Dr. Seuss, the wife of a logger, a furniture manufacturer, and a local citizen (not a logger) who supports the book ban.

Owner of Logging Company:

What is your major source of income?

From your point of view, what role in the logging industry do consumers of wood and paper products have?

Why do you think *The Lorax* is harmful to young children?

What contribution does your company make to the community?

What would happen to the community if your company closed?

Local Citizen (not a logger), Supporter of Academic Freedom:

How do you feel about censoring books?

Why should *The Lorax* be read in Laytonville schools?

What should students be taught in school?

How can academic freedom be retained while addressing the concerns of the loggers?

Teacher

What is academic freedom and why is it important?

How can you be sensitive to the issues of loggers and still read *The Lorax?*

How would your job be different if every book that offended someone were censored?

Should children be exposed to real life controversy in school?

Why is it important to read *The Lorax?*

Sierra Club Member:

How are trees important to wildlife?

What message from *The Lorax* is important to you?

How do you feel about loggers?

What are your concerns about how people effect the environment?

What are your concerns about logging?

Dr. Seuss:

Why did you write this book?

How do you feel about logging?

What responsibility do consumers of wood and paper products have in this controversy?

What are your environmental concerns?

What did you want young people to think about when they read this book?

Wife, Husband or Partner of a Logger:

What are your concerns about your child's education?

What is the role of the school?

What conflict is created for your family by reading *The Lorax?*

How could the concerns of loggers be presented in school?

How do you feel about literature that influences your child with a political message?

Furniture Manufacturer:

In what ways is it hypocritical for people to buy furniture from your store while opposing logging?

Why do you think *The Lorax* is unrealistic?

If Dr. Seuss is so concerned about the environment, why wasn't the book printed on recycled paper?

What is the responsibility of environmentalists who oppose logging but buy wood products?

Why are the images in *The Lorax* bad?

What should furniture be made from, if not wood?

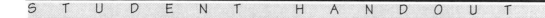

Local Citizen (not a logger), Supporter of Book Ban:

What will happen to the community if the logging business closes?

Why don't people recognize that we use and need wood products?

Why should political perspectives be introduced to young children (or not be introduced to them)?

Why is reading persuasive books harmful to the community?

Why are the images in *The Lorax* bad?

Local Resident, Member of Earth First!

How does putting up blockades so loggers can't do their work help the community in the long term?

Why is cutting down all the trees bad for the logging industry and the environment?

Why do humans sometimes have to make sacrifices to save the environment?

Resources

Ballin, Amy, Jeffrey Benson, and Lucile Burt. *Trash Conflicts: A Science and Social Studies Curriculum on the Ethics of Disposal*. Cambridge, MA: Educators for Social Responsibility.

Trash Conflicts is a curriculum that explores the environmental problem of solid waste management. Students who participate in the entire curriculum are exposed over a few months to the science and social studies concepts and skills involved in this controversy. They learn about the size of the waste problem, what has and can be done with waste, and what social forces influence public policy about trash. The lessons include learning about decomposition, natural resources, natural cycles, recycling, composting, source reduction, hazardous waste, the history of garbage disposal, mapping current disposal, and learning about the effects of race, class and discrimination on public policy.

Creus, Kimberly A. and Patricia Cancellier, ed. *Connections: Linking Population and the Environment*. Washington, DC: The Population Reference Bureau, 1991.

The *Connections* teacher's guide and student resource books include activities and readings on many environmental issues around the world and their impact on human population. There are many opportunities to highlight competing needs, power struggles, differing points of view, and to help students understand conflict in many cultures.

Seager, Joni, ed. *The State of the Earth Atlas*. New York: Simon & Schuster, 1990.

The State of the Earth Atlas includes 36 visual displays of global environmental data offering rich material to investigate conflict, point of view, power dynamics, and cultural differences. Look for the most recent edition.

Gathering Activities

Gathering Activities are short, five-to-ten minute activities that set the stage for conflict resolution lessons by giving students a safe and fun way to share with each other. Gathering Activities are intended to be positive, community building experiences. Use your judgement in choosing the activities you think are most appropriate for your students. Students should have the opportunity to pass if they so desire. The Gathering Activities here were developed by and are used with permission of New York Metro Educators for Social Responsibility, Resolving Conflict Creatively Program.

Go-Rounds

Many of these Gathering Activities are what we call "Go-Rounds." A Go-Round gives every student a chance to respond to a statement or question. If possible, have students sit in a circle. Students speak in turn, going around the circle. Introduce the topic of the Go-Round in the form of a statement or question. The topic can be a general one that most students will be able to comment on (for example, "What is something you've enjoyed about today's lesson?") or it can be a way to introduce the content of the lesson. Students have the right to pass when it is their turn to speak. After everyone has had a chance to speak, you may go back to someone who passed to see if he or she has thought of something to contribute. Some Go-Round topics:

- What is something that makes you feel happy?
- What is one of your most treasured possessions?
- What do you usually do when you see a fight?
- Something I do differently than I used to is...
- A time I helped out a friend or relative who needed some assistance was...

Group Clap

Ask everyone to close their eyes and begin to clap in whatever way they want. You can tell them that at first it will seem like a mess, but to stick with it and they will notice something happening. (Usually this begins very chaotically, but then gradually students start to synchronize the sounds they are making.)

Guessing Box

Place an object into a box that you can close. The object should be something that in some way represents conflict or conflict resolution. Ask students to guess what's in the box. The guesses can be as wild or silly as they choose. Reveal the object, and ask a few volunteers how they came to think of the objects they guessed.

"I'd Like to Hear..."

Have students say something positive they'd like to hear another person say about them. For example: "I'd like to hear someone say I'm a great dancer."

"If Conflict Were a Color..."

Lay out an array of colored paper on a table or the floor. Ask students to choose a color of paper that represents "conflict" to them. Say, "If conflict were a color, it would be..." and have them get up and pick out a piece of paper. (Be sure to have lots of red paper as that is the color most students choose.)

"I Got What I Wanted..."

Have students complete the following sentence: "A time I got something I wanted was when..."

Initials

Have each student say their whole name and then say positive adjectives using their initials. For example, George Frost—generous, friendly.

Mirroring

Have students work in pairs. One person is A, the other is B. Partners should stand, facing one another. First B reflects all movements initiated by A, head to foot, including facial expressions. After a short time, call "Change," so that positions are reversed. Then B initiates the actions and A reflects. Have students discuss what it was like to mirror another person's actions.

Name Game with Motion

Have the group form a circle. Ask students to say their names and make a gesture that goes with their name. After each person says his or her name and makes a gesture, everyone in the group repeats the name and the gesture. Model the activity first, then go around the circle.

New and Good

Have students comment on something new and good that is happening in their lives. It can be anything—a good movie, a good time with a friend or family, a new idea, finishing a project for class. Model the activity for the class by speaking first.

Nonverbal Birthday Line-Up

Challenge students to line themselves up according to the month and day of their birthdays without talking. You will need to tell them where the line begins and where it ends. When the line is completed, ask them to say their birthdays aloud.

Putting Up a Fight

Go-round the group and have students answer: "What is something you have that you would put up a serious fight for—even risk your life for—if someone tried to take it away?" (This can be a material thing, like a gold chain, or something intangible, like a good reputation.) "Why is this so important to you?"

Something Beautiful

Ask each person to say something interesting or beautiful that he or she has seen lately and how that made them feel. Before anyone speaks, however, he or she must paraphrase what the previous student said. You can begin modeling the activity.

Standing Up

Have students say a time they felt they were being taken advantage of and they stood up for themselves.

Strong Feelings

Ask students to describe a strong feeling they have been having in the last week and some reasons for that feeling.

"You Like, I Like..."

Give students a question they can answer briefly. Going around the circle, each person must repeat what the student before them said in response to the question before making their own statement. For example, if the question is, "What are your favorite things to wear?," and the first person who speaks says, "I like to wear jeans and big shirts with hoop earrings," the next person would say, "She likes to wear jeans and big shirts with hoop earrings, and I like to wear patched overalls and leather jackets."

"What's Important in a Friend?"

Ask students: "What do you think are the most important qualities in a good friend?"

"What Would You Do...?"

Go around the group having students respond to this question: "If you saw a fight starting in the street between two people you didn't know at all, what would you do?"

"When I'm in a Conflict..."

Going around the group, ask each student to complete the sentence, "When I get into a conflict, I usually..."

Whip

A whip is a positive, incomplete statement that is completed in turn by each person in a circle. It goes quickly with each person answering in a short phrase. Some possible whips are:

- Something I'm good at that ends with "ing"...
- I feel good about myself when...
- Something I like about my cultural or ethnic background is...
- A hiding place I had when I was a child was...
- Something that usually makes me happy is...
- One word that describes how I feel today is...
- One word that describes a strength of mine is...

Closing Activities

Closing Activities celebrate the time the group has spent together and conclude the lesson's activity on a positive note. Like Gathering Activities, they are good for building community in a classroom and bring a sense of closure to the lesson. These Closing Activities were developed by and are used with the permission of New York Metro Educators for Social Responsibility, Resolving Conflict Creatively Program.

Appreciation

Set the timer for three minutes. Tell the students they have the opportunity to say something they appreciated about the class today or about the group. Model by speaking first, then whoever is moved to speak may do so.

Connections

Set a timer for two minutes and ask the class what they appreciated about the class or about the day. Model the activity first, then whoever feels moved to speak can do so.

Encouragement Cards

Distribute index cards. Ask students to write anonymously one sentence expressing words of encouragement they might offer another student in the class. Collect the cards and redistribute them for a go-round of reading.

Good-Bye/Hello

Ask students some of their behaviors or thoughts they would like to say good-by to and what new behaviors or thoughts they would welcome. Go around with each student completing the blanks in the statement, "Good-bye _____, hello _____."

Go-Rounds

Closing Go-Rounds are like the Gathering Activities. Have the class stand or sit in a circle. Going around the circle have students respond to a question or a statement. Some closing go-rounds that you might try:
- What quality do you possess that you would be willing to share with the group that would help us work as a group more easily?
- What's one word describing an important quality your favorite hero or "she-ro" might have?
- What's one word that expresses how you are feeling right now?
- What's a new idea or awareness that came to you today?
- What quality do you have that would make you a good negotiator?
- What quality do you have that would make you a good mediator?

- What is a food from your cultural background that you especially enjoy?
- What's a time when someone has helped you or another person?

I Used to...

Go around and have students complete the blanks in the following statement: "I used to think (feel) _____, but now _____."

Rainstorm

The goal of this activity is to simulate the sound of a rainstorm. Have the group sit or stand in a circle. One person is the facilitator who begins by rubbing hands together in front of one person in the circle. That person imitates the motion. Then the facilitator continues around the circle until everyone is rubbing hands together.

The second time around, the facilitator clicks fingers in front of one person. Everyone else should continue to rub hands together until the facilitator comes around with clicking fingers. As the facilitator comes to each person, he or she stops rubbing hands and starts clicking fingers.

The third time around the facilitator makes a loud pattering sound by slapping his or her thighs. The fourth time around the facilitator gets all participants stamping their feet. This is the height of the rainstorm.

Next the facilitator directs the subsiding of the storm, going around and changing stamping to pattering, to clicking to hand rubbing to silence.

Telegram

Distribute index cards. Ask students to write on the cards one thing they would like to remember about today's lesson if they forget everything else. Collect the cards and redistribute them for a go-round of reading or, if time is short, select and read a few.

Yes!

Ask students to stand in a circle and hold the hands of the people on either side. Everyone bends over, hands almost touching the floor. Start saying "Yes" together softly and get louder and louder as you slowly rise, exploding into a loud, energetic "Yes!"

Guidelines for Role-plays

What is Role-playing?

Role-playing is temporarily taking on a new role in a practice situation for the purpose of learning new skills or exploring new ways of relating to others.

In conflict resolution, role-playing lets students practice and experiment with new skills and behaviors to see how they feel, how the behavior "works," and what problems come up. It gives you, the teacher, the opportunity to give feedback and assess how well the student is acquiring and using new skills and understandings.

The Teacher's Role

The teacher sets up the role-play environment and explains the rules. The teacher also facilitates the discussion at the end of the role-play. This discussion is very important, for this is where students receive feedback on their use of a particular skill.

To do this you need to:
- Instruct the class in how to give appropriate feedback;
- Demonstrate feedback skills;
- Praise students when they give appropriate feedback.

Try to model the following feedback behaviors. You may also need to point out to students what you are doing, so they will learn to give similar types of feedback.

1. Talk about the behavior, not the person. Role-plays are designed to promote behavior skills, so it is important that feedback be directed at the behavior. For example, instead of saying: "You sounded like you wanted to solve the problem," say: "You said 'Let's work it out' and that let the other person know you wanted to solve the problem."

2. Be specific. Tell students exactly what they are doing right or what could be improved. For example, instead of saying: "That was good," say: "You asked the other person what he or she wanted in the situation."

3. Emphasize what was done well, and suggest improvements for next time. For example: "You did a good job of looking her in the eye. Speaking up a bit more might be helpful next time."

4. Suggest choices rather than giving instructions. Explore the consequences of the new choices. For example, instead of saying: "Ask her when she'll be finished with the tape recorder," say: "What do you think would happen if you asked her when she would be finished with the tape recorder? Give it a try."

5. The types of questions you ask will influence the kind of feedback you get. Use the suggestions that follow.

Questions for Processing the Role-play

Ask each actor

How did you feel playing the role?

What did you notice yourself doing?

How did the other person(s) respond to your action?

What do you think you did well?

What might you have done differently or better?

Ask the observers

How did you feel as you watched the role-play?

How did the conflict develop? How did it escalate?

What stands out about how the actors talked/behaved?

Why do you think they behaved as they did?

What did they do that made the conflict better or worse?

What might they have done differently?

For everyone

Have you ever been in a situation like this one?

How did you handle it? How did it turn out?

What might be another way to handle this situation?

End the discussion by summarizing the major issues. Tie these issues to the purpose of the role-play.

Running Role-plays

1. Begin by explaining the purpose of the role-play, such as practicing problem-solving, trying new ways of communicating in conflicts, or practicing mediation. To learn from the role-play students need to know why they are doing it. Review the rules of role-plays.

ROLE-PLAY RULES:
- Stop everything when the teacher says "Freeze!"
- No booing
- No swearing
- No physical fighting—real or pretend

2. Next explain the role-play situation and the characters needed, as well as the type of role-play it will be.

TYPES OF ROLE-PLAY:

Small groups	Three or four per group, with actors and observers.
Hassle Line	The group forms two lines. Each actor stands opposite a partner. Everyone in each line plays the same role.
Whole Group Role-Playing	The class is divided into large groups. Everyone in the group plays the same role.
Audience-Actors	The class observes role-plays as a group of actors.
Skits	Usually uses the "Audience-Actors" format, with scripted lines.

In the beginning, it is best to use structured role-plays where you give the students a lot of information about the situation, the characters, what you want them to do, etc. You may even want to give them a script. I usually start with skits that use an Audience-Actors format. This gives the students practice in role-playing, giving feedback, and problem-solving. Then, as I think they are ready, I give them practice in other types of role-play and role-play techniques.

ROLE-PLAY TECHNIQUES

Role Reversal	Actors reverse roles half-way through the role-play.
Fish Bowl	The audience forms a circle around the actors and comments on the action or motivations of the actors.
Replacements	As the actors role-play, observers from the audience may tap them on the shoulder and replace them.

3. The format I use is as follows:

STARTING AND MONITORING THE ROLE-PLAY:

- Describe the purpose of the role-play to students.
- Assign roles to players, taking care not to choose someone who might over-identify with the part. Give the roles fictional names.
- Brief the actors. Be sure they understand what the conflict is.
- Brief the audience. As observers, what should they look/listen for?
- Review the role-play rules.

- Start the action. Intervene or coach only if absolutely necessary.
- If the role-play doesn't come to a natural end, cut it off gently.
- Thank the role-players, using their real names.

4. Once students are experienced with simple role-plays, they can begin to develop their own role-plays.

DEVELOPING ROLE-PLAYS:

- Have the class brainstorm situations.
- Choose one situation and develop the problem or issues of the role-play.
- Develop the specific roles: their age, gender, names, characteristics.
  How do the characters feel about each other? The situation?
- Develop the background to the situation: What has led up to the current situation, what is the current situation, etc.
- Decide on any supporting or secondary characters and develop them, defining their roles in the situation.
- Choose a beginning point for the role-play.

Instructional Strategies

Mini-Lectures

Throughout the curriculum you will present students with vital information through mini-lectures. Mini-lectures serve as either introductions to or summaries of some kind of experiential activity. They are designed to be short and quick and often have accompanying visuals or handouts.

Mini-lectures are indicated throughout the curriculum by a dialogue balloon.

Brainstorming

A great way to help students think creatively, come up with many solutions to a problem, or generate ideas quickly is through brainstorming. Be sure to adhere to the following rules when brainstorming:

- Accept and record all ideas without criticism or comment. Evaluation comes later.
- Encourage students to say whatever comes to mind, no matter how silly or outrageous it may seem at first.
- Push for quantity, not quality.
- Establish a time limit before beginning.

Microlabs

Students can learn about themselves and others through sharing their thoughts and experiences in microlabs. In small groups of three or four, students respond to a series of questions. They each take turns speaking, while the other members of the group focus their attention on listening, but do not respond. A pre-determined time limit should be specified for each student to share. In order for everyone to get an opportunity to speak, it is important that all groups be the same size. For suggestions on dividing students into groups for microlabs, see "Group Formation."

When introducing a microlab, discuss the importance of confidentiality. Remind students that everything that is shared during a microlab should not be repeated outside of the classroom.

Web Charts

Web Charts are an effective way to explore an idea by brainstorming in a way that links related ideas. You'll also benefit from learning more about the prior beliefs and associations your students are bringing to a given concept.

To make a web, circle a core word on the board. Ask students for the first words or phrases that come to mind. Write their contributions on the board, connecting them with lines to the core word or related words. Continue this process until you've fleshed out and recorded all of the student's ideas. See Conflict Skill Lessons 2 for an example of using webs.

Group Formation

Much of this curriculum calls for students to be broken into small, cooperative working groups. Here are a few ways to break up students randomly. There are countless other ways to make this task both fun and effective.

- Have students count off. To make nine groups of three in a class of twenty-seven, have students count off from one to nine three times. Then have all the ones, twos, threes, fours, (and so on) come together as a group.

- Cut up pictures or create puzzle pieces on index cards. Students then mill around the room looking for others who complete their puzzle.

- Playing cards are useful for making groups of four. For example, if you have 24 students, you would separate out six suits from the deck for students to draw from. Then have those students holding the same suit come together as a group.

Written Tests

Test 1 Understanding Conflict: Vocabulary and Concepts

Name _____

Part One – Fill in the Blanks

Fill in the blanks with the following words:

Solve the problem	Triggers	Concerns
Paraphrase	Bulldozing	Values
Point of View	Mediation	Disagreement
Above It All	Ammunition	Global Statements
Win-Win	Color	Aggression
Compromise	Cues	Misunderstanding
Culture	Demands	Escalate
Attention	Prejudice	Feelings
PEAR	Collaborative	Experiences
ReallyNeeds	Arbitration	Power
Desires	Potholes	Agree to Work It Out
Goals	Influence	Character

1. When conflicts get worse they _____.

2. P.O.V. stands for _____.

3. Give two types of conflict escalating behaviors: _____, and _____.

4. Three ways diversity can lead to conflict escalating are _____, _____, and _____.

5. A conflict is a dispute or a _____ between two or more people.

6. Things that make us angry are called anger _____.

7. PEAR stands for _____, encourage, pay _____, and reflect feelings.

8. The physical signs that we're angry are called anger _____.

9. The formula for de-escalating conflict is Cool Off, _____, share P.O.V. on the Problem, and _____.

10. Solving a conflict with the aid of a third party is either _____ or _____.

11. The four suits in the Diversity Deck are _____, _____, clout and _____.

12. Negotiation, mediation, and arbitration are all examples of _____ approaches to conflict resolution.

13. When both parties give up something that is called a _____ solution.

14. _____ are the things that people say they want in conflict.

15. A solution that meets the needs of all the disputants is called _____.

16. Needs, _____, _____, and fears are why people make their demands in conflicts. Another word for these is _____.

17. _____ means attacking or trying to hurt another person with actions or words.

18. A person's _____ is made of a combination of their PIES, which stands for _____, _____, and economic status.

19. Three things that color a persons P.O.V. Glasses are _____, _____, and _____.

20. Behaviors that get in the way of communication are called _____.

Part II—Multiple Choice

21. Which of the following are aspects of good conflict resolution? (Check as many as apply)

    a. _____the disputants' relationship improves as a result

    b. _____it's nonviolent

    c. _____the disputants never have another conflict

    d. _____the disputants' needs are met

    e. _____one person feels that he or she "beat" the other

    f. _____all of the above

22. Which of the following behaviors are likely to escalate a conflict?
(Check as many as apply)

a. _____ saying "You always do this..."

b. _____ swearing

c. _____ digging up the past when it's not relevant

d. _____ attacking the other person's weak points

e. _____ anything with the words "Your mother..."

f. _____ all of the above

23. A mediator needs which of the following?

a. _____ to be neutral, fair, and unbiased

b. _____ an ability to keep things confidential

c. _____ a baseball bat to keep the disputants in line

d. _____ listening skills

e. _____ self-control

f. _____ all of the above

24. Mark and Shawna are working together on a cooperative social studies project about the civil war. They must present the material in a joint project. Mark wants them to put the information into a skit. He likes performing. Shawna hates this idea. She doesn't like getting up in front of people and tries to avoid situations where she might be teased. She wants to write a report—no big dramatics, but no risks either. Mark wants to do something dramatic, partly because his grades in social studies haven't been too good. He wants to "wow" the teacher and get an A.

Label the following either "D" for Demands, "R" for ReallyNeeds, or "S" for solutions.

Mark says, "I want to...

_____ get a good grade.

_____ put on a skit.

_____ get attention from everyone
else in the class.

_____ do something I'm good at.

_____ present a dramatic reading.

_____ perform in front of the class.

_____ make a video and do narration.

Shawna says, "I want to...

_____ avoid being teased.

_____ do something safe.

_____ write a report.

_____ get a good grade

_____ not do a skit.

_____ write a report that Mark presents
as a reading.

_____ divide up the tasks so we each do
what we like.

25. Read the following situation. Identify the conflict style being used at each stage. Use the following indicators: Ag-Aggression, Cl-Collaboration, Cp-Compromise, G-Give in, A/D-Avoid or Delay, Ap-Appeal to Authority

Two nations are having a dispute over a piece of land that borders both of them. Both nations claim that the land is theirs.

_____   In the past ownership of the land was determined by who invaded and defeated whom.

_____   Ten years ago, both nations took their dispute to the United Nations which decided that temporarily the land would be neutral territory under the protectorship of the UN.

_____   Since that decision, nothing has been done to further the discussion about who will ultimately own and control the land.

_____   One national leader has seriously considered just giving the land to the other so that the disputes will end.

_____   Both nations were recently in negotiations with each other, with the help of a U.N. mediator.

_____   The result of the negotiation is that the disputed territory will be divided equally between the two nations.

© 1997 Educators for Social Responsibility

Answer Key

1. Escalate

2. Point of View

3. Global statements, above it all, bulldozing

4. Ammunition, misunderstanding, prejudice

5. Disagreement

6. Triggers

7. Paraphrase, attention

8. Cues

9. Agree to work it out, solve the problem

10. Mediation, arbitration

11. Character, color, culture

12. Collaborative

13. Compromise

14. Demands

15. Win-Win

16. Concerns, desires, ReallyNeeds

17. Aggression

18. Clout, power, influence

19. Values, goals, experiences, feelings

20. Potholes

21. a, b, d

22. f

23. a, b, d, e

24. Mark: R, D, R, R, S, S, S
    Shawna: R, R, D, R, D, S, S

25. Ag, Ap, A/D, G, Cl, Cp

Test 2 Applying Concepts: Short Answers/Essays

1. Name three people you consider to be peacemakers. They may be people at school, in the community, or world leaders. Explain why you think each person is a peacemaker, what peacemaking skills each of them has, and how they use those skills.

2. Brainstorm a list of six possible solutions to the following conflict. Describe the possible consequences of each of these solutions.

    Someone accidentally bumped into Mark while he was carrying his tray across the cafeteria. His pizza fell tomato-side down onto George's sweater. To make matters worse, George's girlfriend had just given him that sweater. George is threatening to beat Mark up after school.

3. Choose one of the following conflicts and come up with a solution that would be non-violent, would be likely to meet the needs of the disputants, and improve their relationship.

    Conflict #1 A fight broke out on the basketball court. Cheryl and Jalesa were playing basketball on opposite teams. Cheryl was shooting a basket and claims that Jalesa fouled her and caused her to miss the shot. Jalesa denies this and says she simply blocked the shot. Jalesa also claims that Cheryl threw the ball at her in anger, then pushed her.

    Conflict #2 Daniel and Ramon are in a play together. Ramon has the lead part, which Daniel wanted. Now Ramon is accusing Daniel of distracting him during rehearsal so that he can't remember his lines. The rest of the cast is annoyed with both Daniel and Ramon because they are ruining the play and make rehearsals go on forever. The director is threatening to replace both Daniel and Ramon.

4. Two nations are in a dispute over the location of the border that runs between them. This border has been a source of conflict for many years. At the heart of the dispute is a fertile valley of land, about ten miles wide, that lies between the two nations. Both nations feel that the valley is theirs. The way the border is currently drawn, Nation B owns most of this valley. Recently Nation A began stationing troops at the border. Now Nation B is doing the same thing. Each nation has issued warnings in the press that they are ready to fight.

    Choose five of the following conflict tools and describe how it might be used in this situation:

Conflict escalator	I Messages	Get Help	STARES
P.O.V. Glasses	CAPS	Compromise	Demands and ReallyNeeds

A Sampling of Conflict Resolution Projects

Conflict Tool Kit

Design a tool kit for peacemakers that includes the tools your group thinks people need to resolve conflict non-violently. Try to use objects to represent the tools, but if you can't locate actual objects, make pictorial representations.

Superheroes for Peace

Create a team of superheroes who do not use violence to solve conflicts. Make a poster showing these heroes. Write a description of what powers they have and how they work together as a team.

Design a Peacemaker

In your group identify at least ten qualities you think a peacemaker needs to have. Create a poster that illustrates what such a peacemaker would look like.

Public Service Announcement

Create a public service announcement to convince people that solving conflicts non-violently is cool. Either videotape or present your P.S.A. to the class.

Conflict Resolution Advertisement

Create a T.V. ad to sell the "Conflict Resolution Tool Kit." This kit has the tools people need to solve conflicts nonviolently. Consider making it an infomercial.

Conflict Resolution Rap

Write a rap song that describes some skills people need for conflict resolution and that tries to convince them that conflict resolution is cool. Rehearse and perform your song for the class.

Peacemaker Promotional Spot

Make a T.V. commercial that makes heroes of people who are peacemakers, showing them in a very positive light. Either videotape or present your ad to the class.

Related Resources[*]

Fisher, Roger, and William Ury. *Getting to Yes: Negotiating Agreement Without Giving In*. New York: Penguin, 1981.

Goleman, Daniel. *Emotional Intelligence*. New York: Bantam, 1995.

Kreidler, William J. *Creative Conflict Resolution: More Than 200 Activities for Keeping Peace in the Classroom K-6*. Glenview, IL: Scott, Foresman and Co., 1984.

Kreidler, William J. and Lisa Furlong. *Adventures in Peacemaking: A Conflict Resolution Activity Guide*. Cambridge, MA: Educators for Social Responsibility, 1996.

Lantieri, Linda and Janet Patti. *Waging Peace in Our Schools*. Boston: Beacon Press, 1996.

Ury, William. *Getting Past No: Negotiating With Difficult People*. New York: Bantam, 1991.

Additional Lessons for Specific Classroom Issues

Privacy and Confidentiality

For some students, *Conflict Resolution in the Middle School* may be their first experience with sharing personal experiences and feelings in school. As a result they may be unsure about the limits of such sharing. Some students may need reassurance that they need not share very personal information. The following activity helps students identify for themselves what they wish to keep private, and helps the class establish standards for the group about privacy.

Privacy Lists*

DESCRIPTION Students identify which topics they find easy to talk about, which they find difficult, and which they would prefer to keep private.

MATERIALS Notebook paper, pencils, three large sheets of newsprint, tape, markers

1. Explain to the class that learning conflict resolution skills involves some personal reflection and sharing of personal experiences. However, sharing personal experiences doesn't mean invading privacy. To help establish guidelines for these discussions, in this activity students will be identifying where they "draw the line" about topics they would rather not talk about in class.

2. Have students fold their papers into thirds and label the three sections as follows: "Easy to Talk About," "Difficult to Talk About," and "Private." They should not put their names on the papers. Ask for volunteers to describe one or two topics they might list in the "Easy to Talk About" section. When you think the class understands the task, have students write three or four topics in each section of the paper. Emphasize that while you will be collecting the papers, the activity is anonymous. They may disguise their handwriting if they so desire.

3. When everyone is finished, collect the papers. After class, label three large sheets of paper: "Easy", "Difficult", and "Private." Synthesize the contents of the student papers on the appropriate pages, being careful not to transcribe anything that might be linked to a particular student.

4. Post the large sheets of paper during the next class session and use them as a springboard for discussing appropriate boundaries for personal sharing.

---

* Adapted with permission from *Creative Conflict Resolution* by William J. Kreidler (Scott, Foresman and Co.: 1984).

Throughout the discussion, emphasize the importance of respecting others' privacy.

DISCUSSION
- What makes some things easy to talk about and others more difficult?
- Do you notice any patterns in each of the three lists?
- Why do you think it's important not to force people to talk about private things?
- How does respecting privacy relate to the issue of trust in our class?

Put-downs and Name-calling

Many middle school classrooms are rife with name-calling and other types of put-downs. Under the best of circumstances these are unpleasant, but when you're trying to create a caring and respectful classroom environment they can undo all your best efforts. The following activities are effective ways to initiate a discussion on the put-down problem. In these discussions be careful not to inadvertently teach put-downs. Be sure to put the emphasis on positive statements, not on negative ones.

Put-down Patrol

DESCRIPTION   Students identify common put-downs and think of positive alternatives

MATERIALS   Markers, poster paper, misc. art materials

1. Ask students to keep a record of all the put-downs they hear during a typical middle school day. Caution them not to use swear words or racial or ethnic slurs, even if they hear them. Instead of recording these words they should use a blank or a series of symbols to represent the offending words.

2. Lead a discussion using the following questions:

   - What are some of the results of a lot of put-downs?
   - What might be some benefits of reducing or eliminating put-downs?
   - Some people make a distinction between put-downs and "good natured teasing." Do you agree with this distinction? What makes them different?
   - How can we make our class free of put-downs?

3. Have students work in groups to develop posters or bulletin board displays that promote positive "put-ups" instead of put-downs. Some possible themes and approaches to this include:
   - Use the international symbol for "prohibited" (a circle with a diagonal slash) with put-down statements in the circles;
   - make giant footprints that step on put-downs and call the display "Stamping Out Put-downs;"
   - create a list of "thumbs-up" statements and "thumbs-down" statements (put-downs).

Apples of Discord and Apples of Respect

DESCRIPTION   Students discuss put-downs and think of positive alternatives

MATERIALS   A book of Greek myths that contains the myth "The Apple of Discord," construction paper, scissors, markers

1. Read the myth "The Apple of Discord" to the class. Discuss the long-range negative effects of the apple of discord (among other consequences, it led to the start of the Trojan War). Ask how put-downs might be compared to apples of discord.

2. In Greek mythology, the opposite of the apple of discord is the apple of love. Ask students what they would call the opposite of the apple of discord: respect and caring are two possibilities. Ask the class: "What would be the opposite of put-down behavior?"

3. Have the class make apples of respect on which they write some act or statement that would be the opposite of a put-down and would show respect for others. Display these on a bulletin board labeled "Golden Apples of Respect." You may also have as part of the display a basket of "Rotten Apples of Discord."

Microlab: The Name Game

DESCRIPTION   Students share the stories of their names.

1. Have students form microlab groups of three or four. Each person in the group takes two minutes to talk about his or her name. They can talk about first, middle, and/or last names. Tell students that they don't have to talk about any aspect of their names that they don't want to.

2. List the following questions on the board to help students who become stuck:

    *   How did you get your name?
    *   Were you named after anybody? Who? Why?
    *   How do you feel about your name? Do you like or dislike it?
    *   If you changed your name, what would it be?
    *   Do you have a nickname? How did you get it?
    *   What ethnic background does your name come from?
    *   What does your name mean?

3. Be sure to signal when each two-minute time period is over.

4. Bring the class back together and lead a discussion using the following questions:

    *   What did you observe or learn from this activity?
    *   How do names represent some of the cards from the Diversity Deck? (See p. 238 for the Diversity Deck.)
    *   Was it easy or difficult to talk about your name? Why?

Cooperation Skills

Most of the activities in *Conflict Resolution in the Middle School* are cooperatively structured, requiring that students work in groups to accomplish the assigned task. Some of your students will have had experience working in groups, others will have had little or none. If you think your students don't have much experience working in cooperative groups, or if you think their skills could use brushing up, these activities will help. They can be used at any point in the curriculum.

Group Roles*

DESCRIPTION   Students think about the variety of roles—both negative and positive—played by members of a group and evaluate their own behavior in groups.

MATERIALS   Positive Roles Checklist, Negative Roles Checklist

NOTE   This activity is in two parts. You may not need to use both parts. For some students, a discussion of the positive roles is enough to get the group functioning efficiently. On the other hand, if you see a lot of negative behavior you may want to begin with Part II.

PART I

1. Explain that we all play roles when we are working in groups. There are negative and positive roles. Being able to identify the roles and who is playing which can help a group work together more effectively.

2. Ask students to identify some of the positive roles in groups and record their contributions on the board. If a suggestion is vague, such as "leader," encourage them to explain more fully, e.g.: What does the leader do? What behavior might one see in a leader?

3. Distribute the handout "Positive Roles Checklist." Have students rate themselves in each of the roles listed on a scale from 1 to 5, where 1 is low (you don't like this role nor do you play it very often), and 5 is high (this is a role you find yourself in frequently and is comfortable for you). After they rate their performance in each role, have students list approximately three behaviors that might be observed in the person who plays that role. If students have trouble with this part of the task, tell them to think of someone they know who is good at the role and think of the kinds of things that person does.

4. Give students ten to fifteen minutes to complete the checklist. Then discuss the roles by having the class brainstorm a list of the behaviors for each role which you record on the board.

PART II

5. Ask students to identify some of the negative roles they have seen people play in groups. Record their contributions on the board. Some students may talk about behaviors more than roles. This is not a problem, but as you record the contribution note whether it's a role or a behavior.

---

* Adapted with permission from CITYSERVE Team Leader Manual by Rachel Poliner © 1996 Community Service Learning Center, Springfield, MA.

6. Distribute the handout "Negative Roles." Note that this list is different in format from the previous handout. Explain that sometimes everyone finds him or herself in these roles, at least temporarily. Give students ten minutes or so to think about experiences they have had where either they or someone they know fell into each role. (During the discussion, caution students not to use names.)

DISCUSSION
- Which roles do you find most difficult or annoying when you are in a group?
- What could you do for your teammates to help them avoid these behaviors and styles of working?
- What can your teammates do that would help you when you're in one of these roles?

S T U D E N T   H A N D O U T

Positive Team Roles:
Roles that Encourage Collaboration

Rate Your Behaviors

	Low	—		High	
Initiator	1	2	3	4	5

This go-getter proposes ideas, suggests next steps, has vision, and is willing to experiment.

Organizer/ Coordinator	1	2	3	4	5

Keeps track of who is supposed to do what by when, keeps the group on track and on task.

Seeker	1	2	3	4	5

Identifies what information and resources are needed, does research, synthesizes information.

Encourager	1	2	3	4	5

Looks for ways to encourage everyone's participation and thinking, praises people when they try.

Harmonizer	1	2	3	4	5

Checks in on feelings, tries to resolve conflicts, knows when the group needs a break or a heart-to-heart talk.

Clarifier/ Summarizer	1	2	3	4	5

Pulls together different ideas, clears up confusion, knows when the topic has been discussed enough, offers conclusions.

Negative Team Roles: Roles that Discourage Collaboration

Think about your experiences with these roles:

Distractor

Sometimes known as "the joker": talks about everything except the task at hand, fidgets to get attention, makes jokes, makes fun of people's ideas.

Rebel

Also known as "the blocker": the group's holdout, is negative about every idea, knows the "right" way to do everything, becomes stubborn and won't budge.

Dominator

Has to be in charge, needs to feel more important, more popular, and/or smarter than everyone else, puts down others' ideas, does not like to share the spotlight.

The Silent One

Doesn't share his or her ideas, holds back, isn't involved.

Doom and Gloomer

Expects the group to fail, claims tasks won't work, ideas are bad, the project is boring, speads a sour mood.

Group Vacation*

DESCRIPTION Students practice different methods of group decision-making

HANDOUT *Group Decision-Making Strategies*

1. Divide students into groups of four. Designate a spokesperson for each group. Explain to the groups, "Your group has just won an all-expenses paid two-week vacation anywhere in the world, but you must take the vacation together, and you can only go to one place. Your task as a group is to decide on the one place where you will take your vacation."

2. Explain that they will have 15-20 minutes to discuss the possibilities and come to a decision. If a group fails to come to a decision, they will lose their prize.

3. When the time is up, have a spokesperson report each group's decision and the method(s) used to arrive at that decision. List these methods on the board. When all the groups have reported, review the list with the class. If anyone can identify any decision-making strategies not listed, add them to the list. Discuss the advantages and disadvantages of each method.

4. Distribute the handout *Group Decision-Making Strategies*. Read the handout with the class and compare it to the stratgies listed on the board.

5. You can repeat this activity using other decisions:

   • Your group has just been given $5,000, but the group must give the money away. They may give it to one individual or an organization, but it must be only one.

   • Your group has been given the job of making one major change in your middle school that will benefit both students, teachers, and staff. The change cannot be closing down the school.

DISCUSSION • Which decision-making styles do you use most often when you are with your friends?

   • What does a group need to consider before it chooses a decision-making strategy? (For example: How important is the decision? How much time is there to make the decision? What will the consequences be if some people in the group dislike the decision?)

---

* Adapted with permission from *Elementary Perspectives: Teaching Concepts of Peace and Conflict* by William J. Kreidler © 1990, Educators for Social Responsibility, Cambridge, MA.

Group Decision-Making
Strategies

Voting Decision or Majority Rule

Several choices or solutions are suggested. Each group member gets to vote for the choice he or she likes. The choice that gets the most votes is the one the group chooses.

Consensus Decision

Through discussion, everyone in the group agrees to *consent* to a decision. In other words, every member of the group does not necessarily agree to the decision, but everyone agrees not to stand in the way of the decision. The group members discuss and listen to each other until all members of the group can give their consent.

Compromise Decision

Everybody in the group agrees to give up a little of what they want. The group finds a solution that involves everyone giving up something.

Chance Decision

The group flips a coin or draws straw to choose what it will do.

Arbitration Decision

The group asks an outsider to make the decision for them. The outsider is call the arbitrator. The group agrees to do what the arbitrator decides.

The Leader Decides

The group chooses a leader. The leader hears what everyone thinks about the problem, then the leader decides what the group will do.

Geese As Our Guides[*]

DESCRIPTION   Students examine how well a team is functioning and think about ways to improve.

HANDOUT   *Geese As Our Guides* (two pages)

1. Divide students into teams. Distribute the handout *Geese As Our Guides*. Have the team members and respond to the handout in the spaces provided. Allow 20 minutes or so for teams to complete the handout.

2. Bring everyone back into the large group and discuss.

- What were some of the ideas your team came up with for the first paragraph? The second? The third? etc.
- Which habits of geese do you think will be the most helpful for your team? Why do you think that?
- Are there goose habits that you hope your team won't imitate?

---

[*]   Adapted with permission from CITYSERVE Team Leader Manual by Rachel Poliner © 1996 Community Service Learning Center, Springfield, MA. Neither she nor we have been able to find a source for the handout "Geese As Our Guides." If you have seen this printed elsewhere and/or know the author, please let us know and we will gladly give proper attribution.

Geese As Our Guides

Geese fly in a V-like formation. Scientists who have studied the flight patterns and behaviors of geese have learned some interesting facts. As each goose flaps its wings it creates an uplift for the bird who is following behind it and just a little to one side. Scientists estimate that by flying in this formation, geese are able to fly 70% farther than if each goose flew on its own.

What our team might learn from this is _____

_____

_____

_____

_____

If a goose falls out of formation, it immediately feels increased drag and resistance, so it gets quickly back into formation to take advantage of the lifting power of the bird in front.

What our team might learn from this is _____

_____

_____

_____

_____

Geese take turns being the lead goose who flies at the point of the "V." When the lead goose tires, it moves back in the formation and a new goose moves into the lead position.

What our team might learn from this is _____

_____

_____

_____

_____

Geese as Our Guides (continued)

Scientists have discovered that there are two reasons the geese in the rear of the formation honk. One reason is that their honking encourages the geese up front. Another is that it lets the lead goose know where the tail end of the formation is.

What our team might learn from this is _____

_____

_____

_____

_____

When a goose is sick or wounded it goes down to the ground and two other geese pull out of the formation and join the one in trouble. They stay with it until it is well enough to fly or until it is dead. Then the two (or three) go forward on their own until they find and join another V formation of geese.

What our team might learn from this is _____

_____

_____

_____

_____

Improving Listening Skills

The first lessons in *Conflict Resolution in the Middle School* emphasize the importance of listening. It never hurts to review and refresh student skills in this area. The following activities are proven "middle school pleasers" that will remind your students of the importance of listening while they brush-up their skills. These activities are also good for initiating a discussion on misunderstandings, rumors, and other ways communication break downs can lead to conflict.

Back to Back

DESCRIPTIONS   Students explore how misunderstandings occur when people try to communicate and identify how communication can be faciliated and misunderstandings reduced.

MATERIALS   Pencils, paper, and a set of 3x5 cards with five or six geometric designs on each card. (You will need enough cards for half the class. The arrangement of shapes need not be complicated, but each card must be different. See the two samples at the end of this activity.)

1. Explain that this is an activity to identify some of the factors that influence communication.

2. Have students find partners. If you have an extra person you may have a group of three. Have the partners sit in chairs, back-to-back. Explain that there are two roles in this activity: describers and drawers. The object of the activity is for the describer to accurately describe a series of geometric shapes so that the drawer can reproduce the images.

3. Have students decide who will be the drawer and who will be the describer. Give each describer one of the cards, but tell the describer not to show the card to the drawer. Drawers will need pencil and paper.

4. Once everyone is set up, explain again that the goal is to have the drawer draw what is on the describer's card, but the describer cannot show the card to the drawer. The describer must describe the card in words to the drawer. The drawer can ask questions.

5. When everyone understands the task, begin the activity. Allow ten to fifteen minutes for everyone to complete the task.

6. Now try the activity again, having the pairs switch roles. Before starting again, add one more challenge. Divide the class in half with an imaginary line and explain that in one half of the class the drawers may ask questions of the describer. In the other half of the class, drawers may not ask questions of their describers.

7. Discuss this activity in the large group. Write on the board "Things that Help Communication" and "Things that Get in the Way of Communication." As the discussion proceeds, record student contributions in the appropriate categories.

- What observations, comments, and reactions do you have?
- What was the effect of not being able to ask questions? For those of you who couldn't ask questions, did you figure out other ways to get information you needed?
- As a describer, how did you know if your drawer did or did not understand your directions?
- Did anyone have an experience using very specific language, or language you thought was specific? How did it help or hinder communication?
- As a drawer, what did your describer do that helped you draw?
- Looking back at the activity, what are some things that might have helped the communication process?

The processing aspect of this activity is crucial because this is where students can make the connections between communication, conflict, and conflict resolution. As the class discusses the activity, ask how particular insights could relate to conflict and conflict resolution. Have the drawers discuss their experience first, then the describers.

Sample Cards:

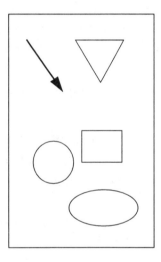
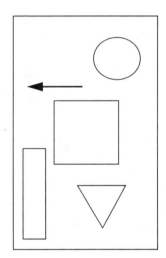

Pete and Repeat*

DESCRIPTION Students practice paraphrasing and reflecting, both skills used in active listening.

1. Have students sit or stand in a circle.

2. The first student finishes to the statement: "My favorite things to wear are…"

3. The student to his or her right paraphrases what the first student has said, then adds his or her own response to the statement. The next student to the right paraphrases what that student has said and then adds his or her own response to the statement, and so on around the circle.

---

* Adapted with permission from William J. Kreidler, *Creative Conflict Resolution: More Than 200 Activities for Keeping Peace in the Classroom* (Glenview, IL: Scott, Foresman and Co, 1984).

Rumors

Rumors spread quickly through the average middle school, and can either lead to a conflict or add fuel to one that has already started. The prevalence of rumors is due, in part, to the interest early adolescents have in relationships. Rumors spread unchecked because young people frequently do not question the content of rumors; they accept and act on rumors without checking them out. These activities help students think about how rumors spread, how they can be destructive, and how they can be stopped.

Rumor Discussion

DESCRIPTION   Students define "rumor" and "gossip" and examine how they can cause conflicts to escalate.

1. Make a web chart around the word "rumor." Ask students: What comes to mind when you hear this word? Record their responses on the board. If the brainstorming lags, try asking:

   - When has a rumor hurt you or caused problems for you?
   - Are rumors always false or negative? What would a positive rumor be like?
   - Is it okay to spread a rumor if you think it's positive?
   - Why do people spread destructive rumors? What do they get from it?
   - Do you think it's true that girls spread more rumors than boys? (Or is that just a rumor?)

   Continue the brainstorming as long as energy is high, usually about five to ten minutes.

2. Ask for volunteers to define the word "rumor" based on the web chart. If needed, here are definitions you can use:

   - A rumor is a story or opinion that circulates without known foundation or authority.
   - A gossip is someone who regularly reveals personal or sensational facts about others, or someone who spreads rumors.

3. After defining rumors, use the following questions to discuss how rumors can cause conflicts to escalate.

   - What are ways that rumors might make conflicts escalate?

   - What are responsible things to do when you hear a rumor?

   - How could you go about checking out whether a rumor is true or not?

Inventing Rumor Mills

Description Students work in teams to examine how rumors spread and identify potential negative consequences of rumors.

Materials Drawing paper; markers or crayons

1. Begin by playing the game "Gossip" as follows. Have the students sit in a circle. Whisper a message into the ear of one student and have him or her whisper it into the ear of the next student. That student whispers to the next, and so on around the cirlce until everyone hears the message. The last student to hear the message says out loud what he or she heard. Use messages that can mutate into serious threats and crises, such as "Sandra's looking for you and she has gum," or "Jerome says he missed your girlfriend."

2. Distribute drawing paper and markers or crayons. Have students work in small groups to design "rumor mills." Rumor mills are imaginary machines that spread and magnify rumors. Students should show how a rumor starts as well as how it spreads and becomes progressively more distorted. Stress that these are imaginary machines so students can be as playful or wild as they want to be. The machines can be Rube Goldberg fantasy creations, or can be based on real machines, for example a spreading rumor can be like a pinball in a pinball machine.

3. A variation on this activity is to have students design posters for the school that have anti-rumor messages, such as:

   - "Rumors Can Be Dangerous—Check Them Out!"
   - "Tame the Rumor Monster"
   - "Rumors—Don't Listen to Them, Don't Pass Them"

Adolescents and Conflict: A Developmental Overview

*by Laura Parker Roerden**

Much has been written about the tumultuous time called adolescence. It's difficult to imagine *Romeo and Juliet* being as poignant had Shakespeare chosen a middle-aged couple as his hero and heroine. Adolescence carries a bitter-sweet sting that we immortalize nostalgically in songs, movies, and theater, and with which we struggle, sometimes painfully, within our schools, classrooms, and homes.

Perhaps no other time in life is so characterized by change as early adolescence. "What happened to my child? Who is this person?" is a familiar refrain from parents. Morally, socially, physically, and cognitively youth ages 10 through 15 are changing—and rapidly. And with this change comes conflict—conflict with peers, parents, teachers, and even with themselves.

Like their parent's attempts to catch up to their newly emerging son or daughter, adolescents are struggling to define themselves. "Who am I? What do I believe in? Am I normal? What will my friends think?" How can we help adolescents with this important stage of development? And how does a conflict resolution program fit in?

Adolescence and Conflict Resolution Programming

Studies show that early adolescence is a critical time for implementing primary prevention efforts such as a conflict resolution and violence prevention programming. Early adolescence may even be our final opportunity to make a significant impact in this area.[1]

Dealing effectively with conflict is an arena where adolescents need help. Feelings of anxiety and conflict in adolescents result in part from the high demands being placed on them. Adolescents also have their own high expectations, but do not yet possess all of the necessary skills and experience to carry out these expectations. And they oftentimes feel that their most important and intimate interests and hopes for themselves are out of synch with those of their school and their community.[2]

Programs that teach conflict resolution can contribute many benefits for this age group. They provide an opportunity for adolescents to develop and enhance cognitive abilities, social abilities, personal identity, independence, and satisfying peer relationships—all the major elements adolescents are concerned with during this developmental stage.[3]

* The author wishes to thank Lisa Sjostrom for her contribution of "Girls' Development: An Overview"; Jinnie Spiegler, Lou Frederick, Mary Edwards, and Sherrie Gammage for their input on racial identity development; and Janine Berkowitz and Eden Steinberg for their research.

Characteristics of Adolescence

SOCIALLY/EMOTIONALLY

- Adolescents make the shift from elementary to middle school just when they are becoming most socially curious. Formerly more defined by their relationships with their parents, teachers, and other adults, peers are becoming increasingly important to their self-definition. Adolescents seek opportunities to make new friendships.[4]

- Adolescents are struggling with ambivalent feelings about independence from and dependence on parents and other adults. They want to be able to turn to parents and other adults, but they do not want to feel suffocated by them.[5]

- Adolescents are trying to develop their own identities and find out what they are good at, what they enjoy, and what they believe in.[6]

- Friendships tend to shift during this age from same sex to cross sex.[7]

- Adolescents are preoccupied with themselves in relation to others. They feel as if they exist on a stage where others are critically evaluating their every move. They watch others intently for cues that they are normal, competent, and likeable.[8]

- Group conformity and peer acceptance are extremely important to adolescents.

- Adolescents are acutely aware of differences. They are learning where they fit in and how they are or are not accepted in the wider society. They are also learning how their gender, race, religion, disabilities, and other characteristics affect how they see themselves and how others see them.[9]

- Far fewer adolescent girls than boys are happy with themselves. Girls are more likely than boys to characterize themselves negatively, saying such things as "I wish I were somebody else" and "Sometimes I don't like myself."[10]

- Rates of depression jump for girls—who show more signs of emotional stress than do boys—during their teen years.[11] Unlike boys, who tend to act out violently and publicly, adolescent girls respond to stress by pulling inward.

MORALLY

- In early adolescence youth begin to formulate and test their own values.[12]

- Adolescents are extremely focused on sorting out right from wrong.

- There are relative gender differences in adolescent moral development. Boys' emerging moral sense is most focused on justice, while girls' is more focused on caring.[13]

Physically

- Adolescence is marked by rapid physical changes. Growth rates vary greatly between peers.

- The rate of physical change relates to perceptions of self. Early maturing boys tend to score high on self-esteem measures. Early maturing girls, on the other hand, tend to be less happy, scoring lower on self-esteem.[14]

- When asked, "What do you like best about yourself?" twice as many boys as girls say their talents. Moreover, during adolescence, girls tend to shift their focus from all the wonderful things they can *do* to how they *appear* in the world. For white, middle-school girls, appearance is the single most important determinant of self-esteem.[15]

- Many teenage girls are unmerciful critics of their own bodies: five in ten girls are unhappy with their bodies by age thirteen; nearly eight in ten dislike their bodies by age eighteen. Up to forty percent of nine-year-old girls are on diets. The number of girls under age twelve seeking help for severe eating disorders doubled in the late 1980s.[16]

Cognitively

- Adolescents have the cognitive maturity to "lead others, meaningfully participate in the workings of their schools and communities, and develop excellent ideas that solve social problems."[17]

- Each adolescent is quite variable in his or her level of apparent cognitive development. A thirteen-year-old, for example, may one day seem to have the cognitive skills of a ten-year-old and another day that of a fifteen-year-old.[18]

- The ten- and eleven-year-old is characterized more by concrete thinking and an ego-centric perspective, a focus on "right now," and on fairly rigid standards of right and wrong. The fourteen- and fifteen-year-old is characterized by more abstract thinking, and the ability to: consider possibilities and not just realities, see things from another person's point of view, allow perceived consequences of behavior to temper the desire for immediate gratification of wants, and consider exceptions to the rules.[19]

Implications for the Classroom

There is much that you can do in your classroom to help middle school students successfully navigate the murky waters of adolescence and learn skillful ways to respond effectively to conflict.

1) Provide opportunities for positive social interactions.

Community-building activities such as gatherings and closings for lessons (see appendices A and B) give students an opportunity to learn about each other in safe, non-threatening, and fun ways. These types of activities also build mutual respect and caring in your classroom. This will help reduce exclusionary behavior and other sources of conflict.

2) Help students explore their identities both by themselves and in small groups.

Journal writing, role plays, and small group discussions (such as microlabs) give students an opportunity to explore their thoughts, feelings, and preferences. Students will be more likely to understand and accept others' points of view if they have practiced listening to varied thoughts and opinions.

3) Model skillful behavior around conflict.

Young people are tuned into the messages that you send through your own dealings with conflict. Model the skills and behaviors that you wish your students to learn.

4) Provide opportunities for practice.

As students learn guidelines and skills for nonviolently resolving conflict, they will need ample opportunity to practice with their peers. Positively reinforce good behavior.

5) Gradually allow for more autonomy.

Include young people in the decision making and problem solving that affects them. As you help youth develop problem-solving skills, gradually provide leadership opportunities. Some examples of leadership and decision-making opportunities are: creating group agreements for classroom behavior, involving students in the selection of topics that will be studied during the year, and implementing a peer mediation program.

6) *Give girls extra encouragement and a safe place to voice their feelings and needs.*

Girls may need to be given extra encouragement to stand up for themselves, speak out, and to value their needs and feelings as much as someone else's. (See "Girls' Development: An Overview" for more information.)

7) *Set clear limits and expectations.*

Clear expectations are helpful to unsure, self-critical young people. Furthermore, in their search for independence, young adolescents often feel immune to risks and dangers, so they require structure and guidance in setting clear limits. Set clearly defined limits, but find ways to involve students in the process of decision making.[20]

8) *Help bridge differences.*

Use the activities in Part III of this curriculum, Dealing With Differences, to help develop an appreciation for differences.

9) *Provide varied opportunities to explore competence and achievement.*

Young adolescents need help finding out what they are good at doing. They can be painfully self-conscious and self-critical and are vulnerable to bouts of low self-esteem. Therefore they require frequent and varied opportunities to be successful and have their accomplishments recognized by others. Furthermore, adolescents are more likely to be tolerant of differences if they experience an environment where different abilities are clearly valued.

Gender and Conflict

Recent research indicates marked differences between girls' and boys' experience during adolescence (see "Girl's Development: An Overview"). These differences in experience have a significant impact on how each sex deals with and is effected by conflict.

- Boys generally respond to conflict with direct confrontation and physical attack, while girls increasingly turn to social ostracism in their conflicts with one another.[21]

- Females focus on conflict at a more intimate level as seen by their focus on caring, while males deal with conflict on more general levels.[22]

- Perhaps because they have a more interpersonal focus,

happened? Annie Rogers describes girls as "entering the borderland," the place between society's conventions of femininity and girls' authentic selves.

As girls' bodies start budding and they make the turn from childhood to womanhood—typically around the age of 11 or 12—girls hear the conflicting messages about what it means to be female. Given lessons in femininity and womanhood from their own families and ethnic communities, as well as from the mainstream culture, girls find it's suddenly not all right to be outspoken, aggressive, angry, messy, or so candidly honest. Girls learn that if they don't look a certain way, people will say they're ugly; if they're clearly smarter than boys in class, they hurt their chances of getting a date; if they don't speak in a particular tone of voice, no one will listen to them. Daily, and everywhere around them, girls hear and see the message, "Tone it down! You're too loud, too loose, too smart, too much."

Yet at this point in their development (11-12 years old), teenage girls don't give in so easily. Girls actively struggle against silencing themselves. They fight hard for the right to shape the world—and their place in it. But without sustained support from adults in their struggle, girls are left extremely vulnerable and at risk for a number of damaging consequences: eating disorders, suicide attempts, disillusionment with education, school dropout, diminished self-esteem, and depression. These self-defeating behaviors might be construed as other ways of speaking—"voices" that adults perhaps will be forced to hear. It is at this developmental point that girls often get pinned with one of a variety of labels: deficit, deviant, high risk, or simply, at risk. As with any kind of "official" classification, these labels can become self-fulfilling prophesies as girls find themselves being treated (as well as termed) differently.

It can be argued that psychological health consists, most simply, of staying in relationship with oneself, others, and the world. Girls need real connections to develop in healthy ways. But to have friendships in the adult world—to please others and avoid "making waves" at any cost—these teenage girls feel pressure to abandon important parts of themselves. Difference and disagreement now become too dangerous to risk. Girls speak of pretending to like people they really don't, and of pretending to agree with others to avoid hurting their feelings.[35] Carol Gilligan sums up this dilemma in girls' development as follows:

> If girls know what they know and bring themselves into relationships, they will be in conflict with prevailing authorities. If girls do not know what they know and take themselves out of relationships, they will be in trouble with themselves.[36]

Many girls give up the struggle for authentic relationships and pursue the feminine ideal—

girls seem more skillful than boys at reaching amicable resolutions. Yet when females are with males they tend to act with power tactics more typical of males.[23]

- Girls tend to have more trouble than boys handling criticism, saying what is on their minds, and standing up for themselves. Girls are also more likely than boys to be overwhelmed by other people's emotional needs when making decisions or taking action.[24] Moreover, the students that teachers report liking least are "aggressive girls."[25]

Racial Identity Development

Identity formation is a central task of adolescence. Part of the process of forming an identity is establishing a racial identity.[26] However, schools, as social institutions, tend to reflect and transmit the views and values of the dominant, Euro-American culture.[27] This creates particular challenges for adolescents of color as they form their racial identities.

At adolescence, racial identity, like other aspects of identity, is in an exploratory phase.[28] Racial identity development is said to begin for many children around the ages of six to nine. At about this time, many children begin to move beyond a childhood understanding of race (as the color of one's skin, for example) to a more sophisticated understanding of race (as a socially constructed power relation). During adolescence, children are further exploring and developing their racial identities.

W.E. Cross defined four basic stages of racial identity development for people of color.[29] The first stage is called "pre-encounter." A student at this stage uncritically accepts the racial images and stereotypes found in the mainstream culture, and may deny or devalue his or her race. The second stage of development is called "encounter." This is a stage of awakening that is often the result of a critical incident (such as an experience of racism) that leads the student to reconsider and reorganize his or her thoughts and feelings about race and society. The third stage of development is called "immersion" and is characterized by an embracing of one's racial group. Students at this stage idealize their racial group and reject the dominant culture. The final stage of racial identity development is "internalization." Students at this stage feel a high degree of self-acceptance and an awareness of the meaning of race while also recognizing and appreciating other ethnic and racial heritages.

It is important to note that the development of racial identity does not end in adolescence. Racial identity can evolve continuously during one's lifetime. Furthermore, each developmental stage may be visited more than once. Young people and adults may repeatedly cycle through the stages of racial identity development.

The fact that schools tend to promote the values of the dominant culture creates a challenge for students of color as they develop their racial identities. Some adolescents of color may feel that they live in two worlds: the white world of school and the world of their neighborhood or home. Some students are able to cope successfully with moving between these two worlds. These students are described as developing a "bicultural identity." Biculturality is the ability to draw simultaneously from the culture of one's ethnic group and from the mainstream culture.[30] Bicultural people actively participate in both cultures, have extensive interactions within both environments, and adopt behaviors that allow them to make the transitions and adjustments between the two.[31]

Other students of color feel less comfort and ease moving between two worlds. Some of these students may view school as a hostile place and may even view teachers as agents of oppression. Some students of color may avoid socializing with white students and seek out same-race friendships to help maintain positive self-esteem.[32] Still other students of color may respond by distancing themselves from their own culture, becoming alienated from it, or internalizing the message that their own culture is inferior to the dominant, white culture.

Teachers and schools can take steps to support adolescents of color as they grapple with their racial identities.[33] The following list describes some starting points.

- Lessen the disconnection between home and school environments by creating school and classroom environments that support cultural diversity. Work to create multicultural curricula that reflect the race and ethnicity of your students as well as the racial and ethnic makeup of the larger society. Multicultural curricula can affirm and strengthen students' relationships to their own cultures. (See Part Three of this curriculum, Dealing with Differences, for lesson plans that directly address diversity.)

- Strengthen in-school support systems for students of color, such as mentoring programs that pair students with same-race role models.

being kind and nice, swallowing their anger, being self-less—at great cost to their own psychological health.

Girls can explain why they aren't speaking—but only for a time. Without active support from adults, girls' self-silencing becomes automatic and unconscious. Girls' speech during adolescence often becomes riddled with the phrase, "I don't know," signaling a covering over or repression of what is too dangerous to say and know in the world.

Girls' bodies often mirror this relational crisis: they adopt self-protective stances and their liveliness seems dulled. Adolescent girls tend to pull in their shoulders, suck in their stomachs, and breath more shallowly—effectively cutting off their breath and feelings from their voices. Once this happens, girls can't speak, know, and think in the same way.

Partnerships Between Girls and Adults

Contrary to common belief, the American Association of University Women survey found that adults have a greater impact on adolescent girls' self-esteem and aspirations than do their peers. The Harvard Project research suggests that relationships between women and girls, in particular, are critical to girls' psychological integrity. Many of the girls who exhibited "ordinary courage" throughout adolescence told of a confiding relationship with a woman who taught them that they could say what they knew and not be thought of as "crazy" or "bad." Sometimes this women was a girl's mother, sometimes an aunt, sister, teacher, or the mom of a best friend. These women not only listened to girls, they also spoke about their own experiences. Many actively coached the girls to resist sexist stereotyping and to see themselves as knowledgeable, resourceful, and entitled to their authority.

Girls need the support of caring adults in all areas of their lives—adults who are aware of girls' strengths and potential, and the dilemmas posed during adolescence. While girls' voices and vision are still powerful, women and men can join girls and encourage open conversations. We can ask and expect girls to be vital, intelligent, creative, and powerful—and thereby support girls' healthy resistance. We can also work to create environments that support girls' healthy resistance. We can seek to create home and school environments that support girls' strength.

- Create small, cooperative, mixed-race learning teams to encourage interracial friendships at school. In these groups, students from different backgrounds study together, working toward a common goal. These types of learning groups allow adolescents from different racial and ethnic backgrounds to learn about their similarities.

- Develop extracurricular activities that will promote the development of interracial friendships and also help children of color feel socially connected to the school environment.

Additional Resources:

Beauboeuf-Lafontant, Tamara and D. Smith Augustine. *Facing Racism in Education*. Cambridge, MA: Harvard Educational Review, 1996.

Delpit, Lisa D. *Other Peoples' Children: Cultural Conflict in the Classroom*. New York: New Press, 1995.

Duvall, Lynn. *Respecting Our Differences: A Guide to Getting Along in a Changing World*. Minneapolis, MN: Free Spirit, 1994.

Hollins, E.R. and J.E. King. *Teaching Diverse Populations: Formulating a Knowledge Base*. Albany, NY: SUNY Press, 1994.

Hopson, Darlene Powell. *Different and Wonderful: Raising Black Children in a Race-conscious Society*. New York: Simon & Schuster, 1992.

Mathias, Barbara and Mary Ann French. *40 Ways to Raise a Nonracist Child*. New York: HarperPerennial, 1996.

Nieto, Sonia. *Affirming Diversity: The Sociopolitical Context of Multicultural Education*. White Plains, NY: Longman Publishers, 1996.

Weis, L. and M. Fine (ed). *Beyond Silenced Voices: Class, Race, and Gender in United States Schools*. Albany, NY: SUNY Press, 1993.

Endnotes

1 Peter C. Scales, *A Portrait of Young Adolescents in the 1990s: Implications for Promoting Healthy Growth and Development.* (Carrboro, North Carolina: Center for Early Adolescence, School of Medicine, The University of North Carolina at Chapel Hill, 1991), 2.

2 M. Csikszentmihalyi and R. Larson, *Being Adolescent: Conflict and Growth in Teenage Years.* (New York: Basic Books, Inc., 1984).

3 J. Anticliffe, "Some Approaches to Conflict with Adolescents in Classrooms," *Maladjustment and Therapeutic Education,* Vol 7(1), Spring, 1989, 39-46.

4 M. Manning and M. Allen, "Social Development in Early Adolescence: Implications for Middle School Educators," *Childhood Education.* Vol. 63(3) (February 1987), 172-176.

5 Peter C. Scales, *A Portrait of Young Adolescents in the 1990s: Implications for Promoting Healthy Growth and Development.* (Carrboro, North Carolina: Center for Early Adolescence, School of Medicine, The University of North Carolina at Chapel Hill, 1991), 8.

6 Ibid., 13-14.

7 M. Manning and M. Allen, "Social Development in Early Adolescence: Implications for Middle School Educators," *Childhood Education.* Vol. 63(3) (February 1987), 172-176.

8 Peter C. Scales, *A Portrait of Young Adolescents in the 1990s: Implications for Promoting Healthy Growth and Development.* (Carrboro, North Carolina: Center for Early Adolescence, School of Medicine, The University of North Carolina at Chapel Hill, 1991), 10.

9 Ibid., 8.

10 Greenberg-Lake Analysis Group, *Shortchanging Girls, Shortchanging America: A Nationwide Poll to Assess Self-esteem, Educational Experiences, Interest in Math and Science, and Career Aspirations of Girls and Boys Ages 9-15* (Washington, D.C.: American Association of University Women, 1991), 4-5.

11 Linda Harris, Robert W. Blum, and Michael Resnick, "Teen Females in Minnesota: A Portrait of Quiet Disturbance," in Gilligan, Rogers, and Tolman, eds., *Women, Girls and Psychotherapy,* (New York: Haworth Press, 1991), 121-122.

12 Peter C. Scales, *A Portrait of Young Adolescents in the 1990s: Implications for Promoting Healthy Growth and Development.* (Carrboro, North Carolina: Center for Early Adolescence, School of Medicine, The University of North Carolina at Chapel Hill, 1991).

13 Carol Gilligan, *In a Different Voice: Psychological Theory and Women's Development* (Cambridge, MA: Harvard University Press, 1982).

14 Peter C. Scales, *A Portrait of Young Adolescents in the 1990s: Implications for Promoting Healthy Growth and Development.* (Carrboro, North Carolina: Center for Early Adolescence, School of Medicine, The University of North Carolina at Chapel Hill, 1991),9.

15 Greenberg-Lake Analysis Group, *Shortchanging Girls, Shortchanging America: A Nationwide Poll to Assess Self-esteem, Educational Experiences, Interest in Math and Science, and Career Aspirations of Girls and Boys Ages 9-15* (Washington, D.C.: American Association of University Women, 1991), 48.

16 Wellesley College Center for Research on Women, *How Schools Shortchange Girls,* 78; and Naomi Wolf, *The Beauty Myth* (New York: Doubleday, 1991), 184-185, 214-215.

17 Peter C. Scales, *A Portrait of Young Adolescents in the 1990s: Implications for Promoting Healthy Growth and Development.* (Carrboro, North Carolina: Center for Early Adolescence, School of Medicine, The University of North Carolina at Chapel Hill, 1991), 17.

18 Ibid., 11.

19 Ibid., 12.

20 Ibid., 13-14.

21 R. Cairns, B. Cairns, H. Neckerman, L. Ferguson, et al, "Growth and Agression: I. Childhood to Early Adolescence," *Developmental Psychology,* Vol. 25 (2) (March), 320-330.

22 Carol Gilligan, *In a Different Voice* (Cambridge, MA: Havard University Press, 1982).

23 C. Schantz and W. Hartup, *Conflict in Child and Adolescent Development* (New York: Cambridge University Press, 1992).

24 *Teenagers Under Pressure,* A report commissioned by Seventeen and the Ms. Foundation for Women, 1996.

25 Sadker and Sadker, *Failing At Fairness: How America's Schools Cheat Girls,* (New York: C. Scribner's Sons, 1994), 13-14; and Wellesley College Center for Research on Women, *How Schools Shortchange Girls,* 60-74.

26 Deborah Plummer, "Patterns of racial identity development of African American adolescent males and females," *Journal of Black Psychology,* Vol. 21 (May 1995): 168.

27 Maxine L. Clark, "Social identity, peer relations, and academic competence...," *Education and Urban Society*, Vol. 24 (November 1991): 41.

28 Plummer, 168.

29 Ibid.

30 Clark, 41.

31 Ibid.

32 Ibid.

33 The following recommendations come from Clark, 41.

34 Findings of the Harvard Project on Women's Psychology and Girls' Development are drawn from Carol Gilligan, Annie G. Rogers, and Deborah L. Tolman, eds., *Women, Girls and Psychotherapy: Reframing Resistance* (Binghampton, NY: Haworth Press, 1991); Lyn Mikel Brown and Carol Gilligan, *Meeting At the Crossroads* (Cambridge, MA: Harvard University Press, 1992); Annie G. Rogers, "Voice, Play, and a Practice of Courage in Girls' and Women's Lives," in the *Harvard Educational Review*, 63(3) (1993); Elizabeth Debold, Marie Wilson, and Idelisse Malavé, *Mother Daughter Revolution* (New York: Bantam Books, 1994); and Jill McLean Taylor, Carol Gilligan, and Amy Sullivan, *Holding Difference, Sustaining Hope: Women and Girls, Race and Relationship* (Cambridge, MA: Harvard University Press, In Press 1995).

35 Ibid., 58-59.

36 Carol Gilligan, "Joining the Resistance: Psychology, Politics, Girls and Women," in the *Michigan Quarterly Review* 29(4) (1990).

About the Author

William J. Kreidler was Educators for Social Responsibility's Senior Conflict Resolution Specialist. A teacher with over twenty years of experience and a nationally recognized expert in conflict resolution, Bill authored *Creative Conflict Resolution, Elementary Perspectives: Teaching Concepts of Peace and Conflict, Teaching Conflict Resolution Through Children's Literature*, and *Conflict Resolution in the Middle School*. He co-authored *The Violence Prevention Curriculum for Adolescents* with Dr. Deborah Prothrow-Stith, *Conflict Resolution in the Middle School: Student Workbook & Journal* with Rachel Poliner, *Adventures in Peacemaking: A Conflict Resolution Activity Guide for School-age Programs* with Lisa Furlong, and *Stop, Caution, Go: A Youth Gang Prevention Curriculum* with Ulric Johnson. In June 2000, *Early Childhood Adventures in Peacemaking*, co-authored with Sandy Whittall, received the special Judge's Award from the Association of Educational Publishers.

A respected writer and trainer in the field of conflict resolution, Bill also served as a speaker and workshop leader, and he collaborated with teachers and students worldwide on issues of violence prevention, diversity, and conflict resolution. In 1997, the National Conference on Peacemaking and Conflict Resolution honored Bill with the Herman Award for Distinguished Contribution to the Field of Conflict Resolution.

William J. Kreidler died on June 10, 2000 after a long battle with AIDS. *Conflict Resolution in the Middle School*, like all of Bill's books, memorializes his lifelong commitment to developing creative and nonviolent solutions to all conflicts.

About ESR

Educators for Social Responsibility, ESR, founded in 1982, aims to make teaching social responsibility a core practice in education so that young people develop the convictions and skills to shape a safe, sustainable, democratic, and just world. We are a national leader in dovoloping and disseminating high quality programs and other teaching resources that help adults teach children to manage feelings positively and resolve conflicts nonviolently, value diversity, understand cultural differences, counter bias and confront prejudice, solve problems cooperatively, think critically and creatively, and take meaningful action. Through a range of programs, ESR offers training for adults in K-12 schools and classrooms, as well as in early childhood and after-school programs. At the core of our work is transforming the climate of schools and other educational settings into safe, caring, respectful, and productive learning communities.

For more information, visit our website at *www.esrnational.org*, or make inquiries at educators@esrnational.org and 1-800-370-2515

ESR Programs and Professional Development Workshops

ESR helps schools to implement comprehensive social and emotional learning programs with a special emphasis in conflict resolution. At the middle school level, our programs include three options:

The Resolving Conflict Creatively Program (RCCP) is one of the largest and longest-standing research-based K-8 programs in the country. RCCP employs a comprehensive strategy for preventing violence and creating caring and cooperative learning commmunities. It features classroom instruction using ESR curricula, a peer mediation program, and specialized training for teachers, administrators, support staff, and parents.

Partners in Learning helps middle and high schools to create safe, respectful and personalized learning environments. The program features a peaceable classroom and school planning process, conflict resolution instruction, student leadership initiatives, and school-community partnerships.

Stories is a K-12 program that explores conflict and character through literature and language arts. **Stories** training provides teachers with avenues to help students develop conflict resolution skills through the discussion of literary works.

All of our programs help school staff to integrate conflict resolution with classroom management and discipline, infuse it into core subject areas, and teach key social and emotional skills and concepts.

In addition to comprehensive programs, ESR offers a wide variety of training and staff development that is tailored to the specific needs of the school or district. Parent trainings and peer mediation trainings are also available.